BRITISH PRESSURE GROUPS

Oxford University Press, Ely House, London W. 1

GLASGOW NEW YORK TORONTO MELBOURNE WELLINGTON
CAPE TOWN SALISBURY IBADAN NAIROBI LUSAKA ADDIS ABABA
BOMBAY CALCUTTA MADRAS KARACHI LAHORE DACCA
KUALA LUMPUR HONG KONG

FIRST PUBLISHED 1958
REPRINTED 1958
REPRINTED LITHOGRAPHICALLY 1966

BRITISH PRESSURE GROUPS

THEIR ROLE IN RELATION TO THE HOUSE OF COMMONS

BY

J. D. STEWART

OXFORD
AT THE CLARENDON PRESS

PRINTED IN GREAT BRITAIN

TO THERESA

PREFACE

In preparing this work I have received assistance from many people. In particular I have been much helped by the officials of a large number of associations, unions, and societies, who have discussed with me the problems of their relations with the government and with Parliament. In addition a number of other organizations have supplied me with valuable information. I have found a readiness to discuss the problems in which I was interested and to help research, an attitude for which I am very grateful. I have also been fortunate in having had discussions on pressure groups with a number of Members of Parliament, from whom I have learnt much. They gave me an opportunity to test out the views I had formed. It would be impossible to name all the people who have helped me.

Mr. David Butler, Mr. Gerald Kaufman, Sir Hugh Linstead, M.P., Mr. John Parker, M.P., Mr. Allen Potter, and Mr. Graham Wootton have been of particular help to me on certain points. Mr. Ian Harvey, M.P., and Mr. Christopher Mayhew, M.P., have given me a good deal of information on the problem of letters to Members of Parliament and advice on the wider issues. Professor Max Beloff, Mr. D. N. Chester, and Mr. H. G. Nicholas have all read the typescript at one stage or another and made helpful comments. Mr. Andrew McIntosh has given friendly advice and assistance in the preparation of this work. To Professor K. C. Wheare I owe an especial debt; without his encouragement and advice I do not think this work would ever have been finished.

The Warden and Fellows of Nuffield College gave me the opportunity to spend two years doing research on the subject of this book, for which I am very grateful.

I must acknowledge with thanks the permission of the Lord's Day Observance Society to publish a letter to parliamentary candidates and a letter to supporters; of the League against Cruel Sports, the National Association of Women Civil Servants, the Officers' Pensions Society, and the United Committee for the Taxation of Land Values to publish letters to parliamentary candidates; of the National and Local Government Officers' Association to publish an extract from the *Local Government Service* of January 1948; and of the Comptroller of Her Majesty's Stationery Office to publish extracts from the reports of the Committee of Privileges, of the Select Committee on Delegated Legislation, of the Committee on Intermediaries of the Royal Commission on Scottish Affairs, of the Select Committee on Estimates, and of the Ministry of Health, and from the 1952 Command Paper on Iron and Steel.

J.D.S.

September, 1957.

CONTENTS

ABBREVIATIONS

A.A.	Automobile Association.
A.B.C.C.	Association of British Chambers of Commerce.
A.E.R.	All England Law Reports.
A.E.U.	Amalgamated Engineering Union.
A.M.C.	Association of Municipal Corporations.
B.D.A.	British Dental Association.
B.E.C.	British Employers' Confederation.
B.I.S.A.K.T.A.	British Iron, Steel, and Kindred Trades Association.
B.L.E.S.M.A.	British Limbless Ex-Service Men's Association.
B.M.A.	British Medical Association.
B.R.F.	British Road Federation.
B.S.A.	Building Societies' Association.
B.U.A.V.	British Union for the Abolition of Vivisection.
C.A.	Chartered Accountant.
C.C.A.	County Councils' Association.
C.E.A.	Cinematograph Exhibitors' Association.
C.L.A.	Country (previously Central) Landowners' Association.
C.P.R.E.	Council for the Preservation of Rural England.
C.S.C.A.	Civil Service Clerical Association.
E.T.U.	Electrical Trades Union.
F.B.I.	Federation of British Industries.
H.C. Deb.	Parliamentary Debates (Commons) 5th Series.
H.L.	Howard League for Penal Reform.
I.R.S.F.	Inland Revenue Staff Federation.
L.D.O.S.	Lord's Day Observance Society.
N.A.L.G.O.	National and Local Government Officers' Association (Previously National Association of Local Government Officers).
N.A.M.B.C.C.	National Association of Master Bakers, Confectioners, and Caterers.
N.A.P.C.	National Association of Parish Councils.
N.C.T.	National Chamber of Trade.
N.E.C.	National Executive Committee.

N.F.P.W.	National Federation of Professional Workers.
N.F.R.N.B.S.	National Federation of Retail Newsagents, Booksellers, and Stationers.
N.F.U.	National Farmers' Union.
N.S.P.C.C.	National Society for the Prevention of Cruelty to Children.
N.U.F.T.O.	National Union of Furniture Trade Operatives.
N.U.M.	National Union of Mineworkers.
N.U.T.	National Union of Teachers.
P.A.G.B.	Poultry Association of Great Britain.
R.A.C.	Royal Automobile Club.
R.D.C.A.	Rural District Councils' Association.
R.I.B.A.	Royal Institute of British Architects.
R.S.P.C.A.	Royal Society for the Prevention of Cruelty to Animals.
T.S.S.A.	Transport Salaried Staffs' Association.
T.L.R.	Times Law Report.
T.U.C.	Trades Union Congress.
U.C.T.A.	United Commercial Travellers' Association.
U.D.C.A.	Urban District Councils' Association.
U.S.D.A.W.	Union of Shop, Distributive, and Allied Workers.
U.T.F.W.A.	United Textile Factory Workers' Association.

CORRIGENDA

Page 48, lines 21–22

for National Dairyman's Union

read National Dairyman's Association

Page 91, lines 27–28

for accountancy . . . Bill.

read County Councils' Association, following its usual practice, approached the Home Office before it approached the sponsor of the Bill.

CHAPTER I

Introduction

THIS book is an attempt to describe the activities of various unions, associations, and societies in relation to the House of Commons. The bodies I shall discuss include the Federation of British Industries, the National Farmers' Union, the Brewers' Society, the National Union of Furniture Trade Operatives, the Pharmaceutical Society, the Automobile Association, the Royal Society for the Prevention of Cruelty to Animals, and the National Temperance Federation among others. These bodies are grouped together under the title 'pressure groups'. The phrase may not be entirely fortunate, but it has established itself too firmly in the language of political science to be worth trying to dislodge.

If I am asked to define the field of study of pressure groups other than ostensively, I must reply by some such formula as Professor W. J. M. Mackenzie's: 'the field of organized groups possessing both formal structure and real common interests, in so far as they influence the decisions of public bodies.'[1] I would prefer myself to amend the last phrase to read 'in so far as they seek to influence the process of government', but all such formulas raise serious problems, as Professor Mackenzie has been the first to recognize. It is put forward merely as a working definition to indicate why it is considered reasonable to group together, in one avowedly coherent study, the various organizations discussed here. All these organizations have this in common: they seek, at several points, to influence the process of government.

It is true that a definition such as that propounded by Professor Mackenzie can cover most organizations that exist and that in studying national representative organizations such as those listed above, one is only studying a part of the field. But the significant point about those and the other similar bodies

[1] W. J. M. Mackenzie, 'Pressure Groups in British Government', *British Journal of Sociology* (June 1955), p. 137.

studied in this book is that they are all organizations whose relations to the process of government are of great importance to them. In studying the national representative organizations one is studying the hard core of pressure groups in this country.

The present study lies in the first approaches to the subject. Although it has been necessary to say something of the general strategy of pressure groups, it concentrates on but one aspect of their activities. Limitation is necessary to bring the subject to manageable proportions. It remains a broad enough field. It is impossible to outline each situation of every pressure group, to explain the peculiar nature of its demands, and the way it uses the House of Commons to overcome its difficulties. All that has been attempted here is an examination of the situations which face pressure groups in order to bring out general considerations with regard to their activities in relation to the House of Commons. There will be, as there must, many groups unnoticed, yet if the work is well done, their position will be illustrated by what is said of other groups.

Two warnings must be given. This is a study of proper, official, and recognized activities. There is nothing written here of the underhand. It may be, though I doubt it, that groups resort to such activities, but the constitutional and open activity is so important and stands so clearly in its own right that there is no space or need to venture into a shadowy half-world.

This is a contemporary study, set in the period 1945–55, though to illustrate a point, or to explain the background, it has sometimes been necessary to examine other periods. It is felt that this period provides material for a coherent and useful study.

The limited scope of this work illustrates the possibility of further study. There is a need for studies of particular groups and of relations between them. There is a need for studies of the history of groups. There is a need for more detailed study of the relations between the ministries and groups. There is a need for studies of group objectives. These needs arise not from the material unexamined, though that is abundant, but from the growing importance of the groups in British politics. Perhaps this book will illustrate these needs.

CHAPTER II

The Process of Consultation

I

THOSE who make decisions for the group will choose that method or combination of methods of pressure which they consider promises to achieve its aims most effectively in the political situation in which it finds itself. It is upon this assumption that the analysis of the behaviour of pressure groups here put forward is based. The group is subject, however, to the restraints put upon it by its ideals and its sense of political responsibility. In certain political situations it is possible that a group might be able to exert considerable influence by means of bribery, without any of the disagreeable consequences that are liable to follow, but it is unlikely it would be considered by any of the groups to be discussed. For these groups have an accepted role in our society, and being fully conscious of this they have accepted the responsibilities of that position. Subject to these limitations, the principle stands that in any given political situation the group will choose that method which it considers to be the most effective.

The judgement made by a group upon the effectiveness of various methods will depend upon the particular political situation faced by the group. A group concerned with the welfare of chemical manufacturers appears to be faced with a different political situation from that faced by a group concerned with the interests of miners. But since both political situations occur in the same political system of the same society, it is not surprising that there are many things in common between the judgements made by the groups and in their consequent strategy. The resemblances are more important than the differences.

At any period and in any country it is possible to discover similarities between the strategies of different pressure groups. The American pressure group tends to find a political situation in which Congress is responsive to pressure and in which pressure on Congress is itself sufficient for the attainment of its aims owing to the degree of independence enjoyed by Congress from control by the administration. It is clear that in this country the degree of party discipline and government control in the House of Commons will influence group strategy. The political situation may vary over time as it does between countries. It is as foolish to expect a twentieth-century British pressure group to behave like a nineteenth-century one as it is to expect it to behave like an American one.

2

The situation faced by groups is in part reflected in the general nature of their aims. A broad distinction can be made between those groups which have major demands and those groups which merely seek to escape the minor frictions that exist and which government intervention can either ease or increase. The society in which many groups have major demands to make is a society of grave discontent, for the demands probably indicate that large sections of the community consider that their interests are not recognized by the state. Such a situation had developed in Britain at the beginning of the century and was reflected in the major demands of trade unions. Discontent of this kind may be increased by the failure of the party system through maladjustment or immaturity to reflect important political issues. Many of the early pressure groups promoted political demands that the party system had failed to present.

But there are also pressure groups which in the claims they advance merely require minor modifications to the existing framework of government action rather than major reform. A society in which most groups are of this type is one in which there are no major organized sections of discontent because all interests of importance in the community are recognized by the government, and the party system is able to deal with most major issues.

Between these two situations there is an infinite series of gradations. In any given situation there will always be some groups which are more discontented than others, some groups whose claims are greater than others.

Yet it is possible to say that there are now fewer major demand groups than there were at the beginning of the century.[1] Most groups are concerned with the administration by the government of a general framework which they accept. They require minor modifications to acts, alterations of administrative procedure, readjustments of licence provisions, and redrafting of regulations. These claims are important, but they do not appear as a challenge to the system of government.

The change is in part due to the widening of the government's concern in society, which has been accompanied by an extension of the role of the party and consequent action to remove major discontent. Recognition has been extended to all sections which can claim important support in society. It is in part a tribute to the action of the groups. The achievement of legislative reform by a group removes a major demand and replaces it by a concern for administrative adjustment.

From its foundations the National Association of Local Government Officers (now the National and Local Government Officers' Association) had among its main objectives the achievement of adequate superannuation provisions for local government officials. In 1937 it finally achieved an Act providing for compulsory superannuation.[2] That Act transformed the situation for the group. Since that date one of its main fields of concern has been the administration of that Act and its successors. From its experience, N.A.L.G.O. prepares the amendments it desires in readiness for the next time the government introduces a bill on the subject.[3] A major demand has been resolved and the group has been left with a watching brief—and that is the position in which many groups, whatever their history, find themselves.

[1] There has been little adequate work done upon the pressure group of this period, but some idea of the different approach followed by groups can be gained from: A. H. H. Mathews, *Fifty Years of Agricultural Politics* (1915) for the Central Chamber of Agriculture, the *N.F.U. Yearbook* for 1922 for the N.F.U., Sidney and Beatrice Webb, *Industrial Democracy* (1897), Part II, chap. IV for the trade unions, and R. A. Brady, *Business as a System of Power* (1944) for information on the early years of the F.B.I.

[2] See N.A.L.G.O., *The Fight for Superannuation* (undated).

[3] At the 1946 annual conference an Executive spokesman stated that a special sub-committee had prepared twenty-seven desired amendments and tha the Association would take the first opportunity of pressing the government to legislate accordingly. *Local Government Service*, July-Aug. 1946, p. 123.

3

One could outline many features of the political situation which groups have to face. To do so would be to enter into a complete description of the British political system. Much must be assumed to be common knowledge. But one feature needs special emphasis, and that is consultation. The nature of group aims makes it especially important.

The government's concern in the various activities of the citizens has laid upon it the necessity of sounding opinions as a guide to action, for the opinions of those concerned is a fact of the situation with which the government has to deal. But the sounding of opinions generally must prove such a difficult task that the government has resorted to the easier method of consulting various representative organizations:

> The justification for trade associations acting in a representative capacity is that, on the whole, it works. It is a physical impossibility for Ministers or their departments to test the opinions or seek the advice of thousands of individuals. They must rely on those individuals who wish to make their views known so to organize themselves that a collective approach to problems becomes possible. That this will result in unanimous opinions being reached on every question is impossible, but the common sense and traditional willingness to compromise shades of view will nearly always result in the adoption of an official policy by the organization which will be supported by its members. Occasional misjudgments may be made, reactions to changes of mind by constituents may at times be too slow, but this cannot be frequent, for trade associations are voluntary organizations, and if their leaders misinterpret their members' views they will soon lead nobody but themselves.[1]

It is not merely the need to sound opinions that leads the government to consultation. The government knows that the groups have particular knowledge, not merely of opinions, but of facts. The statistical and research departments of trade associations and trade unions may be able to supply information. Certainly they will have a technical know-how and an expertize which provide government proposals with a sound test.

In a society in which the major demands appear to have been

[1] Sir Norman Kipping, Director-General of the F.B.I. in a letter to *The Times*, 15 Jan. 1953.

satisfied, both the main political parties realize the necessity of securing co-operation from all sections of society. The government seeks by consultation to build up where possible a responsive attitude to its proposals. It seeks co-operation and elimination of open discontent.

This, then, is the philosophy of consultation as a part of the political system. This philosophy does not imply that the consultation must be with groups, but in fact this was the only way in which it could be kept within reasonable bounds or take place without obvious injustice. The situation worked for the national organizations:

> Trade Associations will grow. Government will in the future take a far greater interest and wield a far greater influence in industry than in the past, and they cannot hope to have an intelligent understanding of industry and trade except through Trade Associations, whether they be organisations of employer or worker, or both.[1]

Thus spoke one trade association leader, and his words contained a large element of truth. Consultation has brought a relationship of confidence and continuing contact between group and government.

For the government, consultation has become a necessity and by government one means not merely the ministers. For most of the consultation takes place well below that level and well below the permanent secretaries of departments. The whole administrative system of government is involved and it is in this sense that one speaks of the importance of consultation to the government. There has been created a widespread machinery which is yet difficult to describe because so little formal expression is given to it in the outward structure of government. For example, it is only to a very limited extent that the system of consultation has been formalized by statute.

Some references to consultation do occur in statutes. The Agriculture Act of 1947 lays upon the Ministers the obligation before holding an annual or special price review to 'consult with such bodies of persons as appear to them to represent the interests of producers in the agricultural industry'.[2] The Act does not constitute a relationship between the government and particular groups, but its meaning was sufficiently understood

[1] Speech by the President of the Motor Agents' Association, quoted in *Wine and Spirit Trade Review*, 2 Feb. 1945, p. 28.

[2] 10 & 11 Geo. VI, c. 48, s. 62 (3).

at the time. Mr. P. H. Collick, the Parliamentary Under-Secretary, made it clear that it referred to the three main farmers' unions:

The practice is, of course, to have in consultation at the annual and the special price reviews the National Farmers' Union representatives of each country, England, Scotland, Wales and Northern Ireland; and, in some cases, of course, bodies like the milk marketing board. They represent, on the whole, the wide interests of producers, and can speak on their behalf. I can imagine nothing more disastrous than to carry an Amendment of this kind which would allow any small dissenting body here, there, or anywhere, to come in under such provisions.[1]

This is the form such references normally take. It would be foolish for an act to name specific bodies since new groups may develop and old ones lose support. It is normally realized, as in this case, which groups are in fact concerned.

The formal recognition of the group rests, not on the references to the need for consultation in statutes, but rather on the advisory committee. The advisory committee is the means by which the pressure group has been given a place in the formal structure of government. Through the advisory committees the leaders of pressure groups have been brought directly into the process of government. This indicates publicly that these groups are regarded as rightful bodies to advise government.

It may be suggested that such an approach is a little fanciful, in that direct appointment by groups to advisory committees is very limited. It is true that on many committees, appointment is left to the discretion of the minister. But even where, as in the case of appointments to the Economic Planning Board, the Minister is apparently, 'not bound to consult anyone at all' (Political and Economic Planning, *Report on Government and Industry*, 1952, p. 132), he did in fact invite the Trades Union Congress for nominations which he then accepted. This P.E.P. report draws a distinction between direct appointment by a minister, selection from group nominations, and direct representation. These distinctions do not necessarily alter the position such a system gives the group. For what is important is the attitude of the member and of his parent group. If a member of an advisory committee regards himself as the representative of a

[1] Standing Committee Debates, Committee A, 13 Feb. 1947, col. 79.

group, then by so doing he brings the group into the advisory committee. By asking a group to submit nominations for a committee, the minister is not trying to save himself the trouble of looking for suitable men, but is asking for the group to be represented by some of its leaders.

The Federation of British Industries and the Trades Union Congress have representatives on a large number of bodies. The conditions covering their membership of the committees may vary, but when one considers the functions of the bodies, it becomes clear that this membership is public evidence of the fact that it is necessary for the government to obtain advice from industry, and that the means by which that advice can best be obtained is through these representative organizations. The National Joint Advisory Council exists 'to advise on matters on which employers and workers have a common interest, and to provide for closer consultation between the Government and organized industry'.[1] On this organization are representatives of the F.B.I., the T.U.C., the National Union of Manufacturers, and the nationalized industries. The T.U.C. states that it appoints its representatives directly.[2] In the case of the National Production Advisory Council for Industry, the Minister asks not for appointments, but for nominations. But in both cases there is the twin recognition of the need for advice from industry and of the fact that such advice can best be obtained from the representative organizations.

But it is not merely the great economic organizations that are represented on these committees. In the same way, the ex-servicemen's organizations are represented on the National Advisory Council on Employment of the Disabled[3] and on the Central Advisory Committee of the Ministry of Pensions,[4] while local authority associations and teachers' organizations are represented on the National Advisory Council on the Training and Supply of Teachers.[5]

Membership of an advisory committee gives outward re-

[1] H.M.S.O., *Government and Industry*; *A Survey of Machinery for Consultation and Co-operation* (1948), p. 10.

[2] *81st T.U.C. Report* (1949), pp. 189–90.

[3] H.M.S.O., *Government and Industry*, p. 14.

[4] H.C. 271 of 1952–3, pp. 83–84.

[5] H.M.S.O., *National Advisory Council on the Training and Supply of Teachers*, 1st Report, 1951.

cognition to a position that is already well established. Such a development could not have taken place unless the government had already developed a certain degree of respect for the advice and position of the group from its previous contacts. It is because of this already existing pattern of consultation that some groups have not been over-anxious to see the constitution of advisory committees. The T.U.C., in discussing the National Joint Advisory Council, stipulated 'that the reconstitution of the Council would not mean any interference with the present contacts which the Trade Union Movement had with various Government departments'.[1] This condition was easily satisfied, for such contact was as important to government as to group, and the advisory committee could never replace it.

5

This relationship, of which advisory committees are the formal expression, is crucial to the political situation in which groups exist, but this does not render it easy to describe. Though the general tendency to uniformity is there, the actual situation faced by each group remains an individual one. Generalizations can be made, but they can only give an indication of the situation faced by most groups.

A second difficulty lies in the sources of information on the subject. This relationship is normally informal. There is no deliberate secrecy about it; it is merely that it is not necessary to its continuance that public attention should be drawn to it or its details. There are many references to consultation in government reports or in the reports by groups of their activities, but they are passing references, not designed to give a complete picture. From these materials there can be gained an idea of the extent of the relationship, the fields which it covers, and the degree of confidence it marks. This is all that can be obtained from a cursory survey, but it is all that is necessary to understand the political situation faced by most groups. A systematic examination of this evidence by research students would reveal many of the factors governing a vital sector of the political system. Until this is carried out all generalization must be a little uncertain.[2]

[1] *78th T.U.C. Report*, 1946, p. 181.

[2] A first approach to this topic was made in Chapter 3 of Political and Economic Planning's *Industrial Trade Associations* (1957), but much remains to be done.

In 1948 the Labour Government, aware of the public concern at the incidents revealed by the Lynskey Tribunal (appointed to inquire into 'Allegations reflecting on the Official Conduct of Ministers of the Crown and other Public Servants'), set up a Committee to investigate the question of intermediaries between the government and the public. It discovered very little that could be called improper, but found that on an official and accepted level, trade associations and other groups were a very important link between the government and the public. Though this investigation was concerned with the problem on a lower level than is dealt with here, in that it was concerned with the day-to-day problems that arise, for example, in connexion with applications for building licences or for pensions, nevertheless it throws light on the whole field, for in explaining the functions of groups in this respect, the Committee drew attention to a general relationship existing between groups and the government:

It is not difficult to understand why these bodies have achieved their present position vis-à-vis the Government. As the scope and extent of Government activity, over many years past, has increased, it has been only natural for the Government to consult bodies which it knew to be representative of the interests which Government activity increasingly affected. Moreover, the need on the part of Government to consult has often produced the instrument of consultation. The Ministry of Food . . . has always dealt with the trade associations in formulating the basis of its policy, and the initiative in forming some of the associations—at any rate as special war-time organisations—came from the Ministry itself. In other instances the mere existence or growth of Government control was sufficient to demonstrate to individual firms the wisdom of combination and collective action. Trade organisations and similar bodies therefore have considerable experience of dealings with Government Departments. It is this experience which specially equips them to perform their intermediary functions—which, however, are usually regarded by the bodies themselves as quite secondary to their main function of advising their own members and, when consulted by it, the Government on questions of policy. In the first place because of that primary function, the organisations have intimate and continuing knowledge of policy. Collectively one of these organisations knows far more of Government policy over a wide field than any individual can hope to attain to . . . . Secondly, there exist between these bodies and the Government Departments with which they principally deal close and friendly personal contacts at all levels. The members and officers of the organisations, senior or junior, know their opposite numbers in the Departments and have ready access to them. This naturally facilitates the despatch of business. Finally there is continuity on both sides. When a civil servant who has been dealing with his opposite number in an organisation on a particular matter moves to other work, his successor will as a matter of course inherit the contact with the organisation, and vice versa.[1]

The report then goes on to examine in detail, on the level with which it is concerned, the activities of the Association of British Chambers of Commerce, the Federation of British Industries, the National Union of Manufacturers, the National Farmers' Union, and the British Legion. Of the latter it says:

The British Legion's staff have grown up with the pensions regulations since the first world war; they know the idiosyncrasies of the Departmental officials and they can often suggest the best ways in which medical advice can be sought. All these are services which in theory the applicant or appellant can perform for himself but which, in practice, a body like the British Legion, with its long experience and its knowledge of the official machine, can perform better.[2]

The knowledge built up by work of this kind has made the British Legion a body whose opinions the Ministry of Pensions and National Insurance is always ready to hear.

This investigation was concerned merely with the problem of intermediaries. Other reports have touched on the wider subject in passing, as it is difficult to deal with governmental problems without at least indicating the phenomenon. They do little more than illustrate the extent of consultation. Thus the Royal Commission on Scottish Affairs (1952–4) was very interested in whether the government took account of public opinion and, in particular, of Scottish opinion. Since for the most part government departments were not aware of there being anything unusual in Scottish opinion, they had set up no special machinery to deal with it. They were therefore compelled to describe their normal machinery. There is no general public opinion about an alteration in the regulations governing furniture control and the like. So for the most part the departments are concerned with the opinion of groups.

[1] Cmd. 7904, pp. 43–44.

[2] Ibid., pp. 48–49.

The Ministry of Transport said:

In regard to shipping matters in particular, Scottish shipping interests are fully represented in the Chamber of Shipping of the United Kingdom and the Shipping Federation Ltd., with whom the Ministry consult regularly on all matters affecting British shipping, such as the formulation of regulations under the Merchant Shipping Acts. Similarly the seafarers' organisations and Lloyd's Register of Shipping, with whom the Ministry is in constant touch, cover the whole country. There are few shipping matters which are of purely Scottish concern. In regard to matters affecting the fishing industry, the Ministry consult with Scottish organisations in the same way as with those which represent other parts of the United Kingdom.

Similar arrangements are in operation on the inland transport side. . . . Examples of the bodies consulted regularly are, on general road transport matters, the Automobile Association, the Royal Automobile Club and the Royal Scottish Automobile Club; on matters relating to public service vehicles, the Passenger Vehicle Operators Association, the Public Transport Association, and the Scottish Road Passenger Transport Association; on highway matters, the County Councils' Association, the Association of Municipal Corporations, the Association of County Councils in Scotland, and the Convention of Royal Burghs of Scotland.[1]

The Ministry of Food said:

In addition to these organisations [advisory panels] many trade associations were set up during the war by the Ministry or by the trade at the instigation of the Ministry. Some perform executive as well as advisory functions on behalf of the Ministry, and all are consulted in the normal course of the Ministry's work. Some of these bodies represent Scottish interests alone. . . . Independent trade associations of longer standing are also consulted.[2]

Similar remarks are found in some of the routine reports made by government departments. The Ministry of Health in an annual report said:

Throughout the year there was frequent consultation with the British Dental Association. It took place not only in correspondence

[1] Royal Commission on Scottish Affairs, *Memoranda submitted by Government Departments*, vol. iii, pp. 59–60.

[2] Ibid., vol. ii, p. 82. Sixty-nine associations—local, Scottish, and national—are listed as being consulted in the normal course of the Ministry's work. They include the Butter and Cheese Association Ltd., the Ice Cream Alliance, the National Federation of Fish Fryers, the Soapmakers' and Fat Splitters Federation, and the Wine and Spirit Association of Great Britain, ibid., pp. 83–84.

and at meetings devoted to particular subjects, but also in regular whole day meetings held at intervals of three months, at which a wide variety of subjects was freely discussed. These included disciplinary procedure, decisions of the Dental Estimates Board, the time limits within which treatment must be completed, arrangements for emergency treatment. . . .

In addition, special meetings were devoted to discussion of the scale of fees, the charges under the 1952 Act, and the list of drugs which may be prescibed under the Service. A revised dental estimate form simplified in a number of respects was introduced at the end of the year after it had been discussed in draft at several meetings with the Association.[1]

The extent to which consultation is practised can also be seen in the annual reports of various groups. All that can be done here is to indicate the type of material available. Annual reports are necessarily concise. Except in very important cases they do not detail the considerations that weigh in negotiations with the government. Nevertheless, regarded in the mass, there is a formidable body of evidence about the relations between groups and government, indicating that the initiative to consultation comes from both sides. In the 1949 Yearbook of the National Farmers' Union, the Hill Farming Committee, just one of the thirty-three committees, found several points worthy of note. During the preceding year it had successfully urged on the Ministry of Agriculture the need to accelerate the procedure for improvement schemes, and also the need for a wider interpretation of the principle that an improvement scheme had to be comprehensive to qualify for a grant. A deputation had been arranged to discuss the marginal production schemes following up a memorandum of the previous year. The usual discussion had taken place with the Ministry on the hill sheep subsidy and on the hill cattle subsidy scheme. Its views on fencing and road grids were communicated to the Ministry.[2]

In the same way the Drapers' Chamber of Trade Executive Council in its annual report for 1950 stated that through the Joint Committee on Retail Margins for Apparels and Textiles it had approached the Board of Trade to secure reconsideration of the margin position. It had successfully pressed for

[1] Cmd. 8933, p. 67.

[2] *N.F.U. Yearbook*, 1949, pp. 57–61.

the removal of price control from non-utility wool cloth and hand-knitting yarns. Representations had been made for a drastic overhaul of purchase tax. To the Board of Trade it had stressed the need for adequate representation of distributors on the Clothing Development Council. It was consulted before the Board of Trade reduced the retailers' margin on carpets, though its protests were unavailing.[1]

These brief descriptions are typical of the reports. Annual reports are only concerned with results. From them emerge references to various methods: the advisory committee, the deputation,[2] the informal meeting, correspondence, and telephone calls. This only serves to illustrate the fact that consultation is a general process adopting various forms at various times.

6

The fullness of the consultation conceded can also be illustrated by studying delegated legislation and legislation proper. For the group here is brought into consultation by the government on matters that are central to the traditional pattern of a parliamentary system. The fact that consultation now lies behind all this activity indicates the place that it has attained in our system of government.

The position of the group in relation to delegated legislation is especially clear, thanks to the Select Committee on Delegated Legislation (1952–3). This Committee circulated a questionnaire which sought to establish the procedure adopted by departments in framing delegated legislation. Several departments took this questionnaire as dealing purely with the internal procedures of the ministry. Others considered that it raised the question of consultation and answered it accordingly as the following extracts show:

The Ministry of Civil Aviation

A proposed new regulation is first discussed with any interested

[1] *Drapers' Chamber of Trade Annual Report*, 1950, *passim.*

[2] One form of this seems almost to have died out—the mass deputation at which formal set speeches were made. An example is given in *Papers and Addresses by Lord Brassey—Imperial Federation and Colonization* (1895), pp. 176–7. The names of over 100 people are given as members of a deputation in 1891 from the Imperial Federation League to the Prime Minister. Today deputations are normally much smaller and hence less formal

bodies, such as Pilots' Associations, aircraft operators, trade unions, aerodrome owners, etc.

The Ministry of Education

No body of regulations is ever put out without full consultation with outside bodies concerned.

The Ministry of Labour

In many instances, of course, subordinate legislation is only initiated after discussion with interested bodies—commonly in our case with both sides of industry.

The Ministry of Transport

In many cases the Minister is required by statute, before making regulations, to consult with representative organisations, and it is settled policy in almost all other cases, before making general regulations, to consult the representative bodies concerned. Consultation includes also any other Government Departments believed to be interested, trade unions and other outside interests.

The Home Office

It is the general practice of the Home Office, that wherever practicable, outside interests which may be affected by the regulations are consulted informally. . . The purpose of all these consultations is to secure that so far as possible regulations are agreed with the interests who will be most affected by them, though of course, in cases of disagreement it is the Secretary of State who decides what provision they shall contain.

The Board of Trade

Regulations were made after lengthy consideration, often after detailed consultation with the interests affected.

The Ministry of Food

There is also consultation with organisations representing the interests affected, such as local authorities and trade organisations.

The Scottish Office

In many cases the regulations are then either published in draft or are the subject of consultation with the appropriate advisory body or with interests affected. In some cases—for example, consultation about Police Regulations with the Scottish Police Council—this consultation is required by the statute. In others—for example, consultation with the Associations of Local Authorities about regulations prescribing the rates of expenses to be paid to councillors—it is undertaken to enable the Secretary of State to consider any representations that may be made.[1]

Throughout a large number of ministries, consultation with 'interests affected' prior to the drafting and certainly prior to the publication of delegated legislation is an established procedure. 'Interests' can generally only mean groups, for groups are the only efficient instruments for representing 'interests', as a government seeking consultation must discover.

7

Consultation generally takes place before bills are presented to Parliament. This does not mean that Parliament's position is undermined. It merely means that consultation with groups at all points is essential to the administrative system, and that without it Parliament would be presented with unworkable bills. It is an accepted fact of political life that such consultation takes place—so much so, that when it is for some reason omitted, it is the subject of comment by way of criticism and excuse.

In introducing the Licensed Premises in New Towns Bill in 1952, Sir David Maxwell Fyfe (now Lord Kilmuir) said:

> I want to make it quite clear that I have had no consultation with the trade about these provisions. May I say at once—and the right hon. Gentleman the Member for South Shields (Mr. Ede), ... would be the first to agree—that that is contrary to modern legislative practice.... Modern legislative practice is to have consultation with those who are affected by the provisions of a Bill. But in view of the feeling which has already been expressed by an hon. Gentleman opposite, and by other people, I felt in these circumstances it was better that I should produce my proposals without that consultation, because they would be my proposals and not the proposals of anyone else.[2]

Groups have come to accept consultation before legislation as part of the established order of things. In 1945 Mr. Ernest Oldmeadow, adviser to the Wine and Spirit Trade Defence Fund, said: 'Two great and grim wars have wrought a change.

[1] H.C. 310 of 1952–3, pp. 170–83, 104, 112, 121, and 61.
[2] H.C. Deb. 496, cols. 1161–2.

No sane Government would now presume to draft any important Bill without ascertaining the opinions and using the experiences of those groups of citizens who would primarily be affected by it.'[1]

Again it is possible to show the extent of this consultation by reference to annual reports and parliamentary statements. It is more difficult to go beyond that and say how important it is, and what features weigh in such consultation. Its frequency provides some measure of its importance.

Important legislation demands consultation. The Agriculture Bill of 1947 was only introduced into the House of Commons after prolonged discussion of the principles governing agricultural policy between the Ministry of Agriculture and outside bodies. It was the product of thought and discussion stretching over a long period. It was from the thought of the groups concerned as much as from the Ministry that the Bill emerged. Mr. Tom Williams, the Minister of Agriculture, quoted the statement of principles propounded by the Royal Agricultural Society, as the basis of the Bill. This had been accepted by farmers, labourers, and landowners. It was therefore natural for the Minister to be able to say:

> In translating those principles into detailed legislation, the Government have been wise enough to keep in close consultation with the main representative bodies of the industry. I refer to the National Farmers' Union, the Central Landowners' Association, the workers' unions, and the professional organisations. We sought, and we used their collective wisdom, and, if Press statements are any guide, they indicated that those bodies welcome the Measure as being a workmanlike, and indeed, a sensible scheme.[2]

Consultation seems part of the atmosphere in such a case, but consultation is even attempted when an issue is more controversial. In the White Paper on Iron and Steel presented to Parliament in July 1952 it is said:

> The Government have discussed their proposals in outline with the Iron and Steel Corporation of Great Britain, the Iron and Steel Consumers' Council, the British Iron and Steel Federation, the Trades Union Congress, the Joint Iron Council and the National Council of Associated Iron Ore Producers. . . . The Government

[1] *Wine and Spirit Trade Record*, 16 Aug. 1945, p. 954.
[2] H.C. Deb. 432, cols. 626–7.

have also had discussions with a number of trade associations on matters affecting their particular section of the industry.[1]

Such consultation is liable to be less harmonious. In this case the T.U.C. reserved its position.

The example had been set by the Labour Government. In 1946, introducing the Transport Bill, Mr. Alfred Barnes, the Minister of Transport, said:

I have had discussions—some of them informal—in the past few months on the subject with a number of organisations representing trade, industry, agriculture and transport. In addition many representative bodies have provided me with information about their transport requirements.[2]

Where there is a definite party attitude, the function of consultation may be limited. Groups are not likely to be consulted on the main principles involved, but only on the best means of implementing those principles.

Where controversy cuts across party, consultation provides the means to its solution, as in the Education (Miscellaneous Provisions) Bill of 1952 which provided a more or less satisfactory result for the long-drawn-out controversies on Catholic and other religious schools, after what the Parliamentary Secretary described as '. . . consultation with those best qualified to speak for the local education authorities, for the teachers and for the denominations'.[3]

The majority of the bills discussed in Parliament do not arouse much controversy either between or within the parties. It is in consultation on such legislation that the group is most influential. For it is in such cases that the government's attitude is most flexible, the legislation in many cases arising out of group representations. The Restoration of Pre-War Trade Practices Bill of 1951 arose out of the advice given to the Minister of Labour upon problems put by him to the National Joint Advisory Council, as a result of which he was able to say: 'Its objects have the support of the British Employers' Confederation, the Trades Union Congress and the nationalised industries, all of which are represented on the N.J.A.C.'[4]

It would be possible to multiply examples of such consultation.

[1] Cmd. 8619, p. 2.
[2] H.C. Deb. 431, col. 737.
[3] Ibid., 509, col. 106.
[4] Ibid., 480, col. 1263.

The Dentists Bill introduced into the House of Lords in 1951 was the subject of consultation with the British Dental Association, 'together with numerous other bodies'.[1] The Local Government (Financial Provisions—Scotland) Bill of 1954 was the result of consultation with the local authorities' associations on the working of the equalization grant.[2] The Baking Industry (Hours of Work) Bill of 1953 was based upon the Reese Committee set up as the result of trade union representations, to which unions and trade associations gave evidence and on whose report consultation took place.[3]

A good example of the extent of this consultation is given by the list of bodies consulted on the Pensions (Increase) Bill of 1946. It includes the Staff Side of the National Whitley Council, the various associations representing local authorities, the National Association of Local Government Officers, the National Union of Teachers, the Educational Institute of Scotland, the Police Federation, and the Chief Constables' Association. In these circumstances it is not surprising that it was claimed that the Bill embodied 'the greatest common measure of agreement that could be arrived at'.[4]

8

That these developments have been challenged is not surprising. Extending as they do throughout the system of government, it might have been thought that they would have been the subject of greater comment. Parliament, supposedly jealous of its prerogative, might have been expected to challenge a tendency to move active debate upon legislation to the offices of government departments. The fear of this has placed one important limit upon such consultation before legislation. It is only in very unusual circumstances that the actual draft of a bill will be discussed between the department and the group. That, civil servants assert, would infringe the prerogative of Parliament. Consultations take place only on general govern-

[1] Cmd. 8655, p. 48. Time was not available for the Bill to proceed to the House of Commons in that session.

[2] Convention of Royal Burghs, Annual Convention, 1953, *Agenda*, pp. 68 and 87.

[3] *Bakers' National Association Review*, 25 Dec. 1953, pp. 2804–5.

[4] H.C. Deb. 431, col. 655.

ment proposals. The amount of detail revealed varies.[1] In 1946, almost immediately before the introduction of the National Health Service Bill and the publication of the explanatory white paper, Mr. Bevan explained the proposals to various organizations such as the Negotiating Committee representing the British Medical Association and other organizations of the medical profession.[2] He placed before them a 12-page document outlining the scheme. Secrecy was imposed on that Committee, which was unable to discuss the proposals with a wider circle.

These limitations on consultation are not sufficient to protect the system from some critics, of whom the most persistent has been Mr. Bevan himself. On three major occasions he has criticized consultation with groups. In 1943 he attacked the position taken up by the Home Secretary on the Workmen's Compensation (Temporary Increases) Bill. He alleged that the Home Secretary wanted the Bill passed, not on its merits, but because it had been agreed by the Federation of British Industries and the Trades Union Congress.

> Now we have reached the position [he said] where the Home Secretary discusses for many weeks with trade union representatives and with representatives of employers a piece of legislation. I do not at that point disagree, because it is good constitutional practice for Ministers to receive representations from specialists on what they think should be the form of legislation. It happens every year when the Chancellor of the Exchequer is preparing his Budget. Deputations are received and are listened to courteously and specialists' advice is taken and various organisations consulted.
>
> But when the Home Secretary proceeds from that point to actual negotiation and agreement with the parties, a position is reached of the gravest constitutional impropriety. Trade unionists and Ministers of the Crown set the Constitution on one side. . . . I do not represent the Federation of British Industries, nor do I represent the Trades Union Congress. I happen to represent the constituents of Ebbw Vale. When I go back to my constituents I expect them to hold me to account for what I have done, and I do not expect if they disagree with anything I have done to be able to explain it away by saying that I did it on the instructions of some outside body.[3]

[1] On the Budget the government will not give any information in consultation as to the proposals to be included therein.

[2] *British Medical Journal*, 2 Mar. 1946 (S), p. 45.

[3] H.C. Deb. 392, cols. 1593–4.

Three years later he was to make the same point in defending himself against the accusation of not having held adequate consultations on the National Health Service Bill:

Of course, the real criticism is that I have not conducted negotiations. I am astonished that such a charge should lie in the mouth of any Member of the House. If there is one thing that will spell the death of the House of Commons it is for a Minister to negotiate Bills before they are presented to the House. I had no negotiations, because once you negotiate with outside bodies two things happen. They are made aware of the nature of the proposals before the House of Commons itself; and furthermore, the Minister puts himself into an impossible position, because, if he has agreed things with somebody outside he is bound to resist Amendments from Members in the House. . . . The House of Commons is supreme, and the House of Commons must assert its supremacy, and not allow itself to be dictated to by anybody, no matter how powerful and how strong he may be.[1]

Behind these criticisms lies a mistaken view. Consultation and negotiation are not clearly separated, but if by negotiation Mr. Bevan implied that ministers enter into binding agreements with outside bodies, he was criticizing a situation that does not and did not exist. For it is the great limitation for groups that the ministers cannot bind themselves. Mr. Chuter Ede has said: 'Is it not quite frequently the continual complaint from people whom the Secretary of State, or the officials meet: "We are expected to act as plenipotentiaries and bind ourselves, whereas you have the get out that if this looks like giving you trouble in Parliament you may throw us over"?'[2] The minister's position in relation to a group is a strong one. If Parliament's position is threatened, it is not because the group can control parliamentary divisions, but because the minister can. If this is a real threat the answer lies not in limiting consultation or negotiation, but in limiting the power of ministers. Consultation and negotiation serve only to assist in preparing workable legislation. They cannot bind, because the group has not the power to bind, as Mr. George Isaacs made clear on the issue dealt with by Mr. Bevan in 1943: 'The parties who negotiated pressed

[1] H.C. Deb. 422, cols. 60–61.

[2] H.C. 310 of 1952–3, q. 633. See also q. 632. 'Is not the usual formula employed in such negotiations. "This is all subject to the final approval of Parliament"?'

their negotiations as far as they could, and when they realised that they had secured the most they possibly could, they decided not to press their opposition any farther, but to allow the matter to go forward. In no circumstances did we reach agreement.'[1]

More reasonable is the criticism that more attention is paid to the views of groups than of M.P.s. Mr. Bevan made this point to the Select Committee on Delegated Legislation (1952–3). Groups can discuss delegated legislation before it is published, M.P.s but rarely:

A further suggestion I would respectfully make is one of even greater substance. It has been said in the course of evidence before your Committee that one of the advantages of present-day legislation is that Ministers consult all sorts of expert opinion and interests especially affected before they present the Orders to Parliament. This is all to the good so far as it goes but it means that the only body which is denied the power to influence an Order except in the ways I have already described, is the House of Commons itself. . . . It should also be kept in mind that it is Parliament's function to protect the general interest, whereas the Minister will have been in consultation with special interests and very often these are of considerable power and influence in the community.[2]

Stronger criticisms of the whole tendency to consultation were voiced by Sir Herbert Williams in 1951. The occasion was an attempt by the Labour Opposition to write into the Home Guard Bill a requirement that consultation should take place with the National Joint Advisory Council before the operative clause of the Bill could come into effect:

After all, who are these people we are supposed to consult? They are a few people who come into being through a body called the T.U.C. and who come into being through certain employers' organisations. They are not elected in any popular way. Their contact with the people is not a tenth as close as that of any hon. Member of this House, and it seems to me that the opinion of Sir Vincent Tewson . . . or of Sir John Forbes-Watson . . . on this issue is worth precisely nothing.[3]

These arguments attack a very important assumption of the system of consultation; that these groups fully represent sections

[1] H.C. Deb. 392, col. 1599.

[2] H.C. 310 of 1952–3, p. 145.

[3] H.C. Deb. 494, col. 1155.

of opinion which cannot express themselves properly through any other channel and certainly not through M.P.s in any direct sense. Upon this assumption—sometimes too readily made—has been built the system of consultation.

However, criticisms of the system are rare as it is fully accepted by both major parties. It is true that several times during the 1951–5 Parliament, Labour M.P.s sought to make out that the Government was reluctant to consult fully with groups and compared unfavourably with the previous Government in this respect. Mr. Harold Wilson made this point on several occasions. For example, in 1954 on the committee stage of the Cotton Bill he said: '. . . on any important question affecting the cotton industry I made it my business to consult the unions and employers personally, and not through officials.' He compared this with the procedure on this Bill:

> During the Recess, in the last two days of September or the first two days of October, the Minister caused two highly responsible officials to meet the legislative council of the United Textile Factory Workers' Association. The council were not consulted in the sense of being informed of what the Government had in mind. They were told that there were a number of courses open to the Government in relation to the future of the Commission and their views were invited. That is all that happened.[1]

But such complaints are part of the routine of parliamentary debate. For example, in 1949 under the Labour Government Sir Thomas Dugdale complained of the lack of consultation on the Sea Fish Industry Bill:

> I should, however, like to ask the Minister that a reasonable time should be given for consultations to take place before we reach the Committee Stage of the Bill. It would appear that up to the present there has been practically no consultation with the various branches of the industry. Perhaps the Minister would inform the House, for instance, whether the British Trawler Federation were consulted in any period before the Bill was introduced; were their views sought before the Bill was in draft form? Turning to another section of the industry, I have a letter in my hand from a federation of one of the principal trades in the industry who say that, far from being consulted, the first notification they had of the Bill at all was the daily Press notices.[2]

[1] Standing Committee Debates, Committee A, 26 Jan. 1954, cols. 371–2.
[2] H.C. Deb. 465, col. 764.

There can never be perfection in consultation and there are always a number of complaints that it has not taken place or that it has taken place at the wrong time or in the wrong manner. These complaints are not made against any one government, though it may be possible that the decrease in legislation and the removal of controls slightly lessened the need for consultation between 1951 and 1955.

These complaints of failure in consultation are, however, few compared with the records of successful consultation. In some cases they are merely complaints about the method of consultation followed. But the important point is that both the complainer and the minister accept the propriety of and the necessity for consultation. It is regarded as a sound and proper complaint in Parliament that groups have not been consulted before members.

9

Most of the groups so far considered are sectional groups.[1] They represent a section of the community: it may be farmers, it may be furniture makers, it may be old age pensioners. Their function is to look after the common interests of that section and their membership is normally restricted to that section. The group's aims and purposes are determined by the common needs of those members.

There is, however, another class of groups best described as cause groups. They represent some belief or principle: it may be the abolition of capital punishment, it may be the welfare of animals, it may be the creation of a strong navy. They seek to act in the interests of that cause. Theoretically their membership is not restricted at all. Anyone can join and by doing so signify his acceptance of the belief or principle. The aims of the group are determined and are not dependent upon the needs of members, though they may be modified by their views.

Many of these cause groups are not admitted to consultation. This does not mean that these groups cannot send in their views to government departments or cannot write to ministers. These things are impossible to stop. But it does mean that these

[1] This phrase is adopted from an article by Mr. Allen Potter entitled 'British Pressure Groups', *Parliamentary Affairs*, Autumn, 1956, pp. 418–26.

groups are not regularly called in for advice and consultation by the government.

The cause group represents only a point of view about the way in which the government or Parliament should act, in many cases a point of view very far from being generally accepted. But even when its viewpoint is accepted, the group cannot expect to be automatically consulted. It is not necessary to the conduct of affairs. The cause group can only ensure consultation by its prestige, by its knowledge, and by its experience. Some have succeeded in doing this.

The National Society for the Prevention of Cruelty to Children secured by parliamentary and other activity the recognition of the principle that it was right and proper for the state to intervene in the interest of children's welfare. The question did not end there. The conception of child welfare is being extended. Also the administration of the law has brought to light new problems, which the N.S.P.C.C. through its inspectors has quickly grasped. But since 1909 it has acted through consultation with the departments concerned. Its knowledge and experience render consultation with it essential to the government.

The Royal Society for the Prevention of Cruelty to Animals and the Howard League for Penal Reform are in much the same position. But bodies like the Lord's Day Observance Society or the National Anti-Vaccination Association have not achieved consultation in the sense that they are regularly admitted by the government into discussions on legislation or problems of administration.

There are some sectional groups which are not recognized by the government for the purpose of consultation, either because the section is not sufficiently important or because the group is felt not to represent the section fully. Sections can be subdivided to such an extent that the government can see little or no point in discussions with groups which represent but fractions of a section otherwise represented.

The claim of certain groups to represent a section may be disputed by the government which does not consider their membership sufficiently large to justify their claim. The struggle of the Engineering Officers' (Telecommunications) Association to obtain recognition from the Post Office, which reached its height in 1950 and 1951, is an example. For though this may be regarded as a special case in that the issue was one of recognition for the purposes of trade union negotiations, nevertheless, the principles and problems are the same though thrown into a sharper light.

Often enough the issue may not be thrown up so sharply. Groups may complain they are not consulted enough, but it is difficult to evaluate their claims. More often than not their claim may be for the shop window rather than for serious attention. Certain it is that many groups are satisfied that they are consulted on most important issues.

10

In this chapter the emphasis has been laid upon the desire of the government to consult, rather than the groups' attitude to consultation, which will be considered later. Enough has been said, however, to show that a relationship exists between groups and government in which both parties feel able to meet freely in discussion of common problems.

It is against the background of this relationship that the problems of group strategy will be considered. For this relationship is the dominant factor in the political situation faced by most groups.

CHAPTER III

Group Strategy

I

THE pressure group adopts various methods to achieve its aims. These methods can be classified according to the institution upon which the pressure is directed. There are, for example, group activities centred on the ministries, centred on Parliament, centred on the press, or centred on public opinion.

The immediate purpose of a group's activities gives no indication of the ultimate purpose. That some activities are directed at influencing public opinion does not mean that the alteration of public opinion is the group's ultimate purpose. Ultimately a group seeks to influence those institutions which carry the power of decision upon its demands, but in order to achieve that influence it may be useful or even necessary to influence other institutions. A study of the locus of group activities illustrates the interrelationships between institutions of which the pressure group makes use. This can perhaps be described as a study of the strategy of the pressure group.

Methods can be taken to mean the particular techniques which the group uses at various centres of activity. Attempts to influence the ministries generally fall within the framework of consultation. Public opinion may be influenced by petition, poster, pamphlet, or public meeting. Parliament may be influenced by the activities of individual M.P.s or the activities of lobbyists. All these techniques may be described as the tactics of the pressure group.

Some writers have used the word 'methods' as a means of describing those factors which may give the groups influence rather than the particular techniques by which they achieve it. For example, Mackenzie has classified as one of the method of groups 'the best information'.[1] It is possible to describe such factors as group methods in that they are matters which are to some extent under the conscious control of the group and it may

[1] Mackenzie, op. cit., p. 142.

be policy to develop them. They can, however, better be described as factors leading to group success.

This chapter is devoted to clearing the ground for an examination of the role of parliamentary activities in the strategy of the pressure group. In order to establish this it is first necessary to say something of the general strategy of the group. It will be useful for this purpose to draw a distinction between discreet pressure and open pressure. This is in part a distinction between pressure direct on the ministries and pressure exerted through one or other institutions. It is a fact that many though not all the techniques of pressure directed—at Parliament, press, or public opinion—involve an open declaration of position. The techniques of pressure direct on the ministries are the techniques of consultation and are in their nature discreet.

The situation is working in favour of consultation, as it is working in favour of discreet pressure. Consultation is a two-way relationship. The government has been seen to be ever ready to take the initiative in consultation, but the group also has problems to raise. The development of consultation to meet a need of the government, has also met a need of the pressure groups. If it is accepted that today the aims of the group are rarely major legislation, but rather minor amendments to a given framework and the safeguarding of the group's interests within that framework, then it is this discreet form of pressure that best meets the groups' requirements. The group is more concerned with the politics of detail than the politics of issues. For many of its needs pressure, other than on the government, would be inappropriate. It would be using a sledge-hammer to crack an acorn. Trade associations and trade unions act for their members on individual cases. If these can be solved merely by taking them along to the ministry it would be foolish and unnecessary to waste time securing an intervention by an M.P. inside or outside the House.

In the same way when problems on, for example, the interpretation of regulations arise it would be sheer inefficiency to try to solve them through banner headlines and mass meetings. The group does not exist for the support of public relations departments. It exists to secure results, not to perpetuate methods. The machinery exists to solve these problems and it is to that that the group will turn.

The appropriate place to challenge legislation (and sometimes delegated legislation) might be thought to be Parliament; for it is there that the formal process of enactment takes place. But the group has the opportunity to raise matters before a bill is drafted for presentation to Parliament. Representation can be made at this point with the minimum of effort and the maximum hope of success. A minister is more likely to be responsive to a suggestion made before his mind is declared, than to accept it when doing so would involve withdrawing from a publicly stated position. A group prefers not to fight against prestige.

Consultation is welcomed by most groups, by most group leaders, and especially by the permanent officials who over time have developed friendly relations with their opposite numbers in the ministries. They are able to take their problems to the ministries and they know that they will be consulted by the civil servants on most of the questions that concern them. They are naturally reluctant to embark on political ventures when the more familiar methods of committees and correspondence are open to them. Often their background is professional or administrative. In some cases they are ex-civil servants. Rare, indeed, is the appointment of a man whose background is political.[1] Even the trade unions are tending to separate more and more their political and their industrial functions. Negotiation has precedence over agitation.

Typical of the attitude of many groups towards consultation is the statement by the Trades Union Congress on its relationship with the Government, after the 1951 election had returned the Conservative Party to power:

It is our long-standing practice to seek to work amicably with whatever Government is in power and through consultation jointly with Ministers and with the other side of industry to find practical solutions to the social and economic problems facing this country. There need be no doubt, therefore, of the attitude of the T.U.C. towards the new Government.

. . . Since the Conservative Administrations of pre-war days the range of consultation between Ministers and both sides of industry has considerably increased and the machinery of joint consultation

[1] Mr. Emrys Roberts, Liberal M.P. 1945–51, later became Director of the Branded Textiles Group, but this example is exceptional. More common are the group officials who later enter Parliament.

has enormously improved. We expect of this Government that they will maintain to the full this practice of consultation.[1]

Significant, too, is the development of the 'right to be consulted'. Though these actual words are rarely used, groups have come to use the language of moral compulsion about consultation, and to protest most strongly at any omission in the protocol. They see consultation as a necessary part of their existence. The right to consultation, though never formally conceded by the government, has been conceded to such an extent in practice that any failure in the normal procedure is treated as an injustice by the group concerned.

In 1951 the Minister of Food announced that in preparing the government plans for slaughterhouses he had consulted the organizations concerned. This claim was soon answered. The secretary of the Association of Municipal Corporations wrote to the Ministry of Food saying:

I am writing to place it on record that no consultation has taken place with this Association. Having regard to the extensive interests of local authorities, and particularly the borough authorities, in the subject of hygiene, meat inspection and slaughtering. . . . I feel that my Association will consider that it is most regrettable that a Government department could have overlooked the desirability of conferring in a matter of this kind with those local authorities upon whom so many statutory duties rest.

The reply from Sir Alan Feavearyear (then Permanent Secretary of the Ministry) stated:

I am sorry that you feel so strongly about our failure to consult your Association before the Minister's statement was made in the House of Commons. I can assure you that this was not due to any deliberate act on our part, and if you feel we have been discourteous I readily apologise.

On the other hand, I am bound to say that I think the right time to consult your Association is now that the broad lines of a national plan for slaughterhouses have been announced.[2]

When in 1946 the Ministry of Works introduced a building materials' priority scheme, it failed to hold prior consultations with the National Federation of Building Trade Employers.[3]

[1] *Labour*, Nov. 1951, p. 65.

[2] *Municipal Review* (Supplement), Dec. 1951, p. 258.

[3] *National Builder*, May 1946, p. 243.

This body protested, pointing out that this was contrary to the normal and desirable practice and in this particular case it claimed that the result had been an unworkable scheme. The Ministry expressed its regrets at the omission.[1] Consultations then took place with both this and other bodies as a result of which the scheme was modified.[2]

The National President of the National Federation of Meat Traders' Associations in giving evidence to the Select Committee on Estimates in 1949 said of the Ministry of Food's consultative machinery:

I should say that on the whole it has worked fairly well. The only point that does arise sometimes is that in attendance on the Consultative Committee decisions are communicated to us, whereas we have many times felt that we should have been in right from the first before decisions were actually taken. Nevertheless, many decisions are taken after consultations have taken place; but on the whole the Consultative Committee does work well.[3]

The significant point about these examples is not that consultation sometimes breaks down—even the T.U.C. has had complaints[4]—but that the groups regard the right to be consulted as of fundamental importance to their activities. For whether admitted to consultation as fully as they would wish or not, they see in it the most effective means of exerting influence. Without it they feel deprived of an important weapon. In 1947 the National Association of Local Government Officers was considering whether or not to affiliate to the T.U.C. It was thought necessary to examine all the advantages and disadvantages of such a step. To this end the General Secretary prepared a report of which one of the sections on the advantages is headed 'Access to Government Departments':

It has been said in the past that NALGO could get all the information it wanted and bring to bear all the influence it needed through direct access to Government departments. This was only true at any time in a very limited sense and in relation to the class of question (superannuation, compensation, etc.) for which precedent is already established; and all such access as NALGO has had in the past, it has in fact retained; but this does not meet the position today

[1] *National Builder*, May 1946, p. 267. [2] Ibid., July 1946, p. 302.

[3] H.C. 283 of 1948–9, answer to q. 1883.

[4] e.g. See Mr. Shinwell's speech on the Home Guard Bill, H.C. Deb. 494, cols. 1151–5.

when the Trades Union Congress is the centre of reference on any wide question of national policy affecting organised workers. Ministers and departments are not willing to refer to isolated bodies on questions of this kind. Why should they, and involve themselves in unnecessary controversy by selecting some and not others, when they can go to the body which is recognised to speak as the voice of the organised salaried and wage-earning classes in general? The tendency in the future, amid the great pressure of legislation, and economic and social change, will be stronger than ever for Governments to consult the large comprehensive bodies; and to think that isolated units can be brought within the range of this kind of consultation is to lose all sense of reality.

If it is the desire of the Association to win prestige by its contributions to any large issues of policy in the world of local government (a question on which the Association has as yet no settled policy) there is no other avenue through which it can effectively do so except the Trades Union Congress. The Association has never yet been consulted on pure questions of policy affecting local government by any Government department, or by the local authority associations. Some if not all of the latter have indeed shown unmistakably that they resent the intrusion of NALGO into the sphere of policy, apart altogether from the question that the Association has itself in many cases, after making a tentative approach to a policy of offering views on questions of policy, thought it wiser not to persist. If the Association feels that the time is arriving when it should have some voice in, or at any rate be allowed to contribute its views upon, any major questions of policy (not politics) affecting the world of local government, then, in view of the attitude of local authorities and their associations, it can most effectively do so by securing its own footing in the Trades Union Congress and being acknowledged there as the voice which should be heard when such questions are under consideration.[1]

2

The permanent officials and the other leaders of the groups who have experienced consultation fully realize its value—perhaps too fully. It induces in them an attitude of distrust towards other forms of pressure, a distrust that can be excessive.

Many of these other methods lack the discreet and routine quality which is one of the attractions of consultation. They imply publicity and a declaration of issues, where consultation

[1] *Local Government Service*, Jan. 1948, p. 9.

means private discussion and the possibility of compromise. To the group leaders the choice appears to be one between subdued and forceful pressure. There is no doubt which they prefer.

On many issues the subdued pressure of consultation is the most appropriate weapon for the group. But there are moments when the group is faced with greater issues and the group must consider whether to supplement its use of consultation with other methods of pressure; to campaign actively and publicly against a decision in an endeavour to make the government change its mind. It is natural for group officials to feel that forceful pressure is unlikely to achieve anything. They are closely in touch with the way departments have been thinking. If it is a matter on which they have been brought fully into consultation, they are likely to feel that they have achieved all that can be achieved.

The *Brewers' Journal* has shrewdly summed up this point. In 1948 Mr. L. R. N. Percey, the Secretary and General Manager of the Licensed Victuallers' Defence League, had spoken at the annual conference of that body about a proposed petition for a reduction in taxation on beers, wines, and spirits and had said that a small sub-committee had considered the proposal and was now awaiting the moment to launch the petition. For 'In the opinion of these men who had experience of such matters the proper time had not yet come for launching the petition'. The *Brewers' Journal*, comparing this proposal with a nineteenth-century petition, said:

> We conceive, however, that Sir Stafford Cripps is made of sterner stuff [than Lord John Russell] and, in any case, the long-winded approach foreshadowed by Mr. Percey can leave the perspicacious Chancellor under no delusion as to the spontaneity of the proposed protest against the beer tax, even though the monster petition be launched at the psychological moment appointed by the experts in these matters. The plebiscitary rejection of the financial expedients of governments, though it still appears to be completely operative in France, is in this country probably to be regarded as obsolete. A reasoned argument against the present excessive figure of the beer duty could derive no added weight from the appending to it of some thousands of signatures.[1]

[1] *Brewers' Journal*, Sept. 1948, p. 373.

On some matters the group leaders know they are faced with a political decision—in the party sense. There may have been consultation, but around and about a principle already decided. Understanding the political factors behind a decision they accept its finality.

In reply to a demand at the annual general meeting of the National Federation of Building Trade Employers in 1948 that meetings should be organized in every locality to bring to the notice of the public and the Government the contribution which private house-builders could make if they were freed from restrictions, Mr. Hearder, the Director-General said: 'It had to be recognised, however, that Mr. Aneurin Bevan was not likely to change his mind readily as to the respective merits, from the political point of view, of local authority and private enterprise housebuilding.'[1]

Similar realism was shown towards the Town and Country Planning Bill in 1948:

> While condemning the confiscatory provisions of the bill, the committee reluctantly concluded that there was no possibility of successfully attacking the main principles on which it was based as these had, to a large extent, been accepted by the previous Government. Having regard to these factors, the Housebuilding Committee decided that, instead of arranging to contest the passage of the bill in Parliament, the efforts of the Federation should be concentrated upon attempting to secure, by direct negotiations with the Minister of Town and Country Planning, some modification of those provisions in the bill which were regarded as being particularly harmful to the future of private enterprise housebuilding.[2]

The fact that consultation is the most appropriate method of dealing with the general run of problems and one that appeals to the leaders of the group, does not explain the degree of distrust for other methods. One must bear in mind the difficulties they involve. It is not easy to use them effectively. Party discipline can provide a barrier to a House of Commons campaign. Public opinion is difficult to arouse. But these and like factors are still not a sufficient explanation. They can to some extent be overcome. One must look elsewhere for an explanation of the degree of distrust.

There is a multiplier effect here. Amongst many groups

[1] *National Builder*, Feb. 1948, p. 147. [2] Ibid., p. 135.

there is a fear that a campaign might destroy the valuable position which they hold in relation to the government. The more important consultation becomes, the more important it is that nothing be done which would disturb it. That this view is exaggerated in that consultation is of value to the government as well as to the group and therefore not lightly to be overthrown, does not matter if the groups in fact think that way. There is substance in their view. Consultation is most effective when it is regarded as apart from the public arena of politics, regrettable though that may be.

The National Federation of Building Trade Employers brought out this point in its journal in 1947:

> Attacks on the Government are usually regarded as news, and the more vicious they are the greater their news value. But it is easier for such attacks to be made by a Federation not represented on the various Government Committees than by one which is. Attacks by the latter must be made with a full sense of responsibility, they must be fully justified if any value is attached to maintaining reasonably good relations with the Ministers and the departments with whom almost daily touch, whether of a formal or an informal character, is maintained. Such relations would soon cease to exist immediately a Federation became political in the party instead of in the industrial sense.[1]

3

The effect of these considerations on the groups can be seen in the gradual alteration of group strategy that has followed the growth of consultation. The decline in the importance of group pressure in Parliament illustrates this. Examples can be found in most groups.

Until the general election of 1945 the British Medical Association used to send questionnaires to candidates for Parliament. The National Farmers' Union regularly promoted private members' bills in the 1920's,[2] besides sponsoring candidates for Parliament.[3]

It is doubtful whether since 1945 the Federation of British Industries has tried to organize any parliamentary campaigns

[1] *National Builder*, Aug. 1947, p. 2.

[2] e.g. in 1922 a bill to amend the Railway Fires Act and a bill to amend the Ecclesiastical Tithe Rent Charges (Rates) Act, the latter being passed. *N.F.U. Yearbook*, 1923, p. 199.

[3] See pp. 173–8.

on the scale of that against compulsory amalgamation of coal-mines in 1938 or that against the national defence contribution in 1937.[1] The T.U.C. has undergone great changes in outlook since the days of the General Strike and its attempt to organize a vast pressure campaign against the Trade Disputes and Trade Unions Act of 1927.

The civil service unions differ from most of the other groups in that their relationship to the government is parallel to that between a trade union and an employers' association. But the government was late in developing negotiating machinery and the first endeavours of civil service unions were advanced by pressure campaigns rather than by the use of the strike weapon.[2] The creation of the National Whitley Council and the growing confidence placed by the government in it have discouraged the use of parliamentary activities by the civil service unions on matters that fall within its scope, although they are still resorted to, in certain cases. The general policy of the Staff Side of the National Whitley Council is to discourage any such activities, since they detract from the importance of the Council, and might destroy the confidence the government has in it.

In 1915 the Webbs described the National Union of Teachers in these terms:

> 'Teachers' Politics' have, in fact, been the most admired and the most condemned of the activities of the NUT; and at particular elections in various constituencies 'teachers' politics' have made a substantial addition to the cross-currents and vocational cleavages that complicate the working of modern Democracy. The 90,000 organised teachers scattered throughout the country, living and working in close intimacy with the most numerous section of the electorate; well-conducted, methodical, through their membership of the NUT experienced in committee work, competent Press writers and frequently clever talkers, are, it is clear, if carefully directed from a centre, able to exercise on the representative system of the country a considerable influence, both as lobbyists and canvassers and as elected representatives. It is this power which has enabled

[1] S. E. Finer, 'The Federation of British Industries,' *Political Studies*, Feb. 1956, pp. 77–78.

[2] See W. J. Brown, *So Far . . .* (1943), pp. 98–105, for a description of a powerful lobbying campaign in 1922–3. The issue was the starting pay of temporary clerks passing into the clerical class, an issue now clearly reserved for negotiation and arbitration.

deputations of the NUT to speak with confidence to Education Ministers, and which has led to the frequent private conferences between the permanent officials of Whitehall and the permanent officials of Mabledon Place.[1]

The interesting point about this quotation is that the Webbs felt the need to explain these consultations and based their explanation on 'teachers' politics'. Today the consultations stand in their own right and teachers' politics, though still present, no longer play such an important part in the life of the union.

In all the bodies mentioned there has been a depreciation in the value placed upon active public or parliamentary pressure. Yet relics of the older viewpoint survive. In many bodies the committee or council which is mainly concerned with negotiating with the government upon bills or other matters is still known as the parliamentary committee. The change in function has not been met by a change in title as it was in the case of the T.U.C. in 1921. Amongst the bodies which fall into this category are the Brewers' Society, the National Farmers' Union, the National Association of Master Bakers, the Incorporated Federated Associations of Boot and Shoe Manufacturers, and the Law Society. Other left-overs of more active days are political funds, many of which, trade unions apart, have become moribund. Indeed, it can hardly be maintained that the political fund has the same importance in the trade unions that it once had. Though from certain points of view it may still be important for the unions to sponsor M.P.s, it is now considered undesirable for general secretaries to be in Parliament. In part it is a question of time, but it also reflects a change from the days when parliamentary activity might be the only means the union had of making representations to the government.

4

It might be surprising that a petition is ever launched, a public protest meeting held, or an M.P. bombarded with letters, apart from the fact that occasionally an issue arises strong enough to break even the restraints felt by group leaders. But there is one general factor working in the other direction. The membership of a group not only likes to get

[1] *New Statesman* (Supplement), 25 Sept. 1915, p. 5.

value for its money; it likes to see itself getting value. It does not see the discussions going on with the government in the way it sees a public campaign. It does not appreciate the value of a letter to an under-secretary as it appreciates a question in the House of Commons.

In 1946 the Deputy Chairman-Elect of the Building Societies' Association felt compelled to defend the Association's attitude to consultation at the annual conference:

Lastly it is said that the Council is in fear of Government departments, particularly the Treasury, the Ministry of Health and the Board of Inland Revenue, to an extent which is contrary to the best interests of building societies; and it has, in fact, been suggested to me that the need to avoid criticisms from such ministerial quarters has been used on occasion to coerce societies into action which they do not desire, or to deter them from a course of action which they desire to take. Opinions on this matter may differ, but I think it cannot be denied that the maintenance of friendly relations with Government departments, as a result of which there is ready access to Government officials, and the policy of negotiation and, if necessary, compromise, have achieved much for which little credit has been given.[1]

But it is in the association or union with a large membership that the pressure for action is greatest. In trade associations representing large firms, most of the members have an outlook similar to that of their leaders, but in other groups the restraints upon action are not so readily appreciated. Their members are further from 'political reality'.

In the years immediately succeeding the war the annual conferences of N.A.L.G.O. were marked by demands for action and yet more action to secure equal pay. The annual conference only demands; it does not need to plan. In 1947 the Executive argued that all possible action had been taken, and if it was not effective, that was not the fault of the Executive:

There were many other campaigners in the field, and the Council took its share in their activities and was associated with practically every movement in the country aimed at securing equal pay. At the same time it was pressing the claim on the National Joint Council at every opportunity; for example, the proposals for the consolidation of salaries omitted all sex differentiation.

[1] *Building Societies' Gazette*, July 1946, p. 262.

But the motion asked for more than this—it called on the Association to take the lead in a national campaign. To start yet another movement was neither necessary nor desirable, and it would involve heavy expense. . . .[1]

But this did not satisfy those members who wanted an immediate victory. They were not prepared to accept the Executive's view of the limitations of the position. They could not believe that a victory was impossible at that time. It is doubtful whether the equal pay campaign would have been supported with such fervour by so many organizations if it had been left to their national executives.

The National Union of Agricultural Workers has found itself in a dilemma that stems from the same source: the different judgements made on the political possibilities of a situation by executives and members. Its members demand action to secure the abolition of the tied cottage. Its leaders believe that they have tried or are trying every reasonable method of securing this aim which they fully accept. Yet the tied cottage is not abolished and the members demand further action to achieve it. The Executive Council must be conscious of the comparative weakness of the Union, and this knowledge may lie behind their reluctance to organize any large-scale public campaign, and some of the strange reasons advanced against it. For example, at the 1950 annual conference, the President reminded delegates that if they acted on the suggestion of lobbying M.P.s county by county, some of them would be talking to Tory members only.[2]

Too often the ordinary member does not consider the situation in which a demand is made. In moving a resolution he is not concerned so much with its practicability as with its desirability. A pressure group moves in a world of restraints, and the member does not always realize this so readily as the leaders. He comes to the annual conference with a list of demands. In his view it is the task of his group to satisfy these demands. Often he merely receives explanations of the difficulties involved, because the demands are not adjusted to the capacity of the group. At the 1946 annual conference of the National Union of Teachers, a member moved a resolution on the subject of

[1] Speech by a member of N.A.L.G.O.'s Executive at the annual conference, *Local Government Service*, July–Aug. 1947, p. 372.

[2] *Landworker*, June 1950, p. 7.

teachers supervising school meals. It called on the Executive to 'take the necessary steps to bring about the deletion from the Education Act (1944) of that part of the Act which places this work on the teachers and makes it compulsory'. There was a demand made; there was no thought given to how it was to be attained. Yet this is the whole problem of the groups. Their problem is not the ordering of society as they would have it; it is how to secure as much of their aims as possible given the limitations of their position. The Executive poured scorn on this resolution, which ignored such points in expressing the simple desires of a branch. The resolution called for the Executive to remove the provision from the Act 'but in that case they had to ask themselves where were their friends? Could they go to Parliament? could they go to the Press? could they go to the public with any real hope of success?' The answer was obvious, at least to the Executive (though there were cries of 'yes' from members), but this did not mean that the situation was hopeless. Only that it was not a simple case of demand and satisfaction. The best course was to approach the Minister of Education, who would secure that local authorities took measures to solve the problem. 'There was no party in Parliament that would accept responsibility for altering the Education Act.'[1]

The supporters of the resolution were even told that the part of the Act they wished to remove was a safeguard for them. What a political world they had left unconsidered; they were even prepared, all unknowing, to undermine their own foundations, or so their leaders said.

No group can satisfy all its demands in consultation. That is a method of compromise. The dilemma of the group lies in its attitude to the unsatisfied demands. How great they are depends partly upon the way the group frames its demands, taking as a basis the greater needs or lightly felt desires. But however demands be framed, groups cannot attain equal satisfaction, nor is it right they should, for they do not represent equally important interests. It is in dealing with the residual discontent that the group's problem arises. It is impossible to say how any one group will solve it. The factors vary from case to case. But the restraints upon a group using more public measures or starting a campaign are great. Too much is at

[1] *Schoolmaster*, 2 May 1946, pp. 408–11.

stake. The campaign is a risk. It has now become abnormal, an action that requires decision and explanation. Consultation is the routine. Its explanation is obvious and it is entered into naturally and automatically. There are factors which lead the other way, of which the attitude of the membership is the most important, but over and above it all is the general rule of consultation first and foremost.

The supremacy of consultation provides the most useful weapon for the analysis of the behaviour of pressure groups in Great Britain. It does not mean, however, that consultation is the only technique of pressure used by the group. There are other discreet methods of pressure apart from consultation; there are, of course, groups which are not even admitted to consultation; there are occasions when the group feels the need for more than discreet pressure. The usefulness of the supremacy of consultation as a weapon of analysis is that it enables examination to be concentrated on these points: the points that require explanation.

It is from this standpoint that the activities of the group in relation to Parliament are examined. In doing so it is important to discuss not merely those activities which are located in the House of Commons itself such as the sponsoring of amendments or those activities in which M.P.s take part, such as deputations to ministers on behalf of the group, but also all those activities which are intended to bring about action by M.P.s or by the House of Commons and those activities on which intervention by M.P.s in the House of Commons is designed to have an effect. In this way the activities of the group in relation to the House of Commons will be given their place in the general strategy of the group.

CHAPTER IV

Enemies and Allies

I

BEFORE beginning to outline the particular problem faced by the groups in relation to the House of Commons, one other general point must be made.

The group cannot ignore the attitude of other groups. It exists in a world of groups. Other groups are making decisions on matters that concern it. Some may be hostile to it, others may be friendly to it. The group must adapt its tactics to these circumstances.

These considerations apply at all levels. Whether the group is consulting with the minister or the ministry, whether it is seeking amendments in the House, whether it is organizing a campaign or endeavouring to secure a friendly passage for a private members' bill, the attitude of other groups is important to it. The groups operate in limited politics, the issues in which are group issues, the standards in which have been set by past group activity. The most powerful argument for or against a group is the attitude of another group.

2

There are some groups which form pairs in hostility. Their whole purpose is to defeat the other group. The policies of the League Against Cruel Sports are in direct opposition to those of the British Field Sports' Society, and those of the Sunday Freedom Association to those of the Lord's Day Observance Society. In many cases one group calls into existence its hostile partner.

It is only in the cause group based upon some common principle, that the singleness of purpose needed for such clear hostility can be found. A sectional group concerned with an economic interest is more likely to find its enemies varying with circumstance. The licensed trade can be said to be pursued with single purpose by the temperance movement, but the clarity of purpose is more on the one side than the other. For the licensed trade as organized for pressure is not a group committed to the cause of 'unrestricted drinking', but to the more complex interests, economic and personal, of the trade and its members. It is not surprising that the temperance movement opposes any relaxation of the licensing hours, but up to a point so does the trade.

It can never be said that two sectional groups are perpetual enemies. A group defined by a cause may be logically opposed to another group. No change of circumstance can alter the fact that to support blood sports is irreconcilable with opposing them. But sectional groups define their spheres differently. They are not based on principle, but upon the needs of their members, which may change with circumstance. These needs are too complex to be expressed in clear-cut hostility.

The division between employer and employee is important and the groups representing one side are often opposed to those representing the other, but on many issues they are brought together. The needs of the industry accomplish this. The Theatre Entertainments Tax Committee was formed in 1954 by all sides of the theatre industry, through their respective groups, to advocate the abolition of that tax.[1] In 1950 the National Union of Agricultural Workers and the Transport and General Workers' Union joined with the National Farmers' Union and the Country Landowners' Association on a deputation to the Ministers of Agriculture and of Town and Country Planning to urge that good agricultural land should not be taken for development.[2] In 1938 the Joint Committee of the Mining Association and the National Union of Mineworkers had an interview with the Secretary of Mines in order to ask him to obtain powers for the coal-owners to exact a levy on all coal produced for the purpose of subsidizing the export industry.[3] Such developments are inevitable.

3

The alliances of the groups are more permanent. This is

[1] Cf. *Manchester Guardian*, 17 Feb. 1955: 'A recently formed committee representing the leading trade union and management organisations of the British theatre, music-hall and circus has appealed to the Chancellor of the Exchequer for the complete abolition of entertainments tax in the living theatre.'

[2] *Farmer and Stockbreeder*, 1 Dec. 1950, p. 3118.

[3] W. A. Lee, *Thirty Years in Coal* (1954), p. 120.

quite natural since the group itself is an alliance. It may be formally a federation, composed of local associations, or it may have individual membership, but its object is to bring together in a national organization a number of individual firms, members, or organizations, with common interests. The organization can never be so formed that complete agreement exists between the component parts. But unity of purpose exists, at least over a defined field.

The purpose can be so defined that the group can represent more or fewer people: according to whether the emphasis is laid upon the matters uniting or the matters separating interests, the pattern of the groups in a given field will be unitary or fragmented.

The fragmented pattern does not mean that the groups do not realize the value of unity. They can form an alliance as groups, where other interests are united in one group. Some groups cover more complex fields than others. This does not mean that unity is necessarily increased. There are differences within the organizations, rather than between them.

The purpose of an alliance between groups may be to express a certain common purpose, which in other situations is expressed by a unitary organization. It is not easy to say how far this principle can be carried. There will come a point in organizations when the concept on which unity is based becomes so general and covers so many differing interests and impulses, that the unity achieved becomes unreal and so much autonomy has to be given to the separate interests that they become separately existing groups.

The Trades Union Congress could theoretically alter its constitution and the trade unions theirs, so that the former became the governing body for the whole trade union world. But in practice it might mean little, since such autonomy might have to be accorded to the separate interests that little useful change would be brought about. There seems to be a point where an interest is sufficiently clear and distinct for it to be best expressed in autonomous existence and since the governing factor in any interest is self-interest, it will seek to achieve that level of expression. Other purposes can then be expressed by alliances between the groups.

The T.U.C. provides the clearest example. So constituted that it does not hamper the activities of the individual unions, its primary purpose is to act as a pressure group on behalf of general trade union interests. Representations by trade unions made separately would lack the coherence and force that comes from a unified viewpoint. The Federation of British Industries,[1] while fulfilling similar functions, differs in structure in that it has as members not merely individual groups, in this case trade associations to the number of 285 in 1953, but also in the same year over 6,600 individual firms. In this it resembles the National Union of Manufacturers, which had in membership 5,400 firms and 75 trade associations.

The common interest which unites the National Road Transport Federation is clearer, because more closely defined. It was set up during the Second World War as a body to represent the common interests of its three member associations—the Road Haulage Association, the Passenger Vehicles Operators' Association, and the Traders' Road Transport Association, all of which were new organizations constituted as a result of a review by the previously existing organizations. It was specifically stated that it would 'take all practicable steps to secure the greatest measure of unified action between the Associations, thereby enabling the industry to speak with one voice on all possible occasions'.[2] The need to secure effective and efficient representation to government or to Parliament is a motivating force in the formation of alliances and the recognition of a common interest. The Conjoint Conference of Public Utility Undertakings, which flourished until the nationalization of the gas and electricity undertakings removed two of the three participants, was another example. The multiplication of statutory regulations necessitated a common approach, from a common pool of knowledge.

[1] The F.B.I. is not the direct parallel of the T.U.C. There is also the British Employers' Confederation which contains in membership the national employers' organizations. Its relations with the F.B.I. are very close. They occupy the same building and in 1947 the F.B.I. approved the principle of amalgamation. On that occasion Lord Baillieu, the President, moving it on behalf of the Council said: 'We have been confronted with a dyarchy which at times has confused our councils and lessened their effectiveness. I doubt whether any business would survive—much less prosper—if its organisation and control were fashioned on the lines of the BEC.–FBI. relationship' (*British Industries*, Jan. 1947, p. 9). Nevertheless, amalgamation had still not taken place in 1956.

[2] *Commercial Motor*, 25 Feb. 1944, p. 73.

In this last example it is clear that the interests were not merely separate, but hostile on some questions. The existence of an alliance does not preclude the possibilities of differences between the groups, differences which may be fought out in the public arena. There have been strong differences of opinion between the National Federation of Off-Licence Holders' Associations and the groups representing the on-licensees, which are the Licensed Victuallers' Defence League of England and Wales and the Licensed Victuallers' Protection Society of London Ltd.[1] Yet for many purposes these groups are allies. Their common interests as retailers are expressed through the National Consultative Council of the Retail Liquor Trade. Their common interests in the licensed trade are expressed through the National Trade Defence Association, that historic body which has been the main defence of the licensed trade against the attacks of the prohibitionists and temperance reformers. Each relationship reflects a different level of interest which members of the groups share with one another.

Organization round an industry of all the sections and groups engaged in it, at least on one side of the employer–employee relationship, is necessary if representation is to be made effective. The pharmaceutical bodies banded together from 1926 to 1943 to support a parliamentary fund. The four associations representing the secondary school teachers act together on most matters in relation to government, Parliament, and public. The Motor Legislation Council represented the motor industry including in membership the Society of Motor Manufacturers and Traders, and the Motor Agents' Society. In the same way federations have been formed among trade unions, such as the Printing and Kindred Trades' Federation, in which all the unions falling under that classification have joined. Most of these federations are primarily, in some cases solely, concerned with the industrial or negotiating function of trade unions. The Staff Side of the Whitley Council is an alliance produced directly by the machinery of negotiation. It has an existence outside that as the representative organization of general civil service union interests. Nevertheless, the Staff Side does not normally pursue forceful pressure activities. These activities are generally carried through by *ad hoc* combinations. At the 1950

[1] See pp. 139–40.

general election, the Civil Service Clerical Association, the Civil Service Union, the Society of Civil Servants, and the Institution of Professional Civil Servants made a joint effort to secure promises from candidates on the subject of equal pay. At the same election, twelve civil service unions combined to approach candidates on the issue of political activities by civil servants. But the Staff Side itself confined its activities to representation through the appropriate machinery.[1]

There is a simple pyramidal pattern in these alliances which pleases the lover of orderly classification. The particular character of these alliances derives from the fact that each alliance is of the same character as the groups within it. They accept the same basic method of classification by trade and industry.

There are some federations which run counter to this system of classification. Their existence can be said to be due to the need to fill in gaps or cover up weaknesses in the basic pattern of groups. The British Road Federation is an organization which in March 1954 had a membership of 107 trade associations, varying in type from the Association of British Chemical Manufacturers to the Caterers' Association, the National Dairymen's Union to the Wholesale Textile Association. It represents the interests these groups have in common on questions of road maintenance and road transport. In other words this alliance is not based on the general functions of the interests represented, but upon one of the factors in the achievement of those functions. The basis of classification is changed. It is true that this is one of the interests which could be represented by the F.B.I., but it was evidently felt that special emphasis was needed.

The Fair Prices Defence Committee is another example of the way in which the configuration of group alliances can depart from the basic pattern, in this case because of attacks upon a particular practice—re-sale price maintenance. The result has been to make all the groups concerned conscious of their common interest and to bring them together in a permanent alliance on that question.

One of the purposes of trade union federation is to enable alliances to be formed on a different pattern from that which

[1] *Red Tape*, Feb. 1950, pp. 148 and 156.

is determined by the divisions between unions. For example, the National Federation of Professional Workers contains sections of such unions as the National Union of Railwaymen or the Union of Shop Distributive and Allied Workers besides complete unions such as the Clerical and Administrative Workers' Union or the Transport Salaried Staffs' Association. This Federation has been active in questions arising out of the Gowers report on non-industrial employment which concern only part of the former unions. Its existence helps those parts to secure representation, which otherwise the pattern of group division might have hindered.

It has been assumed that as far as lines can be drawn, a firm has only one group to join for each interest it wishes represented. Often the firm will only wish to join one group, since that group will itself recognize all the interests of the member, by joining in alliances with other groups. This is less likely to be true of the multifarious interests of the individual person.

But there are some fields in which the whole assumption breaks down. There are fields which seem to breed groups overlapping and competing for the same members and the same supporters. There are four major anti-vivisection societies, and the animal welfare world also contains bodies like the Council of Justice to Animals, Our Dumb Friends' League, the R.S.P.C.A., the Universities Federation for Animal Welfare, and specialist bodies like the National Canine Defence League or the Pit Ponies' Protection Society. It is sometimes suggested that the reason is that it is possible to raise more money with a variety of bodies appealing for public support, than if one body were to do so, but it is doubtful if it is worth the confusion caused by the difference of emphasis and approach used by the groups. These are differences to be settled within rather than between groups.

An incident in the House of Commons, a prelude to the storms which were to beset the National Canine Defence League,[1] is an example of this confusion. Sir Thomas Moore speaking on the Dogs (Protection of Livestock) Bill in 1953 said.

The second criticism comes from the Secretary of the National

[1] At the annual general meeting in 1954 Sir Thomas Moore was elected chairman in circumstances of extreme acrimony. His election and that of the Council were later invalidated by the High Court (*The Times*, 15 June, 1956.)

Canine Defence League. I have been associated with the National Canine Defence League, on its Council and in various other ways for the past 25 years, but I was never consulted about whether this protest should be made and I wonder how many other office bearers were consulted.

The R.S.P.C.A. for whom I have the authority to speak are warmly in support of the principle of the Bill.

He could not spare himself one parting shot at the National Canine Defence League: 'The R.S.P.C.A. believe that they have a duty to the sheep as well as to the dogs.'[1]

This disagreement can hardly have increased the influence of the animal welfare societies. Short of uniting in one group, the best solution seems to be that adopted by the temperance movement. The National Temperance Federation has been created by the various temperance bodies. Dominant among them is the United Kingdom Alliance which, although only one of twenty-two members of the Federation, contributed over a third of the finance in 1952.[2] These groups have agreed to leave the bulk of their parliamentary work to the Federation. This secures a unity in representation which prevents confusion. It is true that since 1951 there has been a Federation of Animal Welfare Societies, but it has not yet been allowed to take over the parliamentary work of the separate associations.

The Council for the Preservation of Rural England and its allies in Wales and Scotland are particularly happy alliances. They unite in membership a variety of bodies, many of them local organizations, some closely concerned in the countryside and some more remotely. They also have an individual membership. The Councils are of importance in their own right, in a way that the National Temperance Federation is not intended to be.

Competition could be said to exist between the motorists organizations but it is hardly a real problem. The Automobile Association, the Royal Automobile Club, and the Scottish Royal Automobile Club have working arrangements, which are carried over into the field of group representation by a joint committee. The dangers of competition between ex-servicemen's organizations are avoided in a different manner. The

[1] H.C. Deb. 512, col. 1767.

[2] *National Temperance Federation Report* (1952), p. 24.

smaller ex-servicemen's organizations have usually been content to leave most issues and especially pensions work to the British Legion.

The National Council of Women is a more complex alliance since, besides containing groups representing women, it also contains a number of cause groups such as the League against Cruel Sports or the N.S.P.C.C. It contains professional bodies such as the Educational Institute of Scotland and political bodies like the Women's Liberal Federation. This variety of constituent bodies seems likely to rob the Council of any clear uniting interests except in the most general terms. It is possible for an alliance to be too wide.

These are but a fraction of the number of alliances. They take a wide variety of forms in federations, working committees, and conferences. Whatever the form, they represent some interest the allying groups share. They are not mere tactical alliances, but alliances based upon an interest. They are in fact pressure groups based upon pressure groups. They may attain a status of their own, beyond the status or importance of the supporting groups.

4

These are the permanent features of the world in which the pressure group lives. Among these features, new situations develop, which necessitate new alliances or bring new enemies. In these situations the permanent alliances are important and the group must learn to use them, but it must also learn to make new alliances.

The first effect of a new situation in which the group needs to make representations either to government, to Parliament, or beyond, is to unite all those with a like attitude. It may be that they are already members of an alliance and then all that is required is that the federation or working committee should reaffirm its position, and those within use it, as a co-ordinating body.

The need for unity is emphasized by the dangers of separate representations. These can do a lot of harm. They can be in their number irritating rather than helpful. It might be thought that a large number of separate expressions of opinion would impress, but a bombardment is not judged by the number of shells, but by their power and accuracy. Both are increased by co-ordinated representation.

It is a common enough phenomenon. After the Gowers report on non-industrial employment, the National Federation of Professional Workers was active in endeavours to secure government action, but realized that these endeavours would be most effective if co-ordinated with other groups. Consequently in November 1952 it arranged for the Non-Manual Workers' Advisory Council of the T.U.C. to represent it. This Council contains representatives of the General Council, the unions concerned, and the Federation.[1] It can be regarded as a subsidiary alliance within the machinery of the T.U.C. and in using it, the Federation was merely demonstrating the value of this alliance.

Similarly, between 1944 and 1947 the policy of N.A.L.G.O. on the question of the transfer of and the compensation for public assistance officers, in view of the various proposals for national insurance and assistance, was co-ordinated with a number of groups closely concerned. In 1944 a joint committee was set up consisting of N.A.L.G.O., the Association of Chief Officers of Social Welfare, the Local Government Clerks' Association, the National Association of Administrators of Local Government Establishments, the National Association of Social Welfare Officers, and the Scottish Association of Welfare Officers.

> The County Public Assistance Officers' Society was precluded by its constitution from membership of the committee, but members of the society gave helpful co-operation. This joint committee was considered to be fully representative of the public assistance officers who would be affected by the social insurance legislation.[2]

The group acts as common sense would suggest in seeking unity of action.

A group will seek to extend its support and win over groups only indirectly concerned or concerned in a different way. The Council of the Rural District Councils' Association, for example, received and considered in April 1947 a memorandum submitted by the Joint Consultative Committee of the National Farmers' Union, the National Union of Agricultural

[1] *N.F.P.W. Report*, year ended 31 Mar. 1953, pp. 6–7.
[2] *Local Government Service*, Feb. 1947, p. 272.

Workers, and the agricultural section of the Transport and General Workers' Union on the subject of rural housing.[1] It agreed to support suggestions made by the British Legion to the Ministry of Health that local authorities should give preference to ex-servicemen for council houses.[2] They decided to take no action on a letter addressed to the Minister of Transport by the Railway Act 1921 Traders' Panel asking for a similar panel to be set up under nationalization.[3]

The extension of a group's support is an important part of its strategy. The resultant alliances are a useful guide in an analysis of the interests involved in any given political situation.

There are some occasions when the support of a particular group can be very effective, as when the British Fields Sports' Society secured the support of the N.F.U. for its campaign against the Bills to abolish hunting.[4] The agreement between the County Councils' Association, the Urban District Councils' Association, the Rural District Councils' Association, and the National Association of Parish Councils provided strong backing for the C.C.A.'s attitude to local government reform.[5] That these Associations had been able to resolve their differences and agree upon a common policy appeared to reflect upon the attitude of the Association of Municipal Corporations.

To win over a former opponent is a great step forward in a campaign to convince the government of the need for action on a group's demands. The government is often reluctant to act where two strong groups oppose each other, as on local government reform. It was to eliminate possible opposition that the N.F.U. engaged in a campaign during the war to persuade industry and commerce of the importance of government action to maintain a prosperous agriculture. It stressed the value of a rural market in approaches to local chambers of commerce and of trade. Its great triumph was when the Manchester Chamber of Commerce, the traditional home of free trade, moved a motion at the annual meeting of the Associa-

[1] *R.D.C.A. Circular*, 1947, p. 87.
[2] Ibid., p. 103.
[3] Ibid., p. 104.
[4] See pp. 132–5.
[5] In 1953 representatives of these Associations prepared a memorandum on local government reorganization which was accepted by the Associations in 1954 subject to certain amendments. *Public Administration*, Summer, 1953, pp. 176–87, and Autumn, 1954, pp. 331–49.

tion of British Chambers of Commerce commending the N.F.U.'s policy and saw it carried.[1] This support was cemented when, not long afterwards, the N.F.U. joined the Association and still further strengthened when, in 1950, it joined the F.B.I.

In particular situations the support of particular groups is important. But there are some groups whose importance in the community is such that to gain their support is valuable on most if not all issues. A group's importance derives largely from the interest it represents and it may be that the interest in question, such as that represented by the F.B.I. or that by the T.U.C., is so crucial to the community that views expressed by these groups are of importance on all issues. But over a period of time it is possible for a group to gain prestige over and above that of the interest represented. The local authority associations are perhaps examples. Whenever a group comes to exercise influence, then that group itself becomes subject to pressures both external and internal with the object of gaining its help. To some extent these groups become channels for pressure; this is not surprising; it is but part of the process of decision-making. The extent to which it takes place emphasizes the influence of the group in question.

The constituent unions of the T.U.C. use its machinery to forward demands for which their own influence is too slight, albeit they are not matters of general trade union interest. At the 1954 conference of the T.U.C. a variety of motions were passed or remitted to the General Council which were of this nature. The National Union of Agricultural Workers obtained the support of Congress for a motion pressing for immediate action to speed up rural water supplies.[2] The Association of Scientific Workers secured the passing of a motion calling upon the Government to take measures to meet the shortage of qualified science teachers.[3] Equity demanded measures to protect the rights of British actors in commercial television.[4] The National Union of Public Employees tried to secure Congress support for the 44-hour week in the national health service.[5] The Women Public Health Officers' Association sought more training facilities for physically handicapped children.[6] The

[1] *A.B.C.C. Annual Meeting Report*, 1945.
[2] *86th T.U.C. Report*, 1954, p. 492.
[3] Ibid., p. 338.
[4] Ibid., p. 475.
[5] Ibid., p. 347.
[6] Ibid., p. 341.

result of the passing of these motions was to secure the representations of the T.U.C. to the appropriate ministries. It is natural that those who have the opportunity should seek to use this great influence when their own is proving insufficient. Perhaps the most important use made of the T.U.C. by subordinate groups in recent years was in 1950 when the Congress, against the advice of the General Council, passed a motion recommending the immediate introduction of a scheme for equal pay. As a result the influence of the T.U.C. swung into the movement with representations to the Government, and the political importance of the equal pay issue was increased.

There is bound to be a large tactical element in the forming of alliances of this nature, yet a group cannot hope to go beyond its own interests, and the patterns of alliance and hostility that are formed on issues are a guide to the balance of interests in the community on any question. The pressure groups draw a map of their world, but it is a map that describes real features of society, even though sometimes it may be a little imperfect.

CHAPTER V

Parliamentary Routines

1

IN laying down the principle that consultation is the main feature of the strategy of pressure groups, it has been allowed that there can be no question of consultation being used alone. There are other techniques of pressure. There are political institutions to be influenced other than minister and ministries. Parliamentary activities clearly have a role to play. In this and the next two chapters these activities will be examined in order to assess the part they play in group strategy—the sort of occasion on which they are used.

A distinction must be made between those actions which result from group activity—such as the tabling of an amendment or the asking of a question—and the actions actually taken by the group to bring this about. Both will necessarily be dealt with in these chapters, but later it will be useful to examine in detail the particular techniques the group uses in order to bring about action by the House of Commons or by M.P.s.[1]

In this chapter various activities will be examined which are examples of discreet pressure in Parliament. They are for the most part associated with consultation, so much so that they seem almost a part of it.

2

There is a stage before consultation. Consultation cannot take place without something to consult about, nor can the government bring to that consultation an open mind: it will have certain predetermined ideas and views, in particular where it takes the initiative in consultation.

A group which wishes to exert as much influence as possible will seek, by a well-designed public relations policy, to influence the formation of governmental opinion. In the last years of the Second World War most sections of the community foresaw a

[1] Chapters VIII and IX.

period of new developments in governmental policy. There was, as a result, a wealth of thought and research upon the fundamental problems facing each group. Agricultural policy provides a striking example. In the period 1943–5 most major agricultural groups published statements of their views on post-war policy. There was a belief that merely by publishing their views, well argued and documented, they were contributing something to the atmosphere in which political decisions are taken.

Many groups influence the formation of governmental opinion through their parliamentary activities. They seek to build up relationships with M.P.s in one or both of the parties that will ensure the group at least some degree of influence. This relationship can take many forms,[1] but whatever form it takes it can endure only as long as it is of advantage to both parties. The M.P. can gain from the group information, research, and a definite point of view upon the detailed issues which take up the bulk of parliamentary time. He may be adding to experience and knowledge already his, he may be responding to the needs of his constituents, or he may, more exceptionally, be entering a completely new field. But whichever it is, a group can be of great assistance to him. An M.P. is in danger of being isolated, unless he has a means of keeping in touch with outside interests. The other sources of information open to him are strictly limited.

This relationship can be important to the group. The views given by a group may be given more or less weight as they are held to represent an important or a minor section of opinion. This, though it is affected by certain other factors, is also a matter for political judgement. Thus the support of M.P.s can be a powerful aid in maintaining the prestige and position of the group.

Some comments by the British Road Federation in its annual report for 1953 show an attempt to influence the formation of parliamentary opinion:

The past year has also been particularly notable for a broadening of the front, so far as Parliamentary interest in road matters is concerned. In Parliament, as elsewhere, what is 'everybody's business' has a tendency to become 'nobody's business' or at best the business

[1] See pp. 152–84.

of a few specialists. But the development during recent months of campaigns for modern road communications, such as in South Wales, Lancashire, the Midlands, London, the Highlands, and so forth, has encouraged an increasingly wide range of Members of Parliament, representing constituencies in the areas concerned, to take a really live interest in road problems which are equally the concern of the British Road Federation.

. . . Such reflection in Parliament of the growing public demand for road improvement has unquestionably been most influential in persuading Her Majesty's Government to take road matters more seriously. . . .[1]

In a more general way the groups seek to keep the whole body of M.P.s informed of their views. This can be done by circulating periodical literature. The British Road Federation circulates to all M.P.s its *Monthly Bulletin*, which gives news on road problems, particularly problems relating to the need for road reconstruction. It is in form a publicity journal, making a great feature of support for its policies in speeches or reports of other organizations and committees. The National Farmers' Union's *Information Service* is of a different type: severely practical, it endeavours to present impartially agricultural problems. There is the *Monthly Bulletin*, a journal concerned with the licensed trade, which hardly deals with any practical problems at all, trying rather, by articles about the good old English inn, to conjure up a general feeling of goodwill among its readers.

These are all publicity journals designed to appeal to outsiders rather than to members. Certain organizations such as the National Union of Agricultural Workers and the British Legion circulate their ordinary journals among some or all of the members of the House of Commons. Then there are organizations which circulate special reports or bulletins upon matters on which they feel M.P.s should be informed. For example, in 1953 the Institute of Fuel circulated the presidential address on 'Fuel and Society'.

Not overmuch importance can be given to these activities. The end of most of these publications is the M.P.'s waste-paper basket, and the groups realize this. But there is always the hope that an occasional point may be read or an article glanced at.[2]

[1] *B.R.F. Annual Report*, 1953, p. 7.

[2] See pp. 219–20 for a further discussion of this point.

3

There are some specific cases where the group has tried to influence the formation of governmental policy on a definite issue by parliamentary action. The problem of the repair of dwellings under controlled rents had long been recognized by all parties to be a difficult one. The National Federation of Property Owners attempted to use this feeling to bring about an agreed solution. It believed that the small majority of the Government in the period 1950–1 would render the parties more amenable to compromise. As a result of its activities, an all-party meeting of back-benchers was held which discussed with the Federation's representatives its policy, out of which came a plan for a deputation to the Minister of Local Government and Planning. This was prevented by the general election, to which the Federation ascribed the breakdown of its policy. 'The change of Government inevitably produced a change of opinion in the House and, though the Federation continued its all-party approach, the chances of success inevitably diminished.' This explanation is a little ingenuous: rather the explanation of the failure is the impracticability of a policy which considers that 'the Rent Restriction Acts . . . should be taken out of the arena of political strife'.[1] Such issues are rather the meat of our democracy.

The local government associations which have been trying to secure support for their version of local government reform face a different situation. Their problem is not one on which the ideologies of party clash. If it is desirable for them to pursue the problem by an all-party approach, then that method is open to them. But there is nothing necessarily valuable about an all-party approach. It would have been striking if the National Federation of Property Owners had really brought it off. No eyebrows are raised on learning that a Labour and a Conservative county councillor are in agreement on local government reform. It would be more surprising if they were not. The divisions have not been formed on party lines. On the one hand, is the Association of Municipal Corporations; on the other, stand the Rest, for the County Councils' Association, the Urban District Councils' Association, the Rural District Councils'

[1] *Property*, July 1952, p. 23.

Association, and the National Association of Parish Councils have been able to agree on proposals for local government reorganization.[1] The M.P. will tend to support whichever group predominates in his constituency. Thus both points of view find ready support in the House of Commons. Besides, there are in the House many active members of local authorities. This means that there has been a lot of discussion which stands the greater chance of being influential because it has taken place prior to the formation of government proposals.

4

More often the group is concerned with an actual decision of government, whether it is a decision to act or a decision not to act. The group is more likely to be concerned with the immediate impact of government policies than with long-term reorganization. In 1943–5 most groups put forward declarations on long-term policies, for the times seemed ripe for making plans; but now the groups are mostly content to accept the framework of action laid down.

It may seem that any attempt to secure a change of attitude in the government's declared policy by parliamentary action might savour of that degree of hostility which must hinder the growth of trust necessary to the proper working of consultation. But this is not so. There has been developed a form of action that still preserves this relationship. It is seen most often in amendments to proposed legislation.

Suppose the government has presented a bill to the House, which represents the considered views of the appropriate ministry or ministries upon the representations made to them. A group's views may not have been accepted. It is possible for that group to have the issue raised in the House of Commons without there being a question of an open challenge to the government. Normally the group does not expect to see its amendment carried against the government; if it is, the group may find the position more embarrassing than helpful.[2] The

[1] In June 1953 they circulated their original proposals to all M.P.s, an example as much of a group giving M.P.s necessary information as of propaganda.

[2] In 1949 an amendment supported by civil service unions was carried against the Government in the Standing Committee on the Superannuation Bill. It was reversed on the report stage and served only to place some of the M.P.s connected

tabling of the amendment does secure, however, that the group's proposal will be looked at again, that the views of some reasonable outsiders will be brought to bear upon it, and that the government will have to state its position clearly, and hence re-examine it to see that it is sound.

The moving of group-sponsored amendments is a very common form of activity, and can take place without any heat, and without any need to rally much support. It is recognized by the ministries as being part of the routine of their relationships with groups. For it is essentially a quiet operation. At its simplest it involves no more than the tabling of the amendment by an M.P. and a slight discussion in a standing committee free from the embarrassment of publicity desired by neither party. Occasionally a ministry will invite a group to arrange for an amendment to be put down to test feeling and to secure discussion. This stage is not a new approach, following on the failure of a previous approach. An amendment in the House may follow consultation, but it is equally likely to accompany it. A close examination of one case may bring out some of the salient points.

5

The Association of British Chambers of Commerce regularly promotes amendments to the Finance Bill. It has developed over the years a set procedure for dealing with the problems presented by the Bill; it has become a routine.

The Association was founded in 1860 and had then in its membership sixteen chambers of commerce. In 1954 it numbered a hundred among its members, including all the larger ones, such as London, Manchester, Birmingham, and Glasgow. Being an association composed of constituent local bodies, each of which has strong support and a healthy tradition, it must needs refer more problems to them than many other associations do to their members. Since the local chambers of commerce include representatives of commerce, trade, and industry, the interests of the Association overlap with other associations. For this reason we find it co-operating with them,

with the unions in an awkward position; cf. Mr. C. Smith's (an M.P. and an official of the C.S.C.A.) speech to the C.S.C.A. Conference.—*Red Tape*, July 1949, pp. 324–5.

and especially with the Federation of British Industries. The Finance Bill provides a good example of that co-operation.[1]

The action of the Association in promoting amendments to the Finance Bill is one stage of a continuous process. The main emphasis in this process is on consultation with and representation to the government. It is only as a part of this process that the promotion of amendments can be understood; without it, such action must be trivial or useless.

The first step normally taken by the Association in preparation for the Budget and the Finance Bill is the deputation and the letter or memorandum to the Chancellor of the Exchequer. The deputation can be dispensed with as in 1946,[2] but the letter or the memorandum is invariable. It is published, and often receives prominent mention from the press and from the B.B.C. More important, because more likely to be effective, is the meeting that takes place—also before the Budget—with officials of the Inland Revenue Department to discuss the more technical problems which fall within the Finance Bill.

After the Budget Speech has been made and the Finance Bill published, the Association is faced with a different situation. The government is now committed, not merely on the general principles of the Budget, but also on the details. It will be prepared to amend, but with far less readiness than before, whether the approach is made inside or outside the House of Commons. Nevertheless, the Association of British Chambers of Commerce, along with many other bodies, considers that the possibilities are sufficiently great to justify action being taken. It first endeavours to secure the views of its constituent Chambers of Commerce and from them to build up a list of amendments required. It endeavours to secure agreement with the Federation of British Industries and as far as possible to act along with it.

The Association's point of view is given public expression in the second reading of the Finance Bill or on the budget proposals, by some M.P. closely connected with the Association. He does not officially express its view, but his position is such

[1] For a general description of A.B.C.C. with special emphasis upon its contacts with the government see *Chambers of Commerce Manual*, 1954–5, pp. 1–11.

[2] It was considered by the Association but too late for action to be taken. A.B.C.C. Council Minutes, Mar. 1946, p. 137.

that his views are likely to coincide with those of the Association. For example, in 1946 the Chairman of the Finance Committee of the Association reported to the Committee both the Chancellor's speech and that made by Sir Arnold Gridley (now Lord Gridley).[1]

For the Association has been fortunate in having M.P.s closely associated with it. Lord Gridley has filled the office of President, and many other M.P.s have served on its Council. These are M.P.s whose connexion with the Association is the normal one, having been appointed to their position by local chambers. There are other M.P.s who have served in the position of honorary secretary or honorary adviser to one of the committees. These, one must surmise, are appointed at least partly because of their parliamentary position. The result is that the Association has no difficulty in securing the expression of its views, for one must assume that a Member of Parliament is unlikely to hold a position in an association from which he differs in attitude.

Views expressed on the second reading must be concerned with more general points and hence are not likely to have a great effect on the government's proposals. For although a government may amend in detail, it is unlikely to be convinced of the fallacy of the main points in a budget. In 1946 the Association sought amendments to raise the earned income allowance and to speed up the payment of post-war credits.[2] These were matters on which the Government had come to a definite policy decision.

However, on questions like the actual application of the excess profits tax, it was more likely that amendment would be achieved provided the Association accepted the actual principle of the tax as a *fait accompli*, and argued on that basis. In May the Association sent representatives to a conference with the Inland Revenue Department at which various such points were discussed.[3]

Not obtaining satisfaction on all points, the Association determined to arrange for the outstanding questions to be raised in the House. This decision can only be regarded as reasonable if we assume that the Association hoped to be able to

[1] Ibid., May 1946, p. 3.
[2] Ibid., June 1946, p. 17.
[3] Ibid.

persuade the Government. It is true that the Association may have merely wanted the issues stated publicly but, though this might reasonably apply to its more general amendments, it seems unlikely in the case of the more detailed ones. These latter amendments can only have been moved as part of the process of persuasion and argument. It is of interest to note that the three amendments covering the more general points sought by the Association were moved by members of the Conservative Party unconnected with it or with the Federation of British Industries. Since they covered questions of such general interest, it is quite likely that the Association had no direct connexion with these amendments. On the other hand, it is possible the Association may have had some influence in getting them full Opposition support. This wider party support may have been gained either through the M.P.s associated with the Association or by direct representations to the Conservative Party's Finance Committee, as happened in 1945 when it was addressed by Mr. Bower, an Association Vice-President.[1] (The Association also expressed its willingness to meet the equivalent Labour group, but in fact the Association generally confines its contacts to members of the Conservative Party.)

These general amendments dealt with post-war credits, earned income allowance, and stocks held by retailers of goods upon which a reduction in purchase tax had been made.[2] The debates on these questions followed the normal party political pattern with the possible exception of the latter, where the Minister conceded the need for a solution.[3] It has been a recurring problem, and in this case the Opposition was not helped by the fact that, though it was supported by the Association, the Minister claimed the support of the National Chamber of Trade (whose interests were very closely concerned) for his clause.

The other amendments which the Association supported were discussed in a very different atmosphere. The first, which was to secure a clarification on a point concerning income tax, was moved by Sir Arnold Gridley, who refrained from making a speech because he considered the point already sufficiently

[1] A.B.C.C. Council Minutes, Nov. 1945, p. 61.

[2] Two were moved by Mr. Osbert Peake and one by Mr. Ernest Marples, H.C. Deb. 424, cols. 397, 427, and 471.

[3] Ibid., col. 423.

discussed.[1] The Opposition divided the House, but failed to carry the point.

Next the Solicitor-General himself moved an amendment to cover a point raised by the Association and referred to by Sir Arnold Gridley and Sir Peter Bennett (now Lord Bennett of Edgbaston) in the second reading. A recent House of Lords decision had appeared to render shareholders in foreign companies liable to a double payment of income tax. The case having been put to them, the Government had admitted the need for a solution.[2]

The first of a series of amendments concerning the excess profits tax was moved by Sir Arnold and sought to spread back 'rehabilitation' costs over the war years.[3] The Chancellor of the Exchequer in reply related this amendment to the series of amendments being proposed. He made it clear that all these amendments must be regarded as a consequence of consultation:

> The Federation of British Industries and the Association of Chambers of Commerce have been in touch with us, and on a number of points we have been able to meet them. On a certain number of points we have not been able to do so. As the Debate proceeds we shall be able to tell the Committee where we have been able to meet them and where not.[4]

This particular amendment he did not accept, but he said that this refusal should be viewed against the new clause he was going to move. In these circumstances Sir Arnold withdrew his amendment, pending consideration of the new clause.

The next amendment supported by the Association was moved by Sir John Anderson (now Lord Waverley) and permitted an extension of the meaning of 'rehabilitation costs', but he withdrew it upon a promise by the Chancellor to reconsider the matter,[5] as did Sir Arnold Gridley after meeting the same response on the next amendment.[6] The next bloc of amendments moved by him was negatived without a division.[7]

The Solicitor-General then moved two clauses[8] which again arose out of representations made by the Association and the Federation of British Industries. These were largely accepted by Sir Arnold, but he moved one amendment which was rejected

[1] Ibid., col. 704.
[2] Ibid., cols. 712–15.
[3] Ibid., cols. 736–46.
[4] Ibid., col. 745.
[5] Ibid., cols. 746–53.
[6] Ibid., cols. 753–9.
[7] Ibid., col. 768.
[8] Ibid., cols. 899–90 and 909–10.

on a division.[1] A new clause moved by Sir Arnold on the issue of rehabilitation costs was not pressed to a division after the Chancellor had promised to reconsider the matter.[2]

A new clause supported by the Association, which was moved by Mr. E. H. Keeling, was accepted in principle by the Chancellor, and on that assurance withdrawn.[3] An amendment moved by Sir John Anderson on the question of estates duty was negatived upon a division.[4]

This was the last of the amendments moved at the committee stage which the Association records as being supported by itself and by the Federation of British Industries.[5] But the process continued, for the Association selected certain points as suitable for consideration on the report stage. The drafting of the amendments to be moved was left to Sir Arnold Gridley in consultation with the F.B.I.[6] At this time Sir Arnold received help from Sir Peter Bennett (a member of the F.B.I. Council), who had been absent from the House during much of the committee stage. In view of the connexion of the two bodies in framing the amendments, it was natural that the two M.P.s most closely associated with the bodies should work together in promoting the amendments.

One of the amendments moved by Sir Arnold in committee had been to secure that replacements as well as repairs could be claimed as a deferred allowance against excess profits tax. The Solicitor-General moved a new clause,[7] which Sir Arnold accepted as meeting his point.

Further problems of the excess profits tax again came up and Sir Arnold moved a new clause on which Sir Peter spoke.[8] Sir Peter himself moved amendments, but all they were able to secure from the Solicitor-General was an assurance that the matter of rehabilitation costs would be gone into more fully next year.[9] Despite the fact that a division was called, nothing more was obtained.

Sir John Anderson had been met at the committee stage by a promise that the period for which concessions for terminal expenses on excess profits tax would be allowed, would be re-

[1] H.C. Deb. 424, cols. 919–26.
[2] Ibid., cols. 1102–18.
[3] Ibid., cols. 1157–9.
[4] Ibid., cols. 1254–74.
[5] A.B.C.C., op. cit., July 1946, pp. 53–56.
[6] Ibid., p. 39.
[7] H.C. Deb. 425, cols. 893–4.
[8] Ibid., cols. 896–9.
[9] Ibid., col. 900.

considered. The result was that an amendment was moved by the Solicitor-General to extend the period, not without limit, as had been asked for, but for one year.[1]

That was the end of the matter as regards the House of Commons, at least for one year. For, though it must be emphasized that negotiation on any bill is a continuous process in which no one part should be regarded separately, in the case of the Finance Bill the phrase 'continuous process' is even more apposite, since what is not achieved one year may be achieved the next. Negotiations may have no immediate effect, but there is always hope for the future.

It has been necessary to separate one particular activity in one particular year from the continuous process of negotiation. This activity does not stand in its own right, but is dependent upon the rest of the process. If the Association had been relying on parliamentary activity to secure its point, it is likely that it would have made a greater effort in that field, trying to widen its support in the House. It was pressure in a subdued key.

6

The most important feature of parliamentary amendments from the group's point of view is that the government is required to give a definite decision, backed up with a statement of its reasons for that decision. It is true that the minister in charge of a bill can say he will consider the point raised, but that does not avoid the necessity for a decision, it only postpones it.

Indecision is often the greatest enemy the group has to fight in consultation. It is possible for a group's representatives to be listened to with care, and yet for the group to feel its points have been passed over. The government cannot give a reply at once and in the short time available between the publication of a bill and its committee stage it is possible for points made to be overlooked—not from malice aforethought but from sheer pressure of work.

It is unlikely that the points will be overlooked completely; that would be both discourteous and inefficient. But the parliamentary amendment gives the group security with the knowledge that not only will its amendments be considered, but they

[1] Ibid., col. 959.

will be considered carefully. The necessity to state a reasoned case induces in the government a fresh approach to a problem. The question is at least faced.

The second important feature is that the government decision is made publicly, which gives greater finality to it. The group has to wait for the bill; it has to wait for decisions on its amendments; it has to wait for any amendments that may be moved in the House. The group knows that public statements have greater finality than private statements. Is it surprising that it uses parliamentary machinery to attain a greater security?

The problem of 'assurances' provides an important example of this. Ministers, reluctant to amend a bill, often give assurances that it will be used in a certain way, that a clause will have a certain meaning placed upon it, or that regulations will be drawn in a particular manner. Though these assurances have no legal value, they have considerable political importance. The tendency to leave the minister considerable discretion in the drawing up of regulations has made the question important. The group unable to achieve the certainty of legal enactment is faced with the problem of achieving certainty in political statement. An assurance given publicly in the House of Commons is a far more binding commitment than an assurance given privately. Though judges will not allow its validity, ministers must, and not merely the minister making the statement, but future ministers too, bound as they are by tradition and precedent.

The third important feature is that the tabling of an amendment means that the problems it raises are looked at from a new angle. The government has got to consider its arguments from the standpoint of Parliament. The point the amendment raises will be discussed in standing committee or in committee of the whole House. It may be discussed in party committees or in other committees in the House of Commons. This discussion will have an influence on the government as much in prospect as in retrospect. The group is not saying to the government, 'All right, we'll see what Parliament says about this—maybe they'll make you change your mind'; rather it is saying, 'We'll see what Parliament says about this', and meaning just that. Calling in a second opinion, assessing parliamentary views puts the group's amendment in a new light. It would be unfair to say that this is an appeal, for the process of consultation is not completed and there is nothing final from which to appeal. It is an activity designed to help the group in that consultation. It is accepted by the government as reasonable and proper behaviour on the part of the group. As a result it is for many groups an accepted part of their routine.

7

The extent to which groups promote amendments and some of the character of this activity can be illustrated by further examples.

The National Union of Manufacturers is an organization which represents similar interests to those of the Federation of British Industries, though tending to have smaller manufacturers amongst its members. There are on its Executive Council several M.P.s. It is therefore natural for the Union to seek their help. In 1952 one of its aims was to secure lower rates of estate duties for the factories, plant, and machinery of manufacturing businesses. A deputation waited on the Financial Secretary to the Treasury in April with a draft amendment, but were later informed that the Government proposed to take no action. Accordingly, Mr. G. W. Odey and Sir Wavell Wakefield, both members of the Executive Council, tabled an amendment which was not, however, called.[1]

The Union then commissioned the Economic Intelligence Unit to evaluate the facts presented by its members, thus obtaining publicity for its case, and a reasoned statement to put before the Government, but when the Finance Bill was brought forward in 1953 it contained nothing to meet the Union's points. The two M.P.s again tabled an amendment and were successful in securing a debate upon it as a result of which the Minister promised to review the estate duties and the anomalies arising from them.[2] It may seem that the Union was over-optimistic in ever pursuing this matter, but the object pursued is not necessarily the object which hard common sense says is likely to be obtained. If a group feels strongly, it does not weaken its position to state its case in full. That is true both of consultation and of representations to Parliament.

[1] *National Union of Manufacturers Annual Report*, 1951–2, pp. 13–14.
[2] Ibid., 1952–3, pp. 15–16.

The Trades Union Congress rarely seeks action by amendments. It is unnecessary in view of the degree of consultation it enjoys and the importance attached to it by the government. To a limited extent the T.U.C. used such methods under the 1951–5 Conservative Government, but the habits of the previous six years were still the governing factor. The T.U.C. likes the chance to stand alone without the support of politicians, even those of the Labour Party. This does not mean that there are never contacts with the Labour Party before the tabling of amendments, but the initiative will come as much from the Labour Party as from the Congress. This contact is much more important to the former than to the latter.

On the Iron and Steel Bill a joint sub-committee of the T.U.C., the Labour Party, the Parliamentary Labour Party, and the appropriate trade unions was set up in December 1952.[1] The actual amendments proposed by the Labour Party were drafted in the light of the discussions of this joint sub-committee. One amendment which the Labour Party proposed concerned the financial interests of members of the proposed Iron and Steel Board. It was feared by the T.U.C. that this might affect the pension rights of any trade unionists appointed, but when it was drawn to the attention of the Labour Party it was found that a new draft had already covered that point.[2]

The separate trade associations and trade unions also promote amendments. For example, the Caterers' Association, faced with the Food and Drugs (Amendment) Bill (1954), arranged for its General Secretary to meet a committee of Members of Parliament for the purpose of explaining certain points in connexion with the proposed legislation on which the Association had strong views.[3]

The Transport Salaried Staffs' Association's sponsored M.P.s moved amendments on its behalf during the passage of the Labour Government's Transport Bill in 1947 and the Conservative Government's Transport Bill in 1952 and 1953.[4] The existence of sponsored M.P.s is a positive incentive to the promotion of amendments, but the National Union of Furniture Trade Operatives, which has no sponsored M.P.s, also works through

[1] *85th T.U.C. Report*, 1953, pp. 251–2. [2] Ibid., p. 255.
[3] *Caterers' Association Annual Report for* 1953–4.
[4] *Transport Salaried Staff Journal*, Apr. 1954, p. 153.

Parliament. In 1952 the Union opposed the D Scheme and the ending of utility furniture, and in its journal describes Mr. Austen Albu as its spokesman in the House on the question.[1]

The Co-operative movement is able to promote amendments through its liaison with the Parliamentary Co-operative Party. In 1943 the Parliamentary Party was asked to put down an amendment to the Disabled Persons (Employment) Bill.[2] On the other hand, the National Committee endorsed the Parliamentary Party's decision not to proceed with opposition to the purchase tax, by way of amendment to the Finance Bill of 1942.[3]

The Magistrates' Association provides an example from a different field. In 1952 Mr. Charles Royle was a member of its Council, and it was through his good offices and those of Mr. H. Hynd and Mr. J. E. MacColl that an amendment was secured to the Children and Young Persons (Amendment) Bill to enable the courts to vary the approved school specified in court orders, in certain special circumstances.[4]

The Howard League for Penal Reform is recognized by the government as a responsible body with views to be listened to on the conduct of prisons. A Chairman of the Prisons Commission described it as an 'official opposition'. The League has always considered parliamentary activity useful and places great weight on its relations with M.P.s. The Penal Reform Group in the House of Commons with which the League is associated seldom meets, but individual members are active, asking questions or raising matters on the adjournment on behalf of the League.[5] Since the Second World War the most important work has been in relation to the Criminal Justice Act of 1948, for which the League pressed very strongly. The most important event was in 1946 when the Penal Reform Group met and passed a resolution urging the early introduction of a Criminal Justice Bill.[6] This resolution was signed by 180 M.P.s and was forwarded to the Home Secretary and then to

[1] *N.U.F.T.O. Record*, June 1952, p. 3.

[2] *Co-operative Union Annual Report*, 1944, p. 94.

[3] *Report of Central Board to the 75th Co-operative Congress*, 1943, p. 84.

[4] *Magistrates' Association Annual Report*, 1951–2, pp. 9–10.

[5] e.g. in 1945–6 Mr. George Benson, Mrs. Paton, Mr. Hector Hughes, and Mr. George Thomas.

[6] *Howard League Annual Report*, 1945–6, p. 4.

the Lord President of the Council (for consideration in the allocation of parliamentary time). Eventually a bill was introduced by the Government. Throughout the time it was before the House, the Committee of the Howard League was in close contact with the Penal Reform Group and originated many of the amendments tabled. Indeed, the Committee claimed a share of the responsibility for about ten important amendments, such as reduction of the minimum period of detention in Borstal from one year to nine months.[1]

The above examples are all cases in which one group alone has been examined, but, as with the Association of British Chambers of Commerce, collaboration between groups is common. The interests of groups overlap, and greater influence can be exerted by presenting a united front. It may be an *ad hoc* collaboration on specific issues, albeit a collaboration often repeated. Circumstances often bring the same groups together. In 1946 and 1947 the General Council of British Shipping collaborated with the Dock and Harbour Authorities' Association and with the Traders' Dock and Harbour Co-ordinating Committee on the Transport Bill. They reached agreement on various amendments.[2] Their interests have often brought them together.

The General Council of British Shipping is itself a body through which various constituent organizations such as the Chamber of Shipping express themselves. The Chamber of Shipping in describing the action taken on the Transport Bill in 1947 records

> its grateful thanks to those Members of both Houses of Parliament and, in particular, to the Hon. J. S. Maclay, M.P., Viscount Swinton and Lord Teynham for their unsparing efforts during the consideration of the Bill to secure that the measure as adopted was best calculated to ensure both the efficient administration of the ports and the safeguarding of the interests of coastwise shipping. The Chamber is also indebted to Lord Leathers and Lord Rotherwick for the invaluable help given by them.[3]

Action by organizations which are composed of representa-

[1] *Howard League Annual Report*, 1947–8, pp. 3–5.
[2] *Chamber of Shipping of the United Kingdom Annual Report*, 1947–8, p. 86.
[3] Ibid., p. 88.

tives of groups with similar interests is quite common. The United Kingdom Forestry Committee was the medium through which the Country Landowners' Association sought amendments to the Forestry Bill in 1951. In this case the main strength was deployed in the House of Lords, though some aid was obtained from the Commons: 'great activity was displayed in providing briefs, framing amendments, meeting officials of the Forestry Commission, and providing expert advice for the Peers who were fighting to improve the Bill'.[1]

A more informal unity is reached by the leaders of accountancy bodies. The Coal Industry (Nationalisation) Bill introduced in 1945 was considered by an *ad hoc* 'Joint Committee consisting of representatives of the leading accountancy bodies'. Parliamentary agents were consulted, and amendments were drafted which, if not accepted by the Government, were to be 'moved in Committee'.[2]

Uniformity of practice does not emerge from these examples. But although the approach of groups to parliamentary amendments varies, it is, nevertheless, an established practice considered, if not adopted, by all groups. It is by no means true that a group whose amendments are rejected by the government automatically promotes them in the House. Practice varies from group to group and case to case. The group's own position in consultation, the likelihood of any change occurring in the government's position, the attitude of M.P.s, and the point of view of other groups are all factors to be considered. Individual groups dealing with individual M.P.s are not likely to create uniformity.

8

One particular set of problems faced by N.A.L.G.O. illustrates this. It is impossible for the government to consult with everyone. A bill may affect interests which fall outside its main purpose. It may be that a group is concerned only incidentally. The ministry itself may not have realized this, but the group certainly will. This group may have no contact with the relevant ministry even though other ministries frequently consult it. In some cases a ministry which has close relations with the

[1] *C.L.A. 44th Annual Report,* Oct. 1951, p. 30.

[2] *Institute of Chartered Accountants Annual Report,* 1945, para. 24.

group may sponsor its proposals, but this is not always appropriate and a Member of Parliament with his ready access to ministries may be used to establish contacts. Alternatively, the group may prefer to have its amendments moved in the House. Shortage of time may make this imperative.

The situation faced by N.A.L.G.O. in 1947 provides examples of the particular problems faced by a group in this position. It found no set solution, but three solutions to three problems. Three Bills were introduced which provided for a transfer of powers from or between local government authorities. They were the Electricity, Transport, and Town and Country Planning Bills.[1] Problems of compensation arose which N.A.L.G.O. felt had not been adequately dealt with, and on which it wished the Bills amended. The tactics pursued to obtain amendments differed in each case. This is not, perhaps, surprising, since it was inevitable that the relationship with the ministry and the time factor would vary from case to case.

In the Transport Bill the main emphasis was on consultation first with the officials of the Ministry of Transport, then with the Minister himself. The Association's Parliamentary Agent drafted amendments to cover the points which the Association wished to raise (as he did for all three Bills). Mr. T. W. Burden, M.P. (now Lord Burden), and the Legal Officer of the Association discussed the amendments with officials at the Ministry of Transport. Arising out of this, there was some correspondence with the Minister in order to clarify some of the issues raised. On all points the Association either received sufficient assurances as to the interpretation to be put on clauses, or was met by amendments in the House of Commons. It was unnecessary for the group to take any parliamentary action.[2]

On the Electricity Bill, the Agent submitted to the Minister of Fuel and Power a number of amendments drafted on behalf of the Association. The Minister, Mr. Emanuel Shinwell replied in a letter which gave satisfactory assurances on most points. On one of the remaining points an Opposition amendment was already tabled; on another, Mr. George Porter sought and gained a satisfactory assurance in the Standing Committee. But N.A.L.G.O.'s main concern was with Clause

[1] For a brief summary see *Local Government Service*, June 1947, p. 343.

[2] *N.A.L.G.O. Annual Report*, 1947, pp. 109–12.

49, a compensation clause which it wished to extend to cover the payment of compensation to those local government officers who were employed for part of their time with an electricity undertaking, and who might suffer pecuniary loss as a result of the transfer to the nationalized board. The Minister reserved his comments, and the Association was forced to put an amendment down. Mr. H. E. Goodrich moved this amendment, and referred to a similar clause in the National Health Insurance Act [*sic*] as a precedent.[1]

The Minister said that the difficulty was that the phrase 'part-time' covered a very large number of people who had only devoted a very small portion of their time to an electricity undertaking. He felt it was a problem which could more satisfactorily be dealt with by regulations. In view of this Mr. Goodrich withdrew the amendment.[2] Mr. Burden was asked to move it again during the report stage because the Council did not wish to drop the amendment without having a perfectly clear assurance that the regulations referred to would indeed cover officers who, while remaining in the employment of the local authority, suffered a pecuniary loss.

Mr. Burden put down the amendment, supported now by the Association of Municipal Corporations, but the Speaker did not call it. During the debate Mr. Shinwell seemed to say that the position could easily be adjusted, but in a letter he said that compensation paid to local authorities should cover it. Mr. Burden was therefore asked to find out, if he could, exactly what the Minister meant. But Mr. Burden was unable to see the Minister before the Bill received the Royal Assent.[3]

On the Town and Country Planning Bill, which came under the jurisdiction of a different Ministry, all the amendments were put down in the Standing Committee. The first of the Association's amendments was moved by Mr. T. Braddock on Clause 94, and was designed to protect the position of officers of district councils.[4] Mr. Braddock also moved an amendment to cover a point raised by N.A.L.G.O. with regard to com-

[1] Standing Committee Debates, Standing Committee E, 15 May 1947, col. 1417.
[2] Ibid., cols. 1417–18.
[3] *N.A.L.G.O. Annual Report*, 1947, pp. 104–9.
[4] Standing Committee Debates, Standing Committee D, 27 Mar. 1947, col. 965.

pensation right created by Clause 31.[1] The Minister did not accept it, having already moved an amendment which he considered covered this point.

He did, however, accept the amendment moved by Mr. Braddock in association with Mr. D. C. Walker-Smith to provide for the transfer and compensation of officers on the dissolution or alteration of a joint planning board. 'Having regard to the very respectable parentage of the Amendment, I have great pleasure in accepting it',[2] as he did a later amendment.

Owing to the guillotine an amendment to the 9th schedule was not reached. The amendment was designed to secure that the repeal of Section 51 of the Town and Country Planning Act (1932), which contained certain compensation provisions, would not affect the rights arising under that section, in consequence of any event occurring before the appointed day. It was taken up with the Minister, who said the point was covered by the Interpretation Act; the amendment would mean undesirable repetition. But a similar point had been taken up on the equivalent Scottish Bill, and the Secretary of State had agreed to move an amendment. In view of this and for other reasons Mr. Burden was asked to approach the Minister suggesting a House of Lords amendment, a suggestion that was effective.[3]

In the action upon this Bill, Mr. Burden's position was crucial. It was through him, one must assume, that Labour M.P.s were persuaded to sponsor these amendments. He held no official position in N.A.L.G.O., although he attended the annual conference to report on his work, but N.A.L.G.O. has always had M.P.s associated with it, if possible from both parties. The work of these M.P.s involves not only putting down amendments, but also helping to secure consultation. The emphasis N.A.L.G.O. lays on their activities is partly due to historical circumstance, since N.A.L.G.O. drew very largely upon the support of private members in its endeavours to secure compulsory superannuation for local government employees.[4]

[1] Standing Committee Debates, Standing Committee D, 27 Mar. 1947, col. 966.

[2] Ibid., 2 Apr. 1947, col. 1055.

[3] N.A.L.G.O., op. cit., pp. 112–13.

[4] See N.A.L.G.O., *The Fight for Superannuation* (undated).

9

Whatever the motives that lead a group to promote amendments, it is not a method without problems. The actual drafting of an amendment should present no great difficulties. Some groups make use of parliamentary agents for this purpose; others rely upon the experience of their own legal departments; but in the end it is the same for all. The monopoly of the government's parliamentary draftsmen is secure, for even if the point of the amendment is accepted the minister will 'not be very happy about the wording' and it will probably be redrafted.

The problem of tabling the amendment is more serious. The examples may have left the impression that it is not difficult for a group to get an amendment tabled by an M.P. Most groups have a number of contacts in the House and normally it is to be expected that with their help supporters will be obtained. The existence of a large number of contacts can be a positive incentive to the promotion of amendments, particularly in the case of trade unions, with their sponsored M.P.s. The National Union of Mineworkers has had well over thirty sponsored M.P.s for many years. It is almost forced to make some use of them. The result can be seen in the committee stage of the Mines and Quarries Bill in 1954. This Bill was to revise the Act passed in 1911, which until then had been the legal basis of all provision for safety in mines. There had been consultation beforehand, but it had stopped far short of agreement. The result was that Mr. William Blyton, an N.U.M.-sponsored M.P., describing the Bill as entirely inadequate said: 'The Minister should not be surprised if he is faced with about 500 Amendments in Committee.'[1] In fact the Standing Committee deliberated from 16 February to 18 May covering 26 sittings in all, with 64 divisions called—both exceptionally high figures. The Labour members of this committee were 21 in number of whom 16 were members of the N.U.M.[2] It is clear that in this case much of the process of consultation centred round the proceedings of the Standing Committee.[3]

[1] H.C. Deb. 522, col. 1398.

[2] Comparative figures for the Coal Industry (Nationalisation) Bill of 1946 and the Miners' Welfare Bill in 1952 were 12 out of 30 and 9 out of 21 respectively.

[3] Standing Committee Debates, Standing Committee A, 16 Feb. 1954 to 18 May 1954.

But the existence of group contacts does not guarantee to all groups that they will be able to get their amendments tabled. The Parliamentary and Legal Council of the motor industry was unable to secure the tabling of an amendment to the Agricultural Marketing Bill in 1949 owing to the Opposition being unwilling to sponsor it. Yet at this time at least one of the constituent bodies of that Council had M.P.s associated with it.[1]

The group has to consider the relationship of its amendments to the party alignment. There are many amendments that do not raise any problem: for example, it is unlikely that an amendment to secure the position of the leading accountancy bodies will be regarded by a party as politically dangerous.

However, many amendments do raise party issues, and then the group must concern itself with the attitude of the party committees either directly or through its own contacts. A wise group will keep in touch with both parties. Apart from changes of government a group has something to gain from both sides of the House. On the government side, committee support is more valuable, but the opposition is more likely to table amendments.

There are cases where an approach to a government party committee is sufficient to get an amendment tabled. In 1948 National Farmers' Union representatives attended a meeting of the Food and Agricultural Group of the Labour Party and the Deputy President and others explained a proposed amendment to the Finance (No. 2) Bill. As a result it was tabled by two Labour back-benchers.[2]

Members of a party committee are often unwilling to promote amendments for which party necessity prevents them voting. Nevertheless they may be anxious to have an amendment tabled in order to speak upon it and to give it informal support. In order to get an amendment moved, where they were unwilling to table one themselves, Conservative M.P.s on occasions between 1951 and 1955 urged trade associations to make contact with the Labour Party. This has merely given support to a tendency that has appeared in many groups,

[1] *Society of Motor Manufacturers and Traders Annual Report*, 1949, p. 14.

[2] *British Farmer*, 31 July 1948, p. 5.

following the example of the N.F.U. in having contacts on both sides of the House. It is a tendency that will grow.

Having secured the tabling of the amendment, the group has to consider what measures to use to support it. Again the party committee is important as are those other committees that cut across party, to any of which the group may explain its amendments. Alternatively, the group may convene a special meeting to put its views to M.P.s. Such a meeting needs to be sponsored by an M.P. In 1952 Mr. Douglas Houghton called two meetings of M.P.s to hear representatives of interested groups explain their attitude to the Pensions (Increase) Bill and their amendments to it.[1]

When a bill is before a standing committee a circular letter may be sent to all its members explaining the purpose of the group's amendments. In 1946 N.A.L.G.O. sought amendments to the National Insurance Bill to ensure that local government staff, in particular public assistance staff, indirectly affected by its provisions should receive compensation. Along with other interested groups, it circularized all members of the Standing Committee, giving them full information as to the effect envisaged and asking for their support for the amendments.[2] Such information is a necessary background to sensible discussion in a standing committee.

Where the group presses its efforts further than this, the issue is taken beyond the process of consultation and becomes a challenge to the government. The line is difficult to draw, but it is clear that parliamentary amendments can be and are often proposed as a part of the consultative process; they are a form of subdued pressure, which the government recognizes and accepts.

10

The other activities of groups in Parliament are not normally very important. The parliamentary question might appear to be important but it has strictly limited uses. While all bills must necessarily come before Parliament and the initiative rests with the government, the group itself must take the initiative in asking a parliamentary question. It does not arise as part of the routine of consultation. Many groups there-

[1] *Whitley Bulletin*, Aug. 1952, p. 114.
[2] *Local Government Service*, Feb. 1947, p. 272.

fore do not consider that any good can come of it. In extreme cases it gives the group a chance to bring flagrant injustices before the public eye. But flagrant injustices are rare and small disagreements are common. In these cases the question as a public challenge is likely to be of little aid. A minister, the groups argue, who is not convinced by argument, is not going to be disturbed by a parliamentary question.

The parliamentary question can be useful to the group within certain limits. The question enables the group to ensure that the government makes public some information. For example, in 1942 the Co-operative movement through a parliamentary question was able to secure a general statement of the expenses of Wholesale Meat Supply Associations, information not previously available.[1] In this way the group secures that the government publishes information previously restricted, for the government is reluctant to be put in the position of refusing Parliament information. It has been known for a government department to ask a group to get a question put down to enable it to give the group information.

The question may be designed to secure a public ruling. On 13 December 1944 Sir Joseph Lamb asked two written questions on behalf of the County Councils' Association, which were designed to obtain statements upon the liability of county councils to reinstate persons serving in the Civil Defence general services, as opposed to the Civil Defence Force, and also persons who left the Civil Defence for the purpose of joining the armed forces.[2] Similarly, on 14 February 1946 Mr. T. W. Burden, acting on behalf of N.A.L.G.O., asked for ministerial endorsement of an agreement made between that Association and local authority representatives and for encouragement to local authorities to adopt it. The value of such rulings depends on their being made publicly; and in the latter case N.A.L.G.O. printed the question and reply in its journal to draw attention to it.[3]

The question is best used as a means of prodding, not as an appeal. It is a weapon against inaction rather than against action. The government has to defend action it has taken and a

[1] *Co-operative Union Report of Central Board to 75th Congress*, 1943, p. 111.
[2] *C.C.A. Gazette*, Jan. 1945.
[3] *Local Government Service*, Apr. 1946, p. 50.

question only increases its obstinacy, but where the government is dilatory a question may help to force a decision. The M.P.s representing unions anxious for action on the Gowers report on working conditions in non-industrial establishments, have persevered with questions. Mr. Fred Mulley, in reporting on his activities in the House to his union—the Clerical and Administrative Workers' Union—said: 'I have endeavoured to do something to speed up legislation on the Gowers Report . . .',[1] and referred to a question he had asked on 26 July 1951.

In 1946 the Board of Deputies of British Jews was disturbed by the failure of the Government to take action about allegations being made that the terrorist campaigns in Palestine were liable to be extended to Britain. It made representations to the Home Office on this matter, and at the same time questions were asked in the House. The Government eventually issued a statement strongly deprecating the allegations.[2]

There are, however, cases where the group appears to regard the question as a means of appeal from the government's decision. In January 1945 the War Emergency Committee of the County Councils' Association considered the Board of Trade's explanation of a refusal to grant to the Kent County Council a licence for the purchase of accounting machinery; it was not impressed by the reasons given, and arranged for a parliamentary question. It was asked on 17 January 1945 by Sir Joseph Lamb, but it was a written question, which meant that no heat was likely to be aroused.[3] It became a formal registration of protest.

Most groups do not usually consider the method worthwhile. Mr. Walter Padley, President of the Union of Shop, Distributive, and Allied Workers, asked only six questions in the session 1951–2. Of these, two were concerned with the Gowers report, one with the failure of the Government to introduce a winter closing order for shops, one with the reference back by the Ministry of Labour of Wages Council decisions, and the other two with non-union matters. Although closely connected with a union, he found little use for

[1] *The Clerk*, Sept.–Oct. 1951, p. 250.
[2] *Board of Deputies of British Jews Annual Report*, 1946, pp. 28–29.
[3] *C.C.A. Gazette*, Jan. 1945.

parliamentary questions. Mr. George Benson, President of the Howard League for Penal Reform, asked three questions in 1951–2, all concerned with problems relating to prisons. Two were requests for statistics of offences in prisons, and the other on the age groups for experimental detention centres. Though closely connected with the League he found little need for questions, and that only to obtain information. Perhaps the parliamentary question provided a surer way of finding it, perhaps a quicker, or perhaps merely a more convenient way. The Howard League may have wished the information to be published. There is, of course, a great amount of variation. But on the whole, M.P.s connected with groups do not ask many questions on their behalf. The following table gives approximate figures relating to the questions asked during the 1951–2 parliamentary session by a number of M.P.s associated with groups in one capacity or another. The figures given in the fourth column give the number of questions which appear to

Name of M.P.	*Name of group*	*Number of questions in 1951–2 session*	*Number of questions in group's field of concern in 1951–2 session*
A. C. Allen	National Union of Boot and Shoe Operatives	0	0
W. G. Cove	National Union of Teachers	0	0
Sir Ian Fraser	British Legion	150	13
E. G. Gooch	National Union of Agricultural Workers	12	4
J. Grimston	Cold Rolled Brass and Copper Association	5	0
R. R. Harris	National Association of Fire Officers	27	3
H. N. Linstead	Pharmaceutical Society	11	2
J. C. Lockwood	R.S.P.C.A.	6	4
F. W. Mulley	Clerical and Administrative Workers' Union	75	3
P. F. Remnant	Brewers' Society	42	1
P. G. Roberts	N.S.P.C.C.	50	0
W. Schofield	Federation of Master Cotton Spinners' Associations	11	6
C. S. Taylor	British Hotels' and Restaurants' Association	23	1
S. P. Viant	National Anti-Vaccination League	26	11
W. A. Wilkins	Typographical Association	2	0

fall in the field covered by the group with which the M.P. was connected. There is, of course, no guarantee that these were asked on behalf of the group.

II

For the most part questions are not important to the group. If it wishes to enlist the support of M.P.s on some issue that has arisen in the course of government policy, it is more likely to approach M.P.s to use their influence informally or by deputation. In 1949 the Honorary Parliamentary Agent of the United Commercial Travellers' Association wrote to the Minister of Fuel and Power in an endeavour to secure an increase in the petrol allowance, and in particular to get him to receive a deputation to urge that point. The Minister regretted that he was unable to meet the request, and hence considered it would be unsuitable to receive the deputation.[1]

The Parliamentary Agent then took the case to the House of Commons, where a meeting of fifty M.P.s under the chairmanship of Mr. D. L. Lipson was arranged to hear him. This meeting passed a resolution instructing Mr. Lipson to inform the Minister that in its opinion a case had been made out, and if a satisfactory response was not forthcoming to arrange another meeting.[2] Some concessions were made, but the Association was not satisfied until the abolition of rationing in 1950.

The Convention of Royal Burghs is the nearest equivalent in Scotland to the Association of Municipal Corporations, and could probably claim to be the oldest pressure group in Britain were it not that it prefers to emphasize its history as a part of the structure of government. It still has a general representative character that many pressure groups have not; its tradition enables it to claim to speak for Scotland. But it is not above the normal activities of the pressure group. In 1952, being dissatisfied with the system of calculating housing subsidies and their amount, and failing to obtain satisfaction from the Secretary of State for Scotland, the Convention determined to invite M.P.s to a meeting in Edinburgh. Difficulty was experienced in arranging this.[3] Instead, meetings were held in London with

[1] *U.C.T.A. Annual Conference*, 1949, pp. 56–59.
[2] U.C.T.A., *Seventy Years* (1953), p. 89.
[3] Convention of Royal Burghs (1953), *Annual Convention Agenda*, p. 7.

the Scottish Parliamentary Labour Group and the Scottish Unionist Members Committee, discussions which were related to the Housing (Scotland) Bill, but which also raised general administrative problems.[1]

Informal aid of this kind can speed the process of consultation and overcome difficulties. M.P.s are ready to listen to a group's viewpoint and to attend meetings where it is being put. They will help to arrange deputations and will support the group's representations to the minister. One example is the work done by Mr. P. Holman and Mr. M. McCorquodale in helping the printing and stationery trades in their negotiations on purchase tax. In 1951 they went with representatives of these trades to the Financial Secretary to the Treasury to discuss the question of evasion of the tax by those buying paper and printing for themselves.[2] There is a great deal of this informal work done by M.P.s.

12

Outside the process of legislation and the occasional question, comparatively little is done through the formal processes of the House (though the problem of purchase tax on printing had been raised on the adjournment by Mr. Holman in 1949[3]). When a group's problems are involved in a debate, appropriate members will be briefed. 'A number of important debates have taken place in both Houses of Parliament on agricultural subjects, including rural water supplies and housing. The Association has supplied briefs to members of the Lords and Commons, and is grateful for the assistance that they have rendered during the year' is the Central Landowners' Association report for 1947–8.[4]

It is only rarely that a group will seek to initiate a debate. Delegated legislation may involve a group in this way, since it may be because of a group's activities that an order is challenged and discussed. The group can hope to do no more than register its objection, but this is sometimes necessary for its self-esteem.

[1] Convention of Royal Burghs (1953), *Annual Convention Agenda*, p. 33.
[2] H.C. Deb. 484, col. 551.
[3] Ibid., 465, cols. 741–8.
[4] *C.L.A. Annual Report,* May 1947–Sept. 1948.

Often enough the group representatives merely intervene in a debate to correct misapprehensions and make clear the group's viewpoint. It is a publicity service. In a debate in 1949 on the London area allowance for teachers, Mr. W. G. Cove said:

> I hope to put clearly and definitely the view of the National Union of Teachers, the main body represented on the Burnham Committee. . . . While the National Union of Teachers welcome the aid of public opinion and particularly of Members of Parliament for an increase in salaries, they are quite clear and definite that nothing should be done to impair the prestige of the Burnham Committee.[1]

But the informal may merge into the formal and the group pass from one approach to the other in situations where a variety of approaches is needed, as when a group seeks to prod the government into action without open challenge or campaign.

The various unions interested in securing the enactment of the recommendations of the Gowers report on working conditions in non-industrial undertakings or premises, have used many methods. The National Union of Agricultural Workers, the Union of Shop, Distributive, and Allied Workers, and the various unions catering for clerical workers have been most concerned. Questions have been used, as already noted. The issue has been brought into other debates, such as the debate on the Shops (Revocation of Winter Closing Provisions) Order (1952), which altered shop opening hours.[2] After a motion had been passed by the Executive Council of U.S.D.A.W. regretting the omission of any mention of this legislation in the Queen's Speech in 1954, a motion was placed upon the order paper to this effect by the Union's M.P.s.[3] Delegations have been formed by M.P.s. In this way attempts have been made to keep the subject before the House and the Government.

13

The by-ways of parliamentary activity have some significance for the groups—private bills and private members' bills. Of private bills there is little new to be said. Private bill procedure

[1] H.C. Deb. 464, col. 586.

[2] Ibid., 507, cols. 1783–1834, e.g. Mr. W. Padley, President of U.S.D.A.W., cols. 1785–7.

[3] *New Dawn*, 1 Jan. 1955, p. 15.

has been fully dealt with elsewhere[1] and the position of pressure groups resembles that of most petitioners against private bills. Pressure groups obtain a *locus standi* before Select Committees on Private Bills by virtue of the standing order which provides that:

> Where any society or association, sufficiently representing any trade, business, or interest in a district to which any Bill relates, petition against the Bill, alleging that such trade, business or interest will be injuriously affected by the provisions contained therein, it shall be competent for the Select Committee to which the Bill is referred, if they think fit, to admit the petitioners to be heard on such allegations against the Bill or any part thereof.

But apart from the actual procedure before the Select Committees private bills have an importance for groups. In order to safeguard their interests in private bills, many groups engage Parliamentary Agents whose main functions as defined by the customs and standing orders of both Houses is the preparation and promotion of private bills or the arrangement of opposition to them, but whose functions may in fact extend beyond private bills to general advice on all legislation.

Groups are concerned with private bills long before they reach the Select Committees. On the Leeds Private Bill (1956) 'From the moment when the Bill was deposited in the House of Commons, officials were concerned in negotiations with interested parties and Government Departments', and the interested parties included the National Farmers' Union and the Leeds and District Property Owners' and Ratepayers' Association.[2]

One reason why a group may be particularly vehement against a clause in a private bill is that it may raise questions of principle beyond the particular case with which it deals. The attempt of a local authority to introduce a new restriction or a new service may provide a precedent for further action perhaps on a national scale. In boroughs and urban districts the group can seek to defeat the clauses it objects to at the statutory town meeting, which is attended by electors in the authority promoting the bill. In 1953 the Automobile Association drew the atten-

[1] See *Sir T. Erskine May's Parliamentary Practice*, 15th edn. (1954), and O. C. Williams, *The History of Private Bill Procedure* (1948–9).

[2] H. V. Wiseman, *The Leeds Private Bill. 1956; Public Administration*, Spring, 1957, p. 30.

tion of its members in Manchester to a Bill that was being promoted by the Corporation in which it sought powers to use parking meters in order to charge for the parking of vehicles in the streets. A letter was sent by the Association to all its 50,000 Manchester members drawing their attention to this proposal and suggesting ways of meeting it, one of which was attendance at the town meeting. The Royal Automobile Club sent out a similar letter. At the subsequent town meeting the clause concerned was deleted from the Bill.[1]

But both the council and the group can appeal to a town poll against the decision at the town meeting. In relation to the Birmingham Corporation Bill of 1954, a clause of which sought to give the Civic Restaurants Undertaking power to build up a reserve fund, the Midland Branch of the Caterers' Association having failed to defeat the clause at the town meeting, requisitioned a poll. Letters were sent to 1,500 caterers, and statements issued to the press. The clause was rejected at the poll by 17,102 votes to 10,829.[2] There were other groups in the field, among them the Birmingham Property Owners' Association (a member association of the National Federation of Property Owners),[3] and five out of six disputed clauses were defeated by majorities ranging from 4,934 to 10,533.[4]

But should local activity prove unsuccessful the group may raise the issue on the second reading in the House of Commons. Such action may be taken not only when the case is a precedent for others, but also when the case itself is of sufficient importance to justify it. The North Wales Hydro-Electric Bill of 1952 seems to merit this description; it certainly found many objectors. In the House of Commons there was, of course, Mr. G. Nabarro, who regarded capital expenditure on these projects as too heavy for the return obtained. There were, too, the countryside preservation societies, ever watchful. There was also the British Waterworks' Association, which considered that this Bill was yet another example of the lack of a policy to conserve the country's resources of water. Mr. (now Sir) Geoffrey Hutchinson was its Chairman, and he put down a motion of instruction to the Committee upon the question.[5] Though he withdrew it, he

[1] H.L. 58–I of 1954–5, pp. 357–62.
[2] Ibid., p. 355.
[3] Ibid., p. 347.
[4] Ibid., p. 167.
[5] *British Waterworks' Association Annual Report*, 1951–2, pp. 11–12.

helped to force a second reading debate, and was one of the forty M.P.s voting against the second reading,[1] though for the most part his protests were ignored in the storm raised by Mr. Nabarro and the countryside protectors.

The County Councils' Association and the Association of Municipal Corporations regarded the Ilford and Luton Corporation Bills in 1953 and 1954 as being preliminary battles over local government reform. These Bills were designed to turn the two local authorities into county boroughs. Each Association tried to secure as much support as possible for its point of view, the County Councils' Association fearing that if Ilford or Luton were to become a county borough, then the same criteria would justify many other boroughs obtaining that status.[2] The second reading debates which have taken place on these Bills have been debates on the general problem of local government reform.

14

The private members' bill is of very limited use to most groups.[3] The uncertainty of parliamentary time and the final sanctions at hand to the government deter a group from entering into the field. Action may be taken as a propaganda method, or as a means of stirring the government into action, but if the bill is intended to become an act, then this method is only of use to the group when the bill deals with a subject that can be separated from the main current of activities. The sphere of action of most groups, certainly of those fully admitted to consultation, is one in which the government is accustomed to initiate legislation, and is normally unwilling to see that prerogative taken from it. To be successful a private members' bill must deal with a side issue of politics: one which will not have too wide repercussions, for that would undermine the government's position. The government should be willing to look benevolently on the bill. At the worst its neutrality must be secured, but at the best it will be a bill which the government, while quite willing to support, has not the time to introduce. The Protection of Animals Anaesthetics Bill (1954), which

[1] H.C. Deb. 498, cols. 1533–4.

[2] Ibid. 525, cols. 671–720.

[3] For details of parliamentary procedure in relation to private members bills see P. A. Bromhead, *Private Members' Bills* (1956).

the British Veterinary Association promoted, is a good example.[1] The Co-operative movement in 1954 promoted the Industrial and Provident Societies (Amendment) Bill to deal with problems such as amalgamation. It was passed without any difficulty.[2]

The private members' bill is used by groups seeking to attain or regulate professional status. The Royal Institute of British Architects, after a long struggle, succeeded in obtaining the Architects Registration Act (1931),[3] promoted by a private member.

The Hairdressers' Registration Council has not been so fortunate. Set up in 1922 by the Incorporated Guild of Hairdressers and the National Federation of Hairdressers in order to promote registration of hairdressers, it was not until 1935 that it decided to draft a parliamentary bill; previously it had attempted to encourage voluntary registration. A Parliamentary Agent was appointed and a Bill drafted which was introduced into the House of Commons in 1937 by Mr. James Compton, who unfortunately died shortly afterwards. An attempt to promote a revised Bill in the House of Lords was obstructed by a memorandum of objections by the Institute of Trichology, as a result of which the Bill was negatived in order to give the Registration Council an opportunity to meet the Institute's objections. The objections of the Institute were met, and in 1939 the Bill was again introduced, but the outbreak of war prevented further action. It was not until 1949 that private members' bills again became possible, and a Bill introduced by Mr. J. A. Sparks passed a second reading. It was, however, defeated on a third reading by a small majority. This was not the end of the matter, and measures have been taken so to revise the nature of the Council and also the Bill, that a further attempt may be more successful. As a result a new Parliamentary agent was appointed in 1953 and a new Registration Bill drafted.[4]

The British Optical Association has long attempted to obtain by Act of Parliament greater professional status for opticians. A parliamentary fund, originally constituted as a result of a bequest in 1906, and augmented by subsequent appeals, exists

[1] M.P.s received a circular inviting them to promote this Bill.

[2] Co-operative Union, *Report of Central Board to 85th Congress*, 1954, pp. 54–55.

[3] *R.I.B.A. Kalendar*, 1952–3; cf. Jennings, *Parliament* (1939), pp. 186–7.

[4] 'Yesterday and Today', a short historical article in a pamphlet (undated) issued by the Hairdressers' Registration Council.

for this purpose, though since 1945 no attempt has been made to use it.[1]

The Pharmacy Act (1953) is different. It was designed to bring the already existing law governing the professional status of pharmacists into line with various changes brought about by the Pharmaceutical Society's new Charter. Its contents were mainly domestic matters of concern to the Pharmaceutical Society, whose Secretary, Sir Hugh Linstead, is a member of the House of Commons. It was due to him that the Bill found a sponsor in Mr. John Hall. Mr. Hall was a member of the House who won a good place in the ballot for private members' bills within a month of his election. None of the bills he was offered appealed to him, and he was unprepared with any of his own. Mr. Hall, hearing by chance that there was a Pharmacy Bill in draft, approached Sir Hugh Linstead about it, and subsequently agreed to sponsor it. The Minister of Health blessed it; a quiet, uncontroversial Bill, it passed without trouble.

The Cremation Society provides another example. Since 1945 it had been anxious to bring about reforms in the laws relating to cremation. An Inter-Departmental Committee had been set up and in making its report in 1950 had outlined some changes required. Although these did not go as far as the Society desired, the report was welcomed as a step forward. In 1951, on the failure of the Government to introduce the required legislation, the Chairman of the Inter-Departmental Committee appealed for the help of the Cremation Society. It thereupon resolved to introduce a bill, and invited Mr. Joseph Reeves, an M.P. associated with it, to help.

As a preliminary to action he secured the support of the Home Office for the measure he intended to introduce, by approaching Mr. Chuter Ede, the Home Secretary. However, being unsuccessful in the ballot for private members' bills, he determined that owing to the general agreement on the subject, the Bill should be introduced under the ten minutes rule.[2] Before this could be done, the 1951 election brought Sir David Maxwell Fyfe to the Home Office and negotiations were re-opened with equal success. In 1952 a private members' bill was

[1] *British Optical Association Yearbook*, 1951, pp. 9–10.

[2] A bill introduced under this rule can only proceed if unopposed, cf. Bromhead, op. cit., pp. 17–20.

passed unopposed on the second reading, and although Mr. G. R. Mitchison supporting the views of the Association of Municipal Corporations secured the deletion of a clause in Committee, the Bill became law.[1]

One of the most interesting descriptions of efforts to promote private members' bills is contained in N.A.L.G.O.'s publication *The Fight for Superannuation* about which Sir Ivor Jennings has already written.[2] The interesting point is that the limitation of this method is shown by the fact that though the 1922 Act was a private members' measure, it was not till the Government introduced the 1937 Act that full success was obtained, despite many attempts to secure a passage for private members' bills on the question.

These are the private members' bills that succeeded, or at least found sponsors. The National Consultative Council of the Liquor Trade sought to promote a Bill to amend the law relating to licensed premises and clubs. In October 1953 it circularized M.P.s asking them to sponsor the Bill: it found no sponsor. A member is only too glad to leave licensing reform to governments, who are themselves likely to take no action.

There are, of course, groups which seek to amend private members' bills. It may be the sponsoring member or group they approach, or they may act directly by amendment in the House, but as often as not it is to a ministry they turn as their normal contact. In 1954, seeking amendments to Mr. Fred Mulley's Bill to secure publication of the accounts of football pools, the accountancy bodies, following their usual practice, approached the Home Office before they approached the sponsor of the Bill.

In 1951 Mr. J. Kinley introduced the New Streets Bill whose purpose was to amend the law relating to the responsibilities of local authorities and owners. The Association of Municipal Corporations appointed a sub-committee to consider the matter, which 'came to the conclusion, however, that if the Bill were to be enacted in the form in which it had been presented it would be a source of considerable difficulty to local authorities in its practical application'. It drew up a series of amendments which were discussed with the Ministry of Housing and Local Government in an endeavour to obtain its assistance.[3]

[1] *Pharos*, Feb. 1952, pp. 2–3. [2] Jennings, op. cit., especially pp. 206–10.
[3] *Municipal Review* (Supplement), June, 1952, p. 136.

Mr. Geoffrey Hutchinson, a Vice-President of the Association, put down a number of amendments, and discussed them with Ministry officials. He arranged a meeting with the Bill's promoters. The promoter of a private members' bill has not the parliamentary control that makes the strength of the government's position in consultation on legislation, and the failure of this meeting prevented effective progress on the Bill. After two sittings the Standing Committee was still dealing with Clause 1, and had had six divisions on Mr. Hutchinson's amendments. Mr. G. R. Mitchison, who was guiding the Bill, moved the adjournment of the Committee: 'My reason for doing so is that there have been discussions between the persons interested, and we are hopeful that, given a little longer time, those discussions may result in a considerable saving of time in our further consideration of the Bill.'[1] Mr. Hutchinson supported him.

Substantial agreement was reached in these discussions, only one A.M.C. point being left unsettled. However, further amendments put down by Mr. Hutchinson on the report stage were accepted, while further amendments were put down in the House of Lords by arrangement with the Ministry.

15

Private members' bills and private bills are side-lines on which some groups play a greater part than others. The main interest of the group is in the government and the measures taken by it or not taken by it. In dealing with this situation the two most important forms of group activity in Parliament are the maintenance of a sound public relations policy and the promotion of amendments through M.P.s. These activities supplement consultation and are dependent upon it, since whether they are used to prepare for it, as part of it, or to smooth over gaps in it, they are dependent upon the relationship of consultation which is foremost in the group's outlook.

They are routine activities pursued without heat or violence. They do not proceed out of dissatisfaction with consultation, or as an appeal from it. They aid its progress. They provide only a formal exception to the supremacy of consultation, since they have become a part of it.

[1] Standing Committee Debates, Standing Committee B, 20 Feb. 1951, col. 683.

CHAPTER VI

The Campaign

I

In a group's relations with the government, there are moments of crisis when the group has to consider whether to adopt more forceful methods. The restraints upon the group are great, but there are moments when discontent breaks down restraint and the group resorts to the campaign.

At such times the group no longer relies upon the arguments of consultation to convince the government.[1] The issue ceases to be a private one between group and government. It is taken away from the process of consultation into the public arena. Having failed to convince the government directly, the group seeks to convince others and thereby bring itself additional support. A campaign involves a declaration of open opposition on certain points.

It is not an attempt to coerce the government; that would be to pass from pressure to revolt. It would not be the expression of a discontent, but of a schism in society.

The campaign rests upon the assumption that the government may respond to opinion, where it has not responded to argument and representation. It is not necessary that it be the opinion of all or of any particular section, that it be the opinion of Parliament or of the press—merely that the government should recognize the importance of opinion external to itself.

The government operates in a climate of politics in which responsiveness to opinion is held a virtue. This virtue is inculcated by the need for the government to seek re-election. But it is more than that. In the same way as the M.P. feels a duty to the constituency, the government feels a duty to opinion.

[1] The group may have succeeded in convincing the ministry with which it has to deal. That in itself is not enough. The ministry concerned must convince other ministries and more often than not the Treasury. A campaign which appears to be directed against the recalcitrant attitude of one ministry may in fact aid that ministry in its arguments with other ministries. That is why it is safer to talk of government than of ministry.

The degree of discontent expressed by the members of the group and the support it receives from other sections of society are new factors in the situation which the government is obliged to consider.

The activities of the government depend upon a certain amount of popular support. It does not rest exclusively on its own powers. Responsiveness to opinion will vary with the degree to which the government, as the party in action, is committed on the question. The mandate stands as the party's justification to opinion, but on many questions the party is not committed.

2

The campaign will make use of such methods as are likely to arouse opinion where it is most effective. They are methods that must be used with care, for they yield no certain results. Yet some groups are led through inexperience to adopt methods which only have meaning in terms of a campaign, at a time when that is unnecessary. They are not possessed of the same judgement on what is attainable, as the more experienced groups.

The British Dental Association was faced in 1946 with the National Health Service Bill. It had not then as close a relationship with the Ministry of Health as has, of necessity, been built up since. The full value and the limits of consultation were perhaps not understood by it. It felt, however, that in this case it had not been adequately consulted—a potent ground for discontent among groups.

Mr. Willink, a former Minister of Health, had held long consultations with it before the publication of the 1945 White Paper on the National Health Service,[1] but Mr. Aneurin Bevan, partly because of the discussions already held and partly because of his views on negotiations with groups, had only very limited discussions before he introduced the Bill. The Consultative Council of the dental profession, on which the B.D.A., along with other dental organizations, was represented, met the Minister twice—once to hear the Government's proposals, the second time to state its reactions. 'In no sense of the word has there been anything in the nature of negotiations.'[2] The B.D.A. was not satisfied with this:

[1] e.g. *British Dental Journal*, 1 June 1945, p. 346.
[2] Ibid., 15 Mar. 1946, p. 210.

It must surely be obvious. . . . that there are a great number of important details needing careful consideration by the Ministry and discussion with a *small* number of dental experts. The attitude of the Ministry is that all these can be considered at a later date after the introduction of a Bill. The profession is entitled to resent this. We are in danger, if we are content to maintain an ineffective defensive attitude, of being put into a position from which it will be extremely difficult to extricate ourselves. If the profession is to surmount this danger we must resist, and the time to make plain that we do not intend to be dominated by any Minister or any Government is *now*.[1]

They were strong words but foolish, since the B.D.A.'s objections were on points of comparatively minor importance[2]—hardly sufficient to justify such strong feelings.

The B.D.A. and the Consultative Committee prepared for action. The latter appointed a Parliamentary Agent and with his help amendments were drafted to the Bill covering the points on which the Committee was in disagreement with the Minister. By the time the Bill was referred to the Standing Committee, the dental organizations stood ready for action.

The Consultative Committee had appointed a 'small Sub-Committee for lobbying purposes, i.e. to meet Members of Parliament who are members of Standing Committee C, which is at present considering the Bill with a view to seeking their support for the various amendments'.[3] An appeal was published stating that any member of the profession who 'feels that he can assist by his personal influence with any Member of Parliament who is a member of the Standing Committee C., is asked to communicate at once with the Honorary Secretary of the Consultative Committee . . .'.[4]

The B.D.A. set up its own Public Relations Committee. It is kindness to ascribe its conduct to inexperience. There was no harm in its holding a series of public meetings, but it went too far in its advice to dentists:

Your patient and thousands of other patients voted <u>your</u> M.P. to Parliament. He wants to retain those votes; he must retain them

[1] Ibid., 5 Apr. 1946, p. 243—from *A Call To The Profession from the Council of the British Dental Association.*

[2] e.g. It wished for increased dental representation on the Central Health Service Committee and it wished to prevent the setting up of separate dental health centres (there being little evidence of a Ministerial desire to do this).

[3] *British Dental Journal,* 7 June 1946, p. 386.

[4] Ibid.

if he is to keep his seat. YOUR PATIENT can be your most powerful ally—he already has confidence in you—he will pay heed to what you say—he may become an active partisan—educate him.

WHAT SHALL I DO?

Seize every opportunity to make your case clear to him. Display the B.D.A. poster in your waiting room—talk to him in your surgery—remind him of your M.P.—his M.P.—encourage him to write a protest.[1]

Such a crude use of the patient's relationship with his dentist would have had dangerous implications had the advice not been doomed to failure. No more unsuitable place for political propaganda than a dentist's surgery can be imagined.

It is not surprising that the dentists found themselves forced back into a more routine pattern. The main contacts of the dental organizations in the House of Commons were on the Government side. There were only two dentist M.P.s—Captain J. Baird and Mr. H. G. McGhee. They were both Labour M.P.s. The Lobbying Committee was closely associated with Captain Baird in the progress of the Bill, though of the eighteen amendments drafted with the help of the Parliamentary Agent engaged by the Consultative Committee, Captain Baird selected only ten.[2] However, he arranged a meeting with the Minister to discuss the other amendments.

After Captain Baird had introduced this deputation, various speakers put the case upon the amendments. The Minister replied at length. He

was not prepared to accept outright any of the amendments to the Bill which were brought to his notice, but he pointed out that the reception of the deputation was unusual and he was glad of the opportunity to explain the points which had arisen though . . . he could not carry on two Committee stages of the Bill, one in his own room, and the other in the House of Commons.[3]

His main point was that he wished to prevent the Bill becoming too precise and he considered that some of the questions raised would be better dealt with by regulations.

The deputation decided to withdraw seven of the amendments. This left the Lobbying Committee with the amendments that Captain Baird had agreed to table and an amendment intended

[1] *British Dental Journal*, 21 June 1946, p. 414.
[2] Ibid., 6 Sept. 1946, pp. 160–1.
[3] Ibid.

to secure that a grant-in-aid could be made to those people who wanted more expensive denture sets than those to be provided by the national health service.

Most of the amendments were treated in the routine manner. It was too routine for the Lobbying Committee which noted that though it could succeed in getting amendments on the order paper, after that their fate lay with the sponsor despite the fact that one member of the Committee always attended the debates in order to keep in touch with Captain Baird and to discuss the amendments with other members of the Standing Committee.[1] Captain Baird was unwilling to push any of the amendments to a division. For the most part he was content to obtain an assurance from the Minister that he would put a certain interpretation on words in the Bill. For example, one of the amendments sought to write into the Bill a scheme to secure a priority dental service for adolescents.[2] The Minister assured the Standing Committee that while there were difficulties involved in priority schemes, he laid 'special emphasis' on the necessity of treating adolescents.[3] In view of this, Captain Baird withdrew his amendment. It is unlikely that the Lobbying Committee, ever seeking concrete results, were satisfied with so vague and informal an assurance. On several points Captain Baird did not even move his amendments. On the question of health centres he had an amendment on the order paper to secure that health centres 'shall not be provided solely for the provision of general dental services'.[4] He obtained an assurance on this point[5] without moving the amendment. The Lobbying Committee clearly found this type of activity unsatisfactory.

Only on the amendment relating to grants-in-aid did the activities of the Public Relations Committee of the B.D.A. have any perceptible effect. This amendment had found no sponsor on the Labour side of the House. Commander T. D. Galbraith (now Lord Strathclyde) of the Conservative Party was approached by Mr. A. H. Condry and Mr. W. G. Senior of the Lobbying Committee, but appeared unwilling to table it; however, after consulting with other members of his Party he indicated that he was willing to sponsor a modified version. Meanwhile the

[1] Ibid.
[2] Standing Committee Debates, Standing Committee C, 6 June 1946, col. 1531.
[3] Ibid., col. 1534. [4] Ibid., col. 1500. [5] Ibid., col. 1515.

activities of the dentists in South Wales had interested Mr. Hopkin Morris of the Liberal Party in the original amendment and he had set it down on the order paper.[1] After a short speech he found the amendment so heavily attacked by Mr. Bevan and Captain Baird that he withdrew it.[2] The use of a Liberal M.P. to sponsor an amendment may relieve a group of some of the difficulties caused by party discipline, but it does not necessarily secure the amendment wide support.

Though further attempts to promote amendments were made on the report stage, the most that the dentists could obtain was assurances. These they could probably have obtained without their attempts at a public campaign. It may have been useful to have them given in the House of Commons, but to secure that there was no need for the waste of energy in their moves towards a campaign. These give the impression of a lack of purpose. The amendments were not sufficiently important to justify them and one can only assume that lack of experience led the dentists to adopt this strategy.

3

Inexperience leads groups to adopt some of the tactics of the campaign, but groups which are far from inexperienced may resort to a campaign, and a full-blooded one at that. These campaigns arise out of major discontents. The restraints are broken down and a group normally content to seek agreement by consultation turns to the campaign. For groups this is no light decision, though there are some like the National Union of Teachers with a greater tendency to believe that solutions can be reached by campaigns. In part this is due to the fact that these groups have certain advantages in a campaign, such as size of membership, and in part to their historical development in which campaigns have been important (for example, a body like the N.U.T. has turned to the campaign where other bodies have turned to the strike, alike in this with many professional organizations and the civil service unions). Even for these groups a campaign involves an important decision. To make it the group

[1] *British Dental Journal*, 6 Sept. 1946, pp. 160–1.

[2] Standing Committee Debates, Standing Committee C, 26 June 1946, cols. 1783–92.

must be able to see some advantage to be gained by a campaign. This means that a campaign must be practical; it must be on an issue upon which feeling is roused, and one on which it is conceivable that some change can be brought about in the government's outlook. It should be an issue of importance to the group, but not to the government. The wise group weighs these factors and only launches a campaign at a favourable moment.

In 1953–4 the National Union of Teachers along with other teachers' organizations vigorously opposed the Government's decision to introduce the Teachers (Superannuation) Bill to increase the contributory rates from 5 per cent. to 6 per cent. of teachers' salaries. To a certain extent the vigour of the campaign may have been due to a failure in consultation. Although the National Union of Teachers had taken part in the Working Party on the subject, it complained that it was not in fact informed of the Government's decision until it was announced in the House of Commons on 21 January 1954. But dissatisfaction with the decision, rather than the way it was announced, was at the back of the campaign. The Executive Committee of the Union unanimously resolved to oppose the Bill, and it was agreed that directions should be sent out to secure co-ordinated action by local associations.[1] At the same time, a letter was sent to all M.P.s which stated that the teachers were being dealt with unfairly in comparison with the rest of the community in being asked to accept what was in effect a cut in salary.[2] A deep dissatisfaction and an arguable case were at the Union's service.

Local associations began to contact M.P.s and the Executive decided that where a personal approach was not possible in the constituencies, the associations would be permitted to send two representatives to London at the Union's expense.[3] The Union headquarters conducted a running argument with the Minister in M.P.s' mailbags, answering point by point his reply to its own case. All these techniques were successful in their primary aim of arousing support from M.P.s. Particularly important was the support among Conservative M.P.s. Perhaps even more impor-

[1] *Schoolmaster*, 5 Feb. 1954, p. 211.
[2] Ibid., pp. 216–17.
[3] Ibid., 12 Feb. 1954, p. 250.

tant than the feeling expressed locally by teachers was the clear marshalling of the case by the headquarters staff of the Union; certainly this was of more importance than the formal expression of opposition by the Union M.P.s in the House.

The campaign gained almost startling success; the influence of Conservative back-benchers on the Government was such that the Bill was withdrawn. It was commonly believed that the Bill would be reintroduced in the next session with minor modifications, but in fact this did not happen. The Union could congratulate itself on at least having postponed the evil hour.

However, a new Teachers (Superannuation) Bill was introduced in the 1955–6 parliamentary session. The Government had made certain concessions, but these were far from sufficient to satisfy the National Union of Teachers or the other teachers' organizations. Despite a renewed campaign of exceptional vigour, the Bill was passed without any more than minor amendment. However, the campaign probably had an effect in bringing about the increase in teachers' salaries which took place at almost the same time as the Bill became law. Thus both campaigns had their successes, though not always direct successes.

A campaign can only hope to be effective if the members of the group are moved by discontent. A campaign must be rooted in members' dissatisfaction. In the case of the National Union of Teachers, each member was affected by the proposal and felt it keenly.

It is a little more difficult to understand the fervour with which the licensed trade fought the Licensing Bill introduced by the Labour Government in 1948. Primarily this Bill was designed to deal with the problem of licensed premises in new towns, which had been first pointed out to the Home Secretary by the Brewers' Society itself.

The reason why the Bill was opposed by the licensed trade was that it proposed an extension of state management to the new towns. The trade feared that this was intended to be an introduction to nationalization. 'It was the first step. The Government were trying to feel the strength of the Trade and to test public opinion. They wanted to see if it was safe to carry through nationalization. The Trade must fight the Bill tooth and nail. The fight would be as a preliminary skirmish to the total war against nationalization',[1] or as expressed by Camberwell licensees:

Your local 'pub'
Under State control
Would be a machine
Without a soul.[2]

The brewers' interest in the issue was direct and obvious and it is not surprising that the *Brewers' Journal* greeted the Bill in these terms:

Hitherto the Trade has loyally supported the Government, but now the time has come when it must declare its uncompromising opposition to these latest proposals. In Parliament the Opposition has tabled a motion for the rejection of the Bill, and this must be followed be an unceasing campaign to prevent such proposals finding a permanent place upon the Statute Book. . . . The only way to break down its determination is for such mass opposition to be brought to bear that no course other than resignation, would be possible except the reconsideration or withdrawal of the Bill.[3]

This was a tall order, and it seems strange that the *Journal* had forgotten its advice of three months before that a reasoned argument could gain little weight from mass support.[4]

The brewers' position was strengthened by the unity of the licensed trade behind them. This unity is part of the tradition of the licensed trade. It is formally expressed by the National Trade Defence Association, which 'exists to protect at all times the general interests of the licensed trade as a whole in and out of Parliament' and has representatives upon its Council of individual firms, and of all the trade associations directly connected with the licensed trade.[5] Following tradition this attack on the brewers' interests was seen as an attack on the whole trade. State management was regarded as a weapon of the temperance movement.

This is the explanation of the feeling throughout the whole trade, which made the strength of the campaign. It is impossible to give full details about the campaign because most of the trade is traditionally reticent about its activities in politics. However, the Wine and Spirit Association, which was a partner in the campaign, is not so secretive. It set up a sub-committee to decide

[1] General Secretary, National Trade Defence Association, *Brewers' Journal*, Dec. 1948, p. 522.
[2] Ibid., p. 523.
[3] Ibid., p. 512.
[4] See p. 34.
[5] *Brewers' Almanack*, 1953, p. 815.

its attitude and, having decided to act in concert with the Brewers' Society, to draft amendments. It circularized all M.P.s with a letter describing the Bill as 'unwarranted, ill-conceived and unnecessary'.[1] All members of the Association received a circular asking them to contact their M.P.s. This was followed up in the January 1949 issue of *Ridley's*, a trade journal, by a list of the members of the Standing Committee and a request from the Secretary of the Association to any who 'are acquainted with any of these Members of Parliament, or who are constituents, to please take a personal interest to see that the Trade point of view is impressed on them'.[2] As a result of these and similar activities, the trade claimed a success in the amendment of Clause 2. This was a clause which because of its loose phrasing was seriously regarded as containing a threat of general nationalization. This threat was removed by amendments.

It was the only success the trade achieved at that time. It was unable to change the main purpose of the Bill as its campaign was unable to make much impact upon the Labour Party. There was no possibility of widespread sympathy for its point of view among Labour M.P.s. The campaign left its mark in trade politics. It reintroduced bitterness. In 1949 the attempt by Mr. Geoffrey Bing to introduce a private members' bill to end the system of tied houses was regarded by the brewers as an attempt to break the unity of the trade. A new agreement between the Brewers' Society and the representatives of the licensees, containing more favourable standard terms for the latter, waylaid any incipient discontent.[3] Though Mr. Geoffrey Bing's Bill was never even debated, the bitterness remained, because the declared object of the trade was still the repeal of the provisions of the Licensing Act relating to new towns. Since this was not likely to be achieved under a Labour government (despite a strange reluctance by the National Executive of the party to give a straight answer on this question in the 1951 election[4]), the licensed trade was committed to working for the return of a Conservative government. The return of such a government led to the almost immediate introduction of the Licensed Premises

[1] *Ridley's*, 16 Dec. 1948, p. 776. [2] Ibid., 16 Jan. 1949, p. 98.

[3] '. . . such little danger as existed that Mr. Bing and his supporters could establish their case on the ground of discontent among tied tenants has been removed' (editorial in *Brewers' Journal*, Jan 1950, p. 3).

[4] Cf. H.C. Deb. 496, col. 1160.

in New Towns Bill, which was strongly opposed by the Labour Party in long acrimonious debates. However, the Bill was passed in 1952 and the trade found itself in a quieter world in which only the routine of consultation was required.

The Automobile Association, along with the other motorists' organizations, has established its position with regard to consultation. Outside the world of trade union and trade association, it is one of the few groups to do so. It has never been reluctant to campaign, and the abolition of the basic petrol ration by the Labour Government in 1947 was a decision which clearly affected all its members and the whole purpose of the Association. It exists to protect the interests of motorists and could not remain unconcerned. Nor were its members quiet and content. Successful campaigns are rarely imposed on members; rather they arise from their discontent to which the executive responds. In this campaign there was more than discontent. The strength of the Association's position lay in the case it was able to state. It claimed that a basic petrol ration was quite possible with existing supplies, provided effective measures were taken to deal with the black market. The motorists' organizations (the Automobile Association, the Royal Automobile Club, and the Royal Scottish Automobile Club) declared 'that in view of the economic crisis the possibility of a reduction could not be ignored, but there was no apparent reason for such a drastic reduction'. They felt that motorists were being asked to make a greater sacrifice than the rest of the community. Having failed to secure an interview for a deputation to the Prime Minister, the Association determined on a campaign along with the other motorists' organizations.

The motif of the campaign was a petition. It gave a positive point to all the activities of the organizations. It was carried by A.A. and R.A.C. patrol men. Garages and filling stations also co-operated.[1] The petition provided a means of expression for the discontent; it kept the issue alive. There was a danger that after the first impact of the decision the fervour would die down. However, the motorists' organizations had realized that a sustained campaign might be needed for success and adjusted their tactics accordingly.

The object was to impress on the Government the strength of

[1] More than 12,000 garages had undertaken to co-operate.

feeling on the issue in the country. They also sought to develop feeling in Parliament. An attempt was made to 'create an informal opposition in the House of Commons by constant contact with members of all parties'. By-elections were exploited, not so much as a means of influencing candidates, but as a means of arousing public opinion and giving it expression.

Formal and informal representations were being made to the Government but, failing a result, the campaign continued with the presentation on 29 October 1947 by Mr. Alfred Edwards (then still a Labour M.P.) of the first million signatures to the petition. Later that day, in a division on petrol policy, the Government's majority fell to 27 (187 to 160), partly due to abstentions.[1] A few weeks later, Mr. L. W. Joynson-Hicks, a member of the Association's Committee, presented the remainder of the signatures to the petition.

The campaign had so far achieved no result. It was a dangerous moment since, with the presentation of the petition, the impetus was lost. The Association asked all its members to inform their trade organizations, the press, and their M.P.s of the hardships that were being caused. It hoped by these means to associate new elements in the campaign and give it renewed vigour.

Early in 1948 the motorists' organizations began to make headway. The Government set up a committee to investigate the black market in petrol. The day after it had reported, the Government announced that it would grant to those who had no other allowance, a basic petrol ration giving about 90 miles a month. It inaugurated the red petrol scheme, which proved as successful as the Association had anticipated, and in October the ration was expanded.

The campaign had been successful because of a combination of pressure by opinion and pressure by well-ordered argument. The motorists' organizations had wisely narrowed their differences with the Government to a practical issue. By continual argument they forced the Government to recognize the possibilities of control of the black market. The public campaign hammered

[1] H.C. Deb. 443, cols. 1043–6. Cf. *The Times*, 31 Oct. 1947: 'a small group of Labour members who were in the House abstained from the division. There seems little doubt that a number of the Labour members who were absent also wished to avoid recording their votes for the Order. They have been made aware of the strong feeling about it in their constituencies.'

home the urgency of the issue. The campaign was an example of well-directed tactics. But there was a very strong case. Motorists felt very strongly on the issue and there was a fair amount of support readily available in Parliament and the press. The support in Parliament was available on both sides of the House.[1]

The National Association of Master Bakers, Confectioners, and Caterers did not find itself in such a strong position in the campaign it waged between 1952 and 1956 for a greater bread subsidy for small bakers. There was no ready support in Parliament or the press. Any support had to be fought for and though its members felt strongly on the issue, the Association lacked a good clear case with which to gain support. Its contention was that the bread subsidy was calculated in such a way as to make it impossible for the small baker to survive. The subsidy was calculated at a level which gave average profits of 5*s.* per sack of flour produced which, if broken down, gave the co-operative bakers average profits of 9*s.* 9*d.* a sack, the multiple bakers 6*s.*, and the smaller bakers 2*s.* 10*d.*[2] The Government contended that the subsidy was fair and that any other basis of calculation would interfere with the prevailing economic tendencies. The small bakers, however, felt their economic survival was threatened and launched a campaign in protest. It continued over a number of years.[3] It was still officially continuing in 1955 and 1956 though the early fervour had faded as hope had died away. For nothing significant had been achieved. In the terms of the prevailing beliefs of society, the bakers had no case, and all their passion could not make up for this.

The highlights of the campaign were meetings which were characterized by deep feeling and strong sentiment. 'The future bread supply of the nation is prejudiced by the rapid elimination of the family baker and immediate action is demanded on the case presented by the National Association of Master Bakers for a graduated subsidy.'[4] This was the motif. Tactics were expressed thus:

We shall not spare them, we shall not leave them alone and we shall not be satisfied with a formal acknowledgement. M.P.s have

[1] *A.A. Annual Report* for year ended 30 Apr. 1948, pp. 2–4.

[2] *N.A.M.B.C.C. Annual Report*, 1953, p. 21.

[3] It was only stopped by the abolition of the bread subsidy in 1956, which left the issue to be settled by economic competition.

[4] Telegram to the Prime Minister, *Bakers National Association Review*, 1952, p. 826.

to come to their constituencies at times and we shall seek interviews with them as long as we are alive to do so. It is time we stopped talking to each other about it. . . . We have been preaching to the converted and we have to convert the heathen. My last word is 'Go thou and do likewise'.[1]

Beyond these fiery mass meetings and contact with M.P.s,[2] the campaign lacked definition. The Association is a loosely knit federation and may have lacked the means to enforce a plan of campaign. Instead there were substituted spontaneous outbursts. A few of the branches achieved success in approaches to local M.P.s in 1952. The Grimsby, Cleethorpes, and District Branch met Mr. Cyril Osborne and obtained his help. He followed up a meeting with the Branch by investigating the case at the Association headquarters. He then arranged for a deputation from the Association to the Ministry of Food.[3] The Newport Association claimed to have had a useful interview with Mr. Peter Thorneycroft, the President of the Board of Trade, who promised to put its case before the Ministry of Food.[4] But this lobbying does not seem to have been general throughout the country.

A few minor concessions were made, but the campaign failed to make the political impact necessary for success. There was no clear case. There was only the anger of the family baker and that was not enough. It was an anger that had to be expressed. A campaign may be tactically useless, but a public expression of discontent still be necessary to the internal health of the group. Perhaps the leaders of the Association could not have prevented the campaign even if they had wanted to.

The Finance Bill annually provides the setting for a number of campaigns. A group representing an interest which faces a declining economic position is only too ready to see in purchase tax or some other tax the cause of the decline. The annual chance to make representations to the Chancellor has advantages for groups, but it is disillusioning if a group experiences a yearly rejection of its representations. Groups which see their representations having no result may feel the need to find some other method of expressing a discontent which grows under the rebuffs. Gradually, from year to year they will seek stronger

[1] *Bakers National Association Review*, 1952, p. 827.
[2] Ibid., p. 506.
[3] Ibid., p. 728.
[4] Ibid., p. 1173.

expression for their views until their activities have the character of a campaign. A general approach to M.P.s in their constituencies can be the first step.

The concern of the National Chamber of Trade about the problem of surplus stocks of goods held by retailers when there is a cut in purchase tax dates back to 1946, since when, in the words of its annual report for 1952–3, it has been 'confronted with the stubborn attitude of Customs and Excise which has consistently opposed the introduction of any scheme of purchase tax rebate, and successive Chancellors of the Exchequer have been ready and willing to be influenced by this point of view'.[1] Confidence had declined since 1946, when the Chancellor was able to claim he had the backing of the National Chamber.[2] This decline had come about from the continual failure of its representations to result in any real benefit for the retailers.

In 1952 the National Chamber approached M.P.s through local chambers to obtain their support for a new clause to the Finance Bill which was moved by Mr. Cyril Osborne, one of the Association's vice-presidents, and seconded by Mrs. Barbara Castle.[3] Yet no help for the retailers was obtained. A further attempt was made to secure support for a clause moved by the Opposition in 1953, but it achieved no more than previous attempts.[4] The Board of Management of the National Chamber did not, however, intensify the campaign. It was restrained in its approach and did not want a full-blooded campaign on this issue. The fact that an independent committee had reported unfavourably on the problem made it difficult to present a convincing case.

The Cinematograph Exhibitors' Association, faced with a similar situation, moved more certainly towards a campaign. It was opposed to the level which entertainments tax had reached and felt that it was threatening the economic position of cinema exhibitors at a time when they were faced with the competition from television. In 1952 the Association relied mainly on routine representations to the Chancellor of the Exchequer and the Financial Secretary to the Treasury, but the only result of prolonged negotiations was a remission of a halfpenny on the nine-

[1] *N.C.T. Annual Report*, 1952–3, p. 17.
[2] See p. 64.
[3] *N.C.T. Annual Report*, 1952–3, p. 17.
[4] Ibid., 1953–4, p. 16.

penny seat.[1] This left the Association completely unsatisfied and it decided to back up its case with an analysis of the state of the industry, which it instructed its auditors to draw up. When prepared it was submitted to every member, to the Chancellor of the Exchequer, and to the Customs and Excise Department.[2]

In 1953 this report provided the background to all the Association's activities. On the national level its representations to the Government were coupled with discussions with the Conservative Film Committee and also with an all-party group interested in the film industry. Seven Labour M.P.s tabled a motion which the Association supported.[3] A collection of documents giving the Association's case was sent to all its members, together with a letter urging them to contact their local M.P.s during the parliamentary recess.[4] For the most part this was organized by the local branches which met M.P.s in their constituencies or sent deputations to the House of Commons, as did the North Lincolnshire, North Staffordshire, and Notts and Derby Branches among others.[5] Since no immediate effect was seen, the campaign for the session of 1953–4 started in September, using the same methods.[6] It achieved some degree of success in the Budget of 1954 when the Chancellor of the Exchequer made some concessions on the entertainments tax, amounting to an average reduction of about 10 per cent. in the level of tax.

For a time, this concession if not satisfying the Association at least induced a quieter mood. But it was not for long. The growing competition from television made the entertainments tax an increasing burden. By the 1956–7 parliamentary session, the Association along with other organizations representative of the cinematograph industry was conducting a vigorous campaign. Among the various methods used to attract public attention was a film made by one of the newsreel organizations which high-lighted the closure of many local cinemas and urged those watching the film to write to their M.P.s demanding the abolition of the entertainments tax on the cinematograph industry. Some cinemas displayed posters and advertisements proclaiming the plight of the industry and ascribing it to the entertainments

[1] *C.E.A. Annual Report*, 1952, p. 4.
[2] Ibid., pp. 4–5.
[3] Ibid., 1953, p. 4.
[4] *Kinematograph Weekly*, 8 Jan. 1953, p. 4.
[5] *C.E.A. Annual Report*, 1953, pp. 40–84.
[6] Ibid., p. 4.

tax. The 1957 Budget made further concessions, but still left the industry dissatisfied.

All these campaigns have been concerned with what were, to the groups, major problems. They arose as much from the discontent of the members as of the leaders, although some of them were associated with what was regarded as inadequate consultation—a more potent influence on a group's leaders than on its members—but in most cases the discontent has been based on the economic threat to the welfare or even the existence of the groups' members. The cinema exhibitors saw in the reduction of the entertainments tax a means of countering a serious threat to their existence. The small local bakers saw themselves threatened by the large concerns. To the teachers the Teachers (Superannuation) Bills were in effect an attempt to cut their salaries, with all that meant in memories to that profession. There can be no doubt that for the groups these were major problems; but there was not a complete campaign. The relations between group and government did not break down. Sometimes negotiations went on alongside the campaign. After all, when all was over, group and government would have to live together.

4

Only when the threat to the group is an immediate and direct threat to its existence through the destruction of the interest it represents, or the group believes the system of consultation to have already broken down, can all restraint be abandoned. For how can restraint be justified when the group's existence is threatened or consultation has broken down? True, the group's existence can be terminated on more favourable terms or consultation be built up again. At the moment of crisis these considerations are not foremost in the leaders' minds: they are hardly present at all in the minds of the members who may themselves carry the group into a campaign.

There is no certain rule. In part it depends on the group. Most of the interests whose existence was terminated by nationalization between 1945 and 1950 did not put up much of a struggle. (The second crop promised to be more unruly, if it came to a harvest.) The gas and electricity authorities, though accustomed to routine parliamentary action, were not likely to sponsor a particularly belligerent campaign. Closely associated with the government, many of them were run by local authorities, to whom such a campaign was impossible, even if it was not for all of them undesirable.[1]

District meetings organized by the British Gas Council in 1946 voted by large majorities against the principle of nationalization but in favour of co-operation with the Ministry of Fuel and Power if nationalization were to be effected.[2] In pursuance of this policy the Council submitted to the Ministry a memorandum on 'The Organization and Regional Boundaries of a Nationalized Gas Industry'. 'This represented the tentative views of the Council without prejudice to its opposition to nationalization, for the accomplishment of which the Council was not to be regarding as having submitted a plan.'[3] While the Bill was going through the House 164 amendments were tabled by Opposition members at the request of the Council, who supplied them with detailed briefs and memoranda.[4] But at no point can the Council be said to have organized a strong public campaign against the Bill.

The Mining Association early came to the conclusion that 'while they preferred private rather than public ownership nevertheless because of the result of the General Election and the acceptance by Parliament of the contents of the Gracious Speech they did not propose to continue their opposition to the principle of nationalisation of the coal industry'.[5] The moment for opposition in principle had passed and the Association confined its representations to the question of compensation. If there had been a time for action, it was during the election period, but it is significant that McCallum and Readman[6] do not make any mention of any group campaigns in their description of the general election of 1945. It was not till 1950 that such campaigns became prominent.

However, the Road Haulage Association along with other bodies threatened by the nationalization of road transport

[1] The active opposition to the nationalization of water supplies has come from the Water Companies' Association representing private owners, not from the British Waterworks' Association, representing public and private owners.

[2] *Gas Journal*, 21 Aug. 1946, p. 307.

[3] *The Gas World*, 26 June 1948, p. 1027.

[4] Ibid., pp. 1028–9.

[5] H.C. Deb. 418, col. 701.

[6] R. B. McCallum and A. Readman, *The General Election of 1945* (1947).

found itself in a campaign in 1946 and 1947 despite the fact that the decision had already been taken and that there was little hope of averting it. It has sometimes been suggested that this type of campaign can best be regarded as a façade—the avowed object being more extreme than the hoped-for object. The concessions made by the Labour Government, especially on the question of the 'C' licensees, would seem to justify the conclusion in this case. But such an analysis ignores the attitude of group members. It assumes that the group's policy is that of the leaders alone.

The leaders of the Road Haulage Association might well have decided on a full-blooded campaign themselves, but much of its vigour was due to the extent to which its membership was aroused. The local branch which franked its envelopes with anti-nationalization slogans and thus earned a rebuke from the Post Office is typical of their attitude.[1] It is perhaps for this reason that the campaign lacked a clear form. It had no clear purpose. The need to give expression to a powerful anger was more important than any design or plan of campaign. A group can rarely hope to be an effective competitor to a political party. A campaign can sometimes be effective when it seeks to influence a government, but when it runs contrary to the main policies of the political party in power it is almost bound to fail. The campaign merely serves as a safety valve for discontent.

However, the threat directed against the group may not be central to the party's policy. In such a case there is more hope for a campaign. In 1945 the National Conference of Friendly Societies, realizing the dangers to its members from the proposals being put forward for a new scheme of national insurance, attempted to safeguard their position by securing support from candidates at the general election. A questionnaire sent out centred round this question: 'If elected to Parliament will you support the Friendly Societies being maintained as the responsible agents of the government under the new scheme of National Insurance in the administration of sickness and allied benefits?' One hundred and ninety-nine of the future Labour M.P.s answered in the affirmative including Mr. G. S. Lindgren, the future Parliamentary Secretary to the Ministry of National Insurance.

[1] *The Times*, 20 Jan. 1947.

The Labour Party later admitted that one of its two instructions to candidates on the subject had read as follows:

Many candidates are receiving questionnaires on the subject of national insurance and approved societies. A factual document on this subject has already been circulated to them, and I submit for your guidance the following additional notes.

NATIONAL INSURANCE AND APPROVED SOCIETIES

The Labour Party is of the view that in our future Social Insurance scheme the system of Approved Societies shall be abandoned with the exception of *bona fide* Friendly Societies and trade unions which have an honourable record of work in both public and voluntary insurance and should be free to come in if they so wish.

The principle of equal benefits for equal contributions, which is a distinctive feature of the Beveridge and White Paper proposals for health insurance should be preserved. This is substantially Liberal and Tory policy, too, though the Tories make no exception for Trade Unions and Friendly Societies.[1]

However, the Labour Government decided not to use the friendly societies in the administrative machinery of the national insurance scheme. Faced with the instruction to candidates various explanations were put forward. The attempt to explain it away as the mistake of a not very experienced young man in Transport House was not impressive.[2] The Government was on happier ground when it said it considered it was now making the right decision, and that that and not so-called pledges was the best test.

It is dangerous to regard election replies as pledges; the group which seeks to use them as such may only succeed in arousing bitterness. The M.P. can only state his opinion at the time the question is asked and does so, perhaps without the necessary amount of thought. He cannot be expected to pledge his future action and most groups, for their own sake, if for no other reason, accept that as being so. But faced with a clear threat the friendly societies were in no mood for such considerations.

The National Conference was roused to action. In January 1946 the Executive, authorized to take any action it considered

[1] Standing Committee Debates, Standing Committee A, 21 Mar. 1946, col. 322, and H.C. Deb. 418, col. 1786.

[2] Standing Committee Debates, Standing Committee A, 26 Mar. 1946, cols. 365–6.

necessary,[1] decided to launch a campaign with special emphasis on mass meetings and a petition.[2] Sir William Beveridge's (now Lord Beveridge) support was enlisted.[3] At a mass meeting in the Albert Hall seven M.P.s spoke (two Conservative, two Labour, two Liberal, and one Independent).[4] It was the support of some Labour M.P.s that gave the edge to the campaign and appeared to give it a chance of success. The most active of these M.P.s was Mr. H. E. Goodrich, himself a member of the National Conference's Executive. The decisive vote on the issue in the House of Commons resulted, however, in a defeat for the friendly societies by 278 to 184 votes.[5]

The most controversial part of the campaign was the use made of the questionnaires, to which members of the Conservative Party were given access and some of which were even taken to the House of Commons to be brought out during debates.[6]

In a breakdown campaign, where the threat to the group is clear, discretion is not an easy virtue. The relationship with the government has broken down and with it the traditional ways. Such a breakdown does not arise only from direct threats. It may arise out of the feeling of a group that its position has been undermined; that consultation, instead of being a help to the group, is taking place on a false basis. The group that distrusts consultation has no feelings of restraint, only the knowledge that drastic measures are needed. Where such a campaign is launched, the group is unlikely to achieve its immediate intent. An angry group cannot beat down a government. Indeed, the impact of the campaign is likely to be greater on the group than on the government. A campaign into which the group throws all its strength must have a cataclysmic effect on the group, if it fails. It must reconsider its position, since its activities have failed to secure it the place and influence it considers itself entitled to.

The outstanding example in recent British politics of a breakdown campaign was the 'pledge dispute' of 1943–4 between the National Farmers' Union and the Government. The actual

[1] *The Times*, 18 Jan. 1946.
[2] Ibid., 22 Jan. 1946.
[3] Ibid., 26 Jan. 1946.
[4] Ibid., 12 Feb. 1946.
[5] H.C. Deb. 423, cols. 616–19.
[6] Ibid. 418, col. 2004. Mr. A. A. H. Marlowe quotes Mr. G. S. Lindgren's reply. Standing Committee Debates, Standing Committee A, 26 Mar. 1946, cols. 385–6. Mr. R. A. Butler quotes Mrs. B. Ayrton Gould's reply.

dispute arose out of the price review by the Government in November 1943, but discontent had been growing in agriculture, for some time. The Government would not commit itself on post-war agricultural policy and declared itself unwilling even to enter into discussions about it. The fear of the farmers that the end of the war would see the end of the period of prosperity, was canalized into a campaign to urge M.P.s to take immediate action to get discussions started. Considerable support was obtained in the House of Commons, but no immediate action resulted. Farmers, faced with this situation, were becoming discontented with the N.F.U. itself. The N.F.U. realized this. Mr. J. K. Knowles, the Vice-President, said: 'Nobody can possibly argue that Britian's largest industry is as strong and articulate as it ought to be. . . . Our councils are divided [and] our counselling is not always coherent to the public.'[1] Measures were being considered to strengthen the Union. New officials had been appointed.[2] Policy was being thought out and an attempt being made to improve public relations by trying to gain the sympathy of chambers of commerce, which were addressed by Union officials as part of a general policy of securing the support of industrial interests.[3] These measures were not sufficient to allay the discontent. Mr. Randolph Tory, in an article in the *Farmers' Weekly*, wrote: 'If the N.F.U. do not get to work and force the Government to state their after-the-war policy very soon indeed, they will lose 40 per cent. of their members.'[4] This could be dismissed if it stood alone, but other evidence shows that morale within the Union was very low. Captain Deakin, the President, was censured at the Norfolk County Branch for his statement that farmers accepted the necessity of government control after the war,[5] and the County Delegate for Norfolk criticized the short time allowed for discussion of the interim report on post-war policy in the N.F.U. Council.[6] Rutland County Branch was dissatisfied with the leadership: 'We are not carrying enough weight and we must have a man of established reputation.' It suggested that the President should be an outstanding personality, such as the Marquess of Linlithgow or Mr. Walter

[1] *Farmers' Weekly*, 29 Oct. 1943, p. 32.
[2] Ibid.
[3] e.g. Captain Deakin's tours, *Farmers' Weekly*, 4 June 1943, p. 15.
[4] Ibid., 12 Nov. 1943, p. 27.
[5] Ibid., 23 July 1943, p. 16.
[6] Ibid., 13 Aug. 1943, p. 12.

Elliot, 'who could go to a government department or anywhere and put their case with exceptional authority.'[1]

Though too much weight should not be put upon such remarks, it is easy to see that the situation in 1943 was far from placid. It is true that at the end of October 1943 Mr. R. S. Hudson (now Viscount Hudson), the Minister of Agriculture, had announced that he was ready to enter into discussions on post-war policy and pledged the Government to a four-year plan. But the impression gained by farmers was that the Government had done this with great reluctance.[2] Until the Union and its members were satisfied with the attitude of the Minister, they could not look forward with any confidence to these discussions on post-war policy.

Such was the atmosphere when the Minister refused to grant the N.F.U.'s request for increased prices to meet an increase in wages. He stated that he did not think it justified in the light of farmers' overall revenue and costs. The Union alleged that the Minister had broken the pledge which had been given to agriculture in November 1940 and October 1941:

> The Government has now decided . . . to guarantee that the present system of fixed prices and an assured market will be maintained for the duration of hostilities and for at least one year thereafter. Prices will be subject to adjustment to the extent of any substantial changes in the cost of production.[3]

The position of the Government was that the pledge had not been broken. There were, in fact, two interpretations of the pledge, the N.F.U. contending that farmers were entitled to full compensation for any increase in costs, and the Government contending that the pledge did not mean that the Minister was prevented from considering the general position of the farmers, both in relation to costs and increased revenue.[4] The N.F.U. also attempted to criticize the Minister's figures and claimed

[1] Ibid., 29 Oct. 1943, p. 21.

[2] Ibid., 5 Nov. 1943. e.g. see editorial, p. 11.

[3] H.C. Deb. 367, col. 92.

[4] This had previously been made clear to the N.F.U. when they were seen by the Chancellor of the Exchequer and the Lord President of the Council. 'On the occasion of each general review of prices it was permissible to consider the whole course of farmers' costs and receipts from that date [1940] up to the time of the review' (H.C. Deb. 396, cols. 721–2). But this interpretation had not been made known to many farmers.

that the farmers' position was not as good as these appeared to show, but it was upon the pledge that it based its stand. The truth was that it did not have the facts which were required to refute the Government's statements on the financial position of farmers or even to challenge them effectively. The N.F.U. had no adequate economic department and therefore was unable to answer the *Farmers' Weekly* editorial which stressed the need for 'specific evidence—seen, counted, checked and verified' to rebut the Government's statements[1] as it was unable to meet other similar requests throughout the campaign. The gravamen of its charge had to be that the Government could not be trusted.

The General Purposes Committee of the Union appealed to the Minister to reconsider his decision on prices in view of the pledge, but without waiting for an answer it began activities which showed that a campaign was beginning. All county branches were instructed to get in touch with their M.P.s and they were urged to do so with these words: 'The pledge of 1940 is withdrawn; . . . That is the background against which we must view the announcement that consultations are to be commenced with the industry on future agricultural policy. . . .'[2] However, the Minister's own statement on the breakdown of the price negotiations was not couched in conciliatory terms: 'I am quite sure that the great body of decent, patriotic and efficient farmers in this country do not ask for anything more than they are obtaining in the price now announced.'[3]

The campaign did not take long to gather force. Within a week three-quarters of the county branches had passed resolutions supporting the N.F.U.'s position. Northamptonshire suggested organized opposition to M.P.s not supporting the farmers' viewpoint; West Sussex passed a resolution of no confidence in the Minister; in Leeds Mr. Hudson, addressing a meeting, invited and had a very stormy passage.[4]

Negotiations were not finally broken off until the end of December 1943, but throughout that month both participants acted as though they had been. Farmers were meeting M.P.s in their constituencies and were making a fair degree of headway,

[1] *Farmers' Weekly*, 3 Dec. 1943, p. 11. [2] Ibid., p. 16.

[3] Ibid., p. 15.

[4] Ibid., 10 Dec. 1943, p. 14: ' "All I can say is that if confidence is such a delicate plant that £3,000,000 on £600,000,000, is going to destroy it then—" the reminder [*sic*] of the statement was lost in interruptions. . . .'

although none of the M.P.s would associate themselves with the demand for the Minister's resignation which some branches were making. Sir William Wayland, M.P. for Canterbury, agreed that the prices were mean but asserted that the Minister was the best that farmers had had for fifty years.[1] More significant, since it drew attention to a weakness in the Union's position, was the reply of Earl Winterton and Mr. L. W. Joynson-Hicks in Sussex. They said that the farmers' contention was a matter of accountancy and, if they would send cost details proving it, they, the M.P.s, would ask for an interview with the Minister of Agriculture.[2]

The highlights of the campaign were the broadcasts. Mr. Hudson made a broadcast stating his point of view. The N.F.U. immediately demanded, as of right, an opportunity to reply. After discussion as a matter of high policy, the B.B.C. granted it broadcasting time and Sir Cleveland Fyfe, the N.F.U.'s General Secretary, put its views before the public.[3]

As a result of the campaign a motion was put down in the House of Commons drawing attention to the inadequate prices. N.F.U. action in the constituencies was now directed at securing support for this motion, so that when negotiations were finally broken off, the impetus of the campaign went on, unaltered. Strong things were said.[4] At a meeting with the Suffolk M.P.s the local branch demanded the resignation of Mr. Hudson with an anger which the M.P.s tried to turn into more productive channels. Like meetings were held throughout the country.[5]

The climax was reached at the annual conference of the N.F.U. which, in the circumstances, became a prolonged protest meeting. It resolved to ask the Prime Minister to receive a deputation before the debate which had now been arranged (though not on the back-benchers' motion). Captain Templeton, the retiring President, sounded a warning note to those who were placing hope in the debate: 'They would see, therefore, that the coming debate in Parliament was not going to get them anywhere. They could not supply members of Parliament with

[1] Ibid., 17 Dec. 1943, p. 14.
[2] Ibid., 23 Dec. 1943, p. 13.
[3] *N.F.U. Yearbook*, 1945, p. 8.
[4] e.g. Mr. Knowles said in Somerset: 'The spectre of betrayal was again haunting an industry that had so much to do for the good of the nation' (*Farmers' Weekly*, 31 Dec. 1943, p. 15).
[5] *The Times*, 12 Jan. 1944 and 13 Jan. 1944.

briefs which would involve the disclosure of information given them by the Government.'[1] Already it had become clear to the N.F.U. leaders that the campaign had resulted in nothing but an outburst of anger. Nevertheless, it continued right up to the debate. M.P.s were circularized with a memorandum and a deputation from the Union attended, by invitation, a meeting of the Conservative Parliamentary Agriculture Committee to give its views on the interpretation of the Government's pledge.[2]

The debate proved to be the end of the campaign which had lasted just under two months. Mr. Hudson made an impressive defence of his position which was accepted by M.P.s. The campaign had failed in its immediate purpose. The N.F.U. attitude was summed up in a statement that

> the dispute remains unsettled. Nevertheless, the debate very definitely contributed to the establishment of a sensibly improved 'atmosphere'. . . .
>
> If confidence is to be restored among farmers, it is essential to get the prices dispute cleared out of the way as quickly as possible; when that has been done the union will gladly enter into discussions with the Minister of Agriculture on the better system of price fixing and other proposals put before the House.[3]

The Times was wiser in its analysis of the debate. It saw that the dispute must be regarded as closed: 'the full debate in the House of Commons on Wednesday should have cleared all minds of misunderstandings about the fulfilment of the 1940 pledge that prices would be adjusted to meet substantial changes in costs of production.'[4]

For Mr. Hudson had taken a firm stand in the debate on the issue of the pledge and the price dispute, making a concession on milk prices alone (in response to a factual case submitted by the Milk Marketing Board). He had offered to re-examine the basis of the price reviews and to renew consultations.[5] This willingness of the Ministry to re-examine its relationship with the N.F.U. was the most satisfactory result of the campaign. It could only be met by the N.F.U. reorganizing itself. The campaign forced it to do just that.

The first important change that occurred in the N.F.U.

[1] *The Times*, 20 Jan. 1944.
[2] *N.F.U. Yearbook*, 1945, p. 8.
[3] *The Times*, 28 Jan. 1944.
[4] Ibid., 29 Jan. 1944.
[5] H.C. Deb. 396, cols. 710–28.

was the building up of the Farm Accounts Scheme. This started in 1944 as a direct response to the demand for a factual check on the government figures in price negotiations. Having been forced to abandon the simple principle that prices should be increased to meet fully every increase in costs, the N.F.U. desperately needed a means of assessing the financial position of farmers. It was hoped 'to receive annually information on the financial results of 10,000 farms of different types and sizes throughout the country'. Towards the end of 1944 an agreement was reached with the Government on the economic basis of the price discussions. Since then the economic department of the N.F.U. has grown, and now agreement is reached between the Ministry and the Union on the economic basis before negotiations begin.[1]

Secondly, the machinery of the Union underwent a striking change. In 1944 a re-organization took place as a result of which Sir Cleveland Fyfe was offered the position of Chief Political Adviser and Advisory Officer. He declined it and left the Union. This left the position of General Secretary open, and it was filled by the then President, Mr. Knowles. The re-organization gave the General Secretary a team of officers directly responsible to him for their departments or groups of department.[2] The most important long-term development was the permanent Presidency of Mr. (now Sir) James Turner. Previously the position changed hands every year, but from 1945 to 1957 he has continued to hold the position. To make this possible the rules of the Union were altered in 1946; but even so it is only possible for him to retain the position if he receives 85 per cent. of the votes cast in an election.[3]

The third important change was in the Union's parliamentary activities. Previously the work in Parliament had been sustained by sponsored candidates. In 1935 the Union sponsored two successful candidates, Sir Joseph Lamb and Major (now Sir) Reginald Dorman-Smith. Faith in this method had been shaken by the defeat at a by-election of Mr. (now Sir) Thomas Peacock, a sponsored Conservative, by a Commonwealth Party candidate.[4] The general election of 1945 was the last attempt to use

[1] *N.F.U. Yearbook*, 1945, p. 34.
[2] Ibid., p. 9.
[3] *N.F.U. Rules*, Rule 34 (as amended 21 Nov. 1946).
[4] *Farmers' Weekly*, 26 Feb. 1943, p. 15, and 5 Mar. 1943, p. 15.

this method. It has been realized that sponsored M.P.s may limit support in the House as much as they promote it. Far more influence is obtained by the methods that the Union has since pursued. A re-organization was begun in 1945 when new officials were appointed to the Parliamentary Department.[1] The Union has made very close contact not merely with the Agriculture Committee of the Conservative Party, but also with the Agriculture Group of the Labour Party. It has also placed emphasis on the selection of candidates within the parties' constituency organizations, urging that N.F.U. members should endeavour to influence this process.

The campaign led to an agonizing reappraisal; measures were taken which raised the N.F.U. from a position where frustration made a campaign of such violence inevitable. The failure of the campaign was necessary to ensure that the attitude existed for that reappraisal to take place.

5

In all the campaigns considered, the House of Commons has played a crucial role. It has been the centre to which the campaigners' attention has been directed. True, many activities have a direct influence upon the government; the spontaneous expression of discontent by a group and the support of the press are obviously important, but even these activities may be formally directed at Parliament. Parliament is seen by the campaigning group as a court of appeal for discontent.

Its role is not merely formal. The government is bound to recognize M.P.s as both mediators of discontent and its active exponents. The extent to which the group succeeds in impressing M.P.s is a test both of the weight of its case and the strength of the discontent. In achieving success in this, the group must rely largely upon its own immediate supporters. They have to carry the campaign. They may be all there is to it. For the groups which try to rouse opinion more widely are not often very successful.

The support of other groups may be obtained and that is important, for the government trained to respect group viewpoints accepts them as a genuine expression of public opinion. The press can be aroused but there are few cases of a group

[1] *N.F.U. Yearbook*, 1946, pp. 84–85.

arousing anything that can be described as opinion at the grass-roots. In 1953–4 the Public Transport Association allied itself with other groups interested in road passenger transport to campaign for a reduction in the level of petrol tax. They placed posters in buses drawing attention to the injustices of this tax and its effect upon bus fares. Almost all these posters contained a request to passengers to write to their M.P.s.[1] It is doubtful whether anybody did. Most groups claim that their campaign is directed at arousing public opinion, but that is a necessary statement in their campaign, rather than a real expression of tactics.

Certainly in the campaign a group relies first on its own strength. It is the opinion of its own supporters and its expression that is important. The response of the government to opinion means the response to the opinions expressed by the group members, the response to Parliament, and in some cases to the press; both the last two are in part dependent upon the strength of group feeling.

Another consideration that is important is to give the campaign a coherent purpose; it should be more than an angry outburst of discontent. It must have a clearly stated object supported with reasoned arguments. There must be a planned use of the group's various weapons. The group must know whom it is going to influence and how. The National Union of Teachers' campaign against the first Teachers (Superannuation) Bill was a well-directed and well-informed campaign which brought influence to bear at the vital point—the Conservative back-benchers—while at the same time securing more general support. The motorists' organizations cleverly sustained the impetus of their campaign outside Parliament while building up an informed opinion inside. For alongside discontent must go a clear and reasoned case. The group must know its facts. Discontent can claim attention but alone it cannot hold it.

The campaign in all its variety is a significant part of British political life. It represents for the group a means of avoiding complete dependence on the government. Whether used or not, for most groups it provides a safety valve by its possibility.

Many groups do not use it. Some do not require to. Their

[1] e.g. in buses of the City of Oxford Motor Services Ltd. in Jan.–Mar. 1954. Leaflets were available at the main bus offices.

position in society is of such importance that they do not need to. The T.U.C. and the F.B.I. stand today outside the world of campaigns. But that is only because the government accords them such full recognition. In 1926 the T.U.C. went far beyond the type of campaign here considered. It still holds the campaign in reserve.

The local authority associations representing interests with a permanent position in our political system are restrained from too public an expression of discontent. Trade associations find in their traditional reticence a powerful restraint. The industrial campaign for better roads conducted by the British Road Federation between 1950 and 1955 was very subdued. But all groups feel some restraint. Most groups can generally find their needs met within those restraints. That does not mean that all their requests are granted, but that they achieve a reasonable proportion. Beyond that, demands would be for more than society could give them. Society cannot capitulate to one group. The campaign merely gives the group a means of ensuring it gets fair shares.

CHAPTER VII

Active Parliamentary Policies

I

THERE are some groups which pursue energetic policies not merely upon occasions, but permanently. These policies do not always reach the intensity of the campaigns described in the last chapter, but they do involve a full use of parliamentary activities.

Perhaps the most common reason for the pursuit of an active policy is the denial of consultation. Groups which have no opportunity to use the techniques of consultation in order to influence ministers or ministries directly must resort to other techniques in an attempt to influence them indirectly.

Groups which are advocates of ideas which are far from acceptance are unlikely to be consulted by the government. Many of them place great importance on their relations with M.P.s. However, this relationship alone cannot bring success. For example, the groups which wish to introduce simplified spelling or abolish vivisection can only hope to achieve success with government approval. These are not merely moral issues which can be left to a free vote in the House of Commons. Parliamentary and public action, even when taken to the stage of promoting a bill, is but a preliminary. This limitation may not be apparent under the forms such action takes, but it is always there. In these activities one watches the preliminaries on a journey that may lead to success. Further problems only arise with initial success in Parliament. Many groups are still seeking that.

The British Union for the Abolition of Vivisection is one of the more important anti-vivisection societies, of which there are four.[1] It might be thought that this dispersal of energy was unfortunate, but in the anti-vivisection campaign this does not really matter since the societies are so far from achieving success

[1] The others are the National Anti-Vivisection Society, the World League against Vivisection and for the Protection of Animals, and the London and Provincial Anti-Vivisection Society.

that the added strength which would come from unity would make no impression. All is done that can be done. The ideas advocated are so far from public acceptance that the groups' activity appears purposeless, as it seeks various methods to pursue its aims.

In 1951 the British Union sent out an election handbill and encouraged local branches to approach their candidates on the question. The branch system was not developed enough for this to be general. When Parliament assembled the Union sent a letter to all M.P.s inviting their support. One new supporter having been gained, a parliamentary panel of ten was formed, which gave help to the Union by asking questions.[1] This parliamentary activity was accompanied by propaganda in the country and legal work to prevent traffic in pets.

In view of the lack of progress made by such groups, the General Secretary of the National Anti-Vivisection Society suggested that candidates should be promoted in by-elections.[2] This could only be useful as a propaganda device. The Society was not the only group to let its thoughts stray in such unrewarding channels—unrewarding even from the publicity point of view.

Some groups have made more headway. They command a greater degree of parliamentary support, and their views have come to be regarded as being at least arguable. Proportional representation and world government have considerable backing in the House of Commons and the movement for the taxation of land values saw some hope of attaining at least some fraction of its aims through the controversies on development charges and town planning in the period from 1945 to 1955.

The temperance movement is long-established.[3] Its great days are past, but it still commands sufficient support to avoid the worst frustrations of weakness. The movement places great weight upon its activities in Parliament, where it has always been sure of support.

The temperance movement expresses itself politically through

[1] *B.U.A.V. 54th Annual Report*, 1952, pp. 13–14.

[2] *Manchester Guardian*, 12 June 1952. He said that the movement was in danger of being ignored. It was boycotted by the press and the B.B.C. while propaganda for vivisection was freely circulated.

[3] Cf. M. H. C. Hayler, *The Vision of a Century* (1953), a history of the United Kingdom Alliance.

the National Temperance Federation. There are twenty-two supporting bodies, of which the most important is the United Kingdom Alliance. The Federation carries out its work in Parliament through a formally constituted Temperance Group. In 1951 the Federation sent out to all candidates, either directly or through interested bodies, such as local free church federal councils, a list of issues considered important, and asked for indications of support. These issues fell far short of a demand for prohibition, and included some, such as restricting drinking by motorists, calculated to win wide support. After the election the Temperance Group was formed on the basis of these issues.[1] Though formally independent of the Federation, the Group was bound to be closely associated with it—a connexion that found expression in the election of Lord Mathers and Mr. James Hudson, the Chairman and Secretary of the Federation, as Chairman and Secretary of the Group.

The Group's activities in 1952 are typical. It decided that it would concentrate on road safety and education policy, the safer subjects. On road safety it determined to seek the support of the Royal Society for the Prevention of Accidents through the latter's Parliamentary Committee. In the meantime, it was agreed to raise the matter in the House and Mr. S. P. Viant (who had won a place in the ballot for motions) proposed a motion calling for measures to improve road safety. He took the opportunity to raise the issue of the influence of alcohol on drivers.[2] This was also brought up by Dr. Somerville Hastings, another member of the Group.[3] Despite the fact that a whip was sent round, 'asking all friends of Temperance to be present at House', nothing was achieved by the debate.[4]

On educational policy the Group relied on an approach to the Minister of Education by a deputation. It urged positive education against alcohol, but despite the sympathy expressed by the Minister, it was made clear that very little action was possible.[5]

The Group also opposed certain proposals in the House. Sir Ian Fraser introduced a Bill under the ten minutes rule to

[1] *National Temperance Federation Annual Report*, 1952, pp. 1–2.
[2] H.C. Deb. 502, cols. 1720–1.
[3] Ibid., cols. 1751–5.
[4] *National Temperance Federation Annual Report*, 1952, pp. 8–9.
[5] Ibid., pp. 14–15.

exempt from the provisions of the Licensing Act (1921) the sale and supply of intoxicants to passengers arriving at airports. The Group having considered this Bill decided to oppose it, with Mr. Charles Gibson as their spokesman, and to send a whip out through Mr. Hudson. On the division a tie of 173 votes appeared, and the Deputy Speaker gave his casting vote in favour of the Bill. The Group made arrangments for each succeeding Wednesday to secure that some member was present in order to prevent the Bill making any further progress.[1]

Later the Group decided to oppose a motion to be proposed in the House by Mr. Stephen McAdden advocating a relaxation of the licensing laws in the interests of encouraging tourists. Some very good whipping was done with the result that Mr. McAdden did not press his motion to a division.[2]

Thus in 1952 the temperance movement relied on its House of Commons activity. The Fraser and McAdden motions were not important. It would have been worthless to widen its activity to cope with threats likely to be repeated each year, but always in such a trivial way. The movement is well-advised to leave matters to a band of ardent men in the House, men with comparative freedom of action. To a certain extent this freedom is due to their concern with private members' bills and motions, but it is also due to the fact that they are allowed by their parties to express their opinions on temperance freely in the House, since those opinions are regarded as matters of conscience.

But what is a group to do which sees no possibility of further headway and yet is strong enough to feel deeply the injustice done to it? The suffragette movement was driven to extremism. There have been signs of extremism in one or two of the minor nationalist movements in Scotland. The dilemma faced by these nationalist movements is that though they enjoy widespread sympathy in Scotland, this sympathy is not sufficient to make people vote for a nationalist candidate in an election. It has been comparatively rare for a nationalist candidate to save his deposit in a fight with both the Conservative and Labour Parties. The only nationalist candidate ever to be elected had a straight fight against a Labour candidate in a wartime by-election. The main political issues are evidently of more importance to electors

[1] *National Temperance Federation Annual Report*, 1952, pp. 19–20.

[2] Ibid., pp. 20–21.

than the nationalist issue. Faced with this frustrating situation it is not surprising that occasionally extremist suggestions for action are made. They provide one road out of the dilemma.

The same dilemma has confronted the Scottish Covenant Association. This Association arose out of the movement started by the Scottish Convention in 1942 and led by Mr. John MacCormick. The objects of this movement were moderate. It sought not the full dominion status demanded by the Scottish National Party, but the creation of a federal structure within Britain. It eschewed electoral action, knowing well the difficulties of that road and turned instead to propaganda and pure pressure activities.

It appeared to meet with great success. Three Scottish National Assemblies called by the Convention between 1947 and 1949 received a fair range of support from local government bodies, the professions, religious bodies, and the like. In 1949 it launched the Scottish Covenant, the signatories to which pledged themselves 'in all loyalty to the Crown and within the framework of the United Kingdom, to do everything in our power to secure for Scotland a Parliament with adequate legislative authority in Scottish affairs'. The Covenant was an immediate success. Within three months half a million people had signed it. Eventually it obtained over two million signatures.

But despite the brilliance of the activities of the Scottish Convention, it remained as far as ever from attaining its objectives. The Labour Government of 1945–51 refused to make any concessions to the movement and the only concessions made by the Conservative Government of 1951–5 were in the field of administrative devolution.

The Scottish Covenant Association (the Scottish Convention renamed) was at a loss to know what to do next. It appeared to have reached the limits of pressure activity. It was unlikely ever to be able to bring greater pressure to bear on the government and that pressure had not been enough. There were signs in 1955 that the Association was turning with reluctance to the idea of electoral action as the only way out of the impasse. It was being forced into hostility to a party system in which it saw its aims frustrated. That hostility was shown by the attempt to make the Scottish Covenant the issue upon which an elector votes Conservative or Labour, an attempt which was made in 1955. This is a technique rarely adopted by groups in Britain.

There have been suggestions of further electoral action though they are not likely to advance its cause. It is difficult to see what alternative the Association has. There is no suggestion that the Association will turn to extremism in action, but the very fact that it is now considering methods it previously eschewed, shows the forces at work driving the various nationalist and home-rule groups away from moderate methods.[1]

The political cause which is too obviously excluded from the political system may turn to extremism. Happily most groups have either hope of success or such a lack of it as not to justify such discontent. It is only when strong support runs counter to party attitudes that extremism may result. Most of the groups considered in this chapter are up against no such formidable obstacles, they battle more with indifference than with anything so positive as hostility.

The time may come when a group's views seem about to win the support of a majority of M.P.s. The group will then seek an opportunity of testing the issue in the House of Commons. The attitude of the government remains crucial. In 1948 the success of those advocating the abolition of the death penalty was snatched from them by the action of the House of Lords and the public outcry. For it is when success is near that opposition hitherto latent may arise. If the Government had committed itself to the abolition of the death penalty it might have overridden opposition; as it was, its neutral attitude ensured the defeat of the abolitionists, for it was neutral between two opinions, and succumbed to that which it considered the stronger. In the same way the hostile attitude of the Conservative Government proved crucial in deciding the issues arising out of the 1955–6 campaign to abolish the death penalty. However, although the Government was able to prevent abolition, the campaign probably pushed it farther along the path of limitation than it would otherwise have gone.

2

However, success can be obtained, as the campaign for equal pay shows. It is true that since the war the problem has not been

[1] For accounts of various Home Rule Movements in Scotland see J. M. MacCormick, *Flag in the Wind* (1955); Sir Reginald Coupland, *Welsh and Scottish Nationalism* (1954); and A. Turner, *Scottish Home Rule* (1952).

to secure the acceptance of equal pay as a principle, but to persuade the government to adopt it in practice. This problem was a serious one to the groups concerned and demanded an active policy as the only means of attaining success. In the early years after the Second World War the campaign lacked momentum and was confused. In part this was due to the setting up of a Royal Commission on the subject, which frustrated campaigning. After the issue of its report the campaign gained impetus.

The existence of two different attitudes at times hindered effective campaigning. In the first place support was centred round the descendants of the suffragette movement; these groups saw the question as one of justice for women. The other groups interested in the question were trade unions, particularly the civil service unions, the National Union of Teachers, and N.A.L.G.O. The civil service unions had sought to raise the matter through the normal Whitley machinery, but that way being blocked, they turned to political action. The others were driven in like manner to pressure tactics. These trade unions centred their activity on the Equal Pay Co-ordinating Committee, while the other groups organized themselves in the Equal Pay Campaign Committee, though some of the unions were associated with both Committees. Confusion arose, as when both bodies sponsored petitions at the same time. There seems to have been little attempt to co-ordinate their activities.

The Campaign Committee explored most tactics over a period of time. It regularly organized lobbying in the House of Commons, constituent societies each being allotted a week in which to send their members to interview their M.P.s. In July 1951 a meeting was held in Trafalgar Square with processions organized by the National Association of Women Civil Servants, the National Union of Women Teachers, and St. Joan's Social and Political Alliance. Elections were welcomed as an opportunity for action, although doubts about the law served as a restraint, with the result that in 1951 the Committee merely asked candidates to sign a declaration pledging themselves to take active steps to secure the introduction of equal pay, and 121 of the successful M.P.s did so. In the 1953–4 parliamentary session it organized a petition. The Committee sought the advice and co-operation of M.P.s.[1] There were few methods that it

[1] From 1951 onwards it obtained special help from Miss (now Dame) Irene

neglected, but out of its actions there emerges no clear plan.[1] The danger of a long drawn-out campaign is drift. The group with no clear idea of how to achieve its object moves from one method to another with hope, but without design.

The Campaign Committee lacked the resources and the organization that were available to the Co-ordinating Committee. This Committee introduced a sense of purpose into its campaigning.[2] Each year the campaign was given a focus. There was to be a climax, and before the members had a chance to feel disillusioned they were given a new aim. The emphasis was generally on parliamentary action, to which outside activities were related. In 1951 Mr. Douglas Houghton, the General Secretary of the Inland Revenue Staff Federation, put on the order paper two motions (one before and one after the election) calling for the beginning of the introduction of equal pay.[3] The Committee organized lobbying—both personal and by letter. It allotted days for lobbying in the House of Commons to various bodies. On 27 November 300 members of the I.R.S.F. lobbied M.P.s. Though this did not include all M.P.s, it was hoped that the others would be seen in their constituencies or at least written to. Branch secretaries were asked to keep a stream of letters going.

Similar tactics were used in the following years, and in 1953 a success was claimed in that a motion calling for the introduction of equal pay at the earliest possible moment was passed unopposed in the House of Commons. But the Government had not spoken and without that nothing had been achieved. For though the campaign was aimed at Parliament and at individual M.P.s, the real object was to convince the Government and the Opposition of the electoral importance of equal pay.

In the 1953–4 campaign season new zest was given to the

Ward. Allen Potter, 'The Equal Pay Campaign Committee' (*Political Studies*, Feb. 1957, p. 51).

[1] *Equal Pay Campaign Committee Annual Statements.*

[2] Cf. *Whitley Bulletin*, July 1952, p. 88: 'For Mr. John Fraser, Organising Secretary of the Institution of Professional Civil Servants, the debate marked the culmination of a remarkably effective campaign for which he was responsible as Secretary of the Equal Pay Co-ordinating Committee. This Committee was set up last summer by the National Staff Side with full responsibility for organising and planning a series of provincial mass meetings and later, of devising schemes to maintain continuous pressure on M.P.s by lobbying.'

[3] *C.S.C.A. Annual Report*, 1951, p. 73.

campaign. It was run with a new efficiency, due in part to the experience gained, but in part also to the engaging of a firm of publicity agents to advise. This firm brightened up the posters and helped to organize branches for action. It was decided to make the centre of the campaign Equal Pay Day which was fixed for the following March. A petition was to be presented then, and was to provide the focus of the campaign leading up to that day. The petition was distributed through constituent organizations and achieved over a million signatures. It was presented against a background of mass meetings, crowded lobbies, and all the paraphernalia that good publicity agents can devise and enthusiasm produce. Excitement was produced within the House as well. By good fortune Equal Pay Day (9 March 1954) turned out to be the Chancellor's day for answering questions, and it was arranged to bombard him with them. Since this was followed up by a private members' bill introduced under the ten minutes rule, a House of Commons success was scored.

Eventually, the campaign recorded a real success. It had produced the political atmosphere in which equal pay became a necessity for electoral reasons. The Labour Party committed itself in 1953 and after that it was only a matter of time before action was taken by the Conservative Government. In fact the Government started to introduce equal pay in the civil service in 1954.

The campaign had laid great emphasis on showing the depth of feeling on the question. The amount of parliamentary support available had been an asset. Besides the women M.P.s there were M.P.s like Mr. Douglas Houghton, who were closely connected with groups advocating equal pay or convinced of its urgency. This parliamentary strength was well used by the groups as no government could strongly object to M.P.s supporting a policy that it professed to accept itself. The support of the T.U.C. obtained at its annual conference in 1950 against the recommendation of the General Council brought additional strength.

The most effective feature of the campaign was its orderliness. Conventional weapons, like petitions, tend to be despised by some observers concerned only with the formal purpose. It is true that Parliament will not pay overmuch attention to a petition unless it gets an abnormal or an unexpected number of signatures. But its importance to the group may not be so much in its direct, as in its indirect, effects. It provides a focus for a campaign, which might otherwise dissipate itself. The person who is asked to talk to his neighbour is less effective for the pressure group than someone who is asked to get his neighbour to sign a petition. It is the definite against the indefinite, the controllable against the uncontrolled.

The equal pay petitions helped to maintain interest, always a major problem in groups faced with long campaigns; and a campaign to urge a new principle upon the government can be very long. For over 100 years there have been campaigns in the baking industry for the abolition or regulation of regular night baking.[1] It is not surprising that at times enthusiasm flagged. There are compensating advantages in the long-term campaign. A campaign against a bill operates within limits imposed by a parliamentary time-table, which may make it difficult for a group to deploy its full strength. A long term campaign knows no such problem.

Eventually success may be attained. It is characteristic of some groups that their whole organization is geared to an active campaign, and with the achievement of their object they lose all purpose. A tale of struggle and achievement may be the whole story of the group.

The Scapa Society was set up in the early part of the century in order to bring about control of unsightly advertisements in town and country.[2] The measure of its achievement lies in the comparision between the roads of Britain and Italy. By the Town and Country Planning Act (1947) it felt that its purpose, which it had forwarded by propaganda and in Parliament, had been fulfilled. Its principles were part of the law. It was true that limited work still existed for the group in ensuring that local authorities used the powers given them, but the Society very sensibly decided to go out of existence as a separate organization, letting the Council for the Preservation of Rural England look after these problems.

3

There are some groups whose whole purpose is devoted to the defence of some cause they feel attacked, either by other groups or by a general tendency in society. Most of these are groups

[1] *Bakers' National Association Review*, 25 Dec. 1953, p. 2084.

[2] See Richardson Evans, *An Account of the Scapa Society* (1926), for a description of the Society's promotion of the Advertisements Regulation Acts of 1907 and 1925.

committed to an active policy. This may be because they feel compelled to meet campaigns with campaigns or because they are not admitted to consultation.

They are always ready to campaign, but they will only be brought into action by the threat of the opposing group or tendency being successful. It is not so much a question of a permanent campaign, but of spasmodic campaigns and their preparation.

The League against Cruel Sports and allied organizations felt themselves in a strong position in the 1945–50 Parliament. They felt that public opinion was with them, and also that a Labour majority in the House of Commons meant support for their point of view. Only the fact that there was no opportunity for private members' bills until the 1948–9 session prevented them from putting the issue to the test.

The group which was the obvious opponent of the League was the British Field Sports Society.[1] At first the Society had difficulty in persuading its supporters that there was a real threat, but it grew quickly to strength when the plans of the opponents of hunting became clear. Real passion was aroused when it was announced that Mr. Seymour Cocks was to promote the Protection of Animals (Hunting and Coursing Prohibition) Bill[2] and that Mr. F. Fairhurst was later to promote the Prohibition of Fox Hunting Bill. The result can be seen in the increase in membership of the Society from 17,709 on 31 March 1948 to 118,357 a year later. The threat had aroused opposition hitherto latent. (Many movements have no ordered opposition now, for example the anti-vivisectionists, but should they appear to be making headway, strong opposition would not be lacking.)

The British Field Sports Society itself was early conscious of the danger. At a meeting in the House of Commons on 6 April 1948 of M.P.s interested in the preservation of fox-hunting, it was agreed that there was a strong likelihood of private members' time being restored before the end of the year, and a resolution was passed urging the Society to launch a campaign with the object of obtaining signatures for a Countryman's Pledge to

[1] *British Field Sports Society Annual Report*, 1948–9, pp. 17–19, for details of the campaign.

[2] The Secretary of the League against Cruel Sports assisted in the drafting of his Bill; cf. *League Doings*, Jan.–Mar. 1949, p. 1.

oppose any attempt to curtail field sports. This method was favoured by the Society as being the best means of dealing with a threat as yet indefinite. For though the Society knew that when private members' time was restored it would probably provide an opportunity for the introduction of a bill, there could be no certainty as to what form that bill would take or when it would be introduced.

The campaign went ahead under the care of an emergency committee. At this stage it had two objects, the Countryman's Pledge and the collection of funds. It was decided to set up local committees and to appoint a representative in every 'Parish, Town and Hamlet.' This operation was scheduled to be completed by 15 June. The rest of June and July were set aside for the distribution of posters and pamphlets calling for financial support.

On 31 July honorary local secretaries were told that the campaign for the Pledge would begin on 1 October, and that they were to be ready with a large empty room for posters and pamphlets for distribution. It was hoped to distribute 500,000 posters and 1,750,000 pledge forms during this part of the campaign. Besides members and supporters they were also to be sent to angling clubs, tackle dealers, gunsmiths, and the like. Until 28 September no public announcement was made. From 1 October the campaign was on, despite the fact that it was to be 25 January 1949 before the threat became definite. Then the emphasis changed to pressure on M.P.s and large protest meetings. For the final stages of the campaign the group was in a very strong position. Over a million people had signed the Countryman's Pledge; the increased membership had brought in £40,000 in subscriptions. The careful preparations had been well justified.

The most important achievement was that the official support of the National Farmers' Union was gained. This had been one of the earliest objectives of the Society, which had directed its local committees to get in touch with their nearest N.F.U. branches.

This campaign led to the defeat of the Protection of Animals (Hunting and Coursing Prohibition) Bill by 214 votes to 101, and the withdrawal of the Prohibition of Fox Hunting Bill. Pressure had brought about a distinct change of attitude among M.P.s. It had also impressed the Minister of Agriculture, who warned the Labour Party that the Bills were untimely and unwise, and would lose the Party support in rural areas. Since it was from the Labour Party that most support for the Bill was expected, this warning was decisive.

4

The free vote leads naturally to campaigns. Nothing can demonstrate this better than a study of the most famous of the opposition groups. Committed like the British Field Sports Society to the defence of the *status quo*, the Lord's Day Observance Society's task is a simple one. It is merely to preserve the laws relating to the Sabbath. The Imperial Alliance for the Defence of Sunday has similar aims, though less striking methods, including among its membership trade unions interested in keeping Sunday a rest day. The Salvation Army and other religious organizations play their part. But the Lord's Day Observance Society is the most important body and that upon which public attention has been focused. Besides its opposition to legislative action, it seeks by youth work and other means to bring about a reverence for the Sabbath. It also endeavours to secure the enforcement of the laws.

There have been three occasions since 1939 on which the Society has been forced to defend its position. On all three (or rather two and a half) of them, it was aided by a free vote.

In 1941 the Government proposed that theatres should be opened on Sundays for the benefit of the forces, a proposal defeated by 144 to 136 votes.[1] In 1950 the proposal to open the festival gardens on Sunday was defeated by 389 to 108 votes on a free vote,[2] though the opening of the festival exhibition was carried by 364 to 148, with the government whips on.[3] In 1953 a Bill introduced by Mr. John Parker to remove most of the restrictions on Sunday activities was defeated by 281 to 57 votes.[4]

The normal activities of the Lord's Day Observance Society provide the basis for its campaigns. It has a system of district organizers whose function it is to campaign against Sunday cinemas in local plebiscites, to prevent illegal Sunday activities, and to preach or speak in churches or at public meetings.[5] An

[1] H.C. Deb. 370, cols. 967–70.
[2] Ibid. 481, cols. 637–42.
[3] Ibid., cols. 1071–6.
[4] Ibid. 510, cols. 1429–31.
[5] 'Raising the standard against threatened encroachment', *Annual Report of L.D.O.S.*, 1951, p. vi.

attempt to form local branches has been made and fifty-five had been formed by 1951. But the public meeting is more important. In 1951 the Society held 2,140, and at these it gained supporters.[1] When a critical issue arises, the Lord's Day Observance Society calls upon these supporters to aid it in its campaign.

The Society, being ever ready to repel an attack, does not let a general election slip by unused. To all candidates it normally sends one simple question: knowing well that such a question might not be answered if it were to come solely from national headquarters, the Society endeavours to get it asked locally. With the help of its records and the answers to this question it was able to assess the views of all but forty-three of those candidates who were elected in 1951. The Society realizes that these answers can only be indications of an attitude, and though the results are filed away, they are only used as a guide to the Society.[2]

But the campaign is what counts. Probably the Society needs a strong attack about every five years to keep its machinery in good condition. So it should be grateful to Mr. John Parker and the Sunday Freedom Association. This Association was the sponsoring body for the 1953 Bill, but its whole strength and importance derived from Mr. Parker who gave it a parliamentary foothold. It had a small individual membership, but the only important support it had came from organizations such as the Variety Artistes' Federation, the English Table Tennis Association, or the National Cyclists' Union, whose activities had been hampered by the laws on Sunday observance. The Association had taken various measures in defence of 'The people's right to do what they wish on Sunday'. In 1951 it circularized all M.P.s asking them to sponsor a motion either calling for an overhaul of the 'chaotic' law, or for a limitation on the power of the common informer in regard to Sunday activities.[3] In 1952, through Mr. Parker, a group was formed in the House of Commons to advocate a brighter Sunday. As a result of this Mr. Parker, backed by Mr. E. Carson, Mr. N. J. Hulbert, Mr. C. Hollis, Mr. W. Nally, and Mr. G. Jeger, tabled a motion in the House of Commons asking for a Select Committee on the Sunday observance laws.

[1] *Annual Report of L.D.O.S.*, 1951, p. vi. [2] See pp. 231–2.

[3] The powers of the common informer were dealt with by the Common Informers Act (1951), an Act unconnected with the activities of the Association.

Despite these activities the Sunday Freedom Association was weak; the Lord's Day Observance Society was strong. If organization, officials, publicity, and finance mean anything, the Lord's Day Observance Society was bound to win in any contest between the two. In 1951 the Lord's Day Observance Society had an income of £29,000.[1] The Sunday Freedom Associations' income was only a fraction of that amount. It would be very easy to conclude that this reflected the volume of support for their respective views in the country, but it would be better to say that their support varied in character.

When Mr. Parker won first place in the ballot for private members' bills and announced his intention of introducing his Bill: 'No time was lost. The Lord's Day Observance Society went into action immediately. The Secretary conferred with Alderman Cyril W. Black, J.P., M.P., C.C., at the House of Commons, and a plan of campaign was agreed upon.'[2] The first step was to send the following letter to all the Society's supporters throughout the country:

Urgent.

Dear Friend,

Mr. J. Parker, M.P., is introducing a 'Sunday Observance Bill' into Parliament. Its object is to repeal some existing legislation in order to make legal Stage Plays, Variety Concerts and other amusements and sports on Sunday. Its Second Reading is to be taken on 30th January, 1953.

The Lord's Day Observance Society is vigorously opposing this Bill, which would result in the complete secularisation of God's Hallowed Day in Britain. BUT WE NEED YOUR IMMEDIATE HELP in the following manner:

1. Write to your M.P. c/o the House of Commons, London, S.W. 1., asking him or her to vote against the Sunday Observance Bill.

2. Obtain as many signatures as you can to the enclosed Petition Forms. We will gladly send more forms upon application. Please ask your minister if he will kindly arrange for the forms to be placed in the church for the congregation to sign. Please return the Forms, when signed, to me, not later than Tuesday, January 20th.

3. Above all, pray that the Bill shall be rejected. Can you organise Special Gatherings for Prayer?

[1] *Annual Report of L.D.O.S.*, 1951, p. viii.

[2] *Joy and Light*, Apr.–June 1953, p. 77.

Let us rise and defend the Lord's Day for the Lord's Glory.

Yours in His Service,

Harold J. W. Legerton, Secretary.

There were 100,000 petition forms sent out, some of these being dispatched to churches, all of which received a communication from the Society. In a period under two months 512,735 signatures were obtained. The Society circularized all M.P.s, and also arranged for the circularization of a letter from forty-eight prominent actors and actresses protesting at the idea of Sunday theatres.[1]

The activity upon which the Society appears to place most emphasis is the letter to the M.P. There is no doubt that M.P.s receive far more than their normal correspondence on this issue. It is difficult to say whether the letters are inspired by the Society for it does not send out cards or even suggest wordings. Indeed, much of the influence of the letters can be ascribed to their apparent spontaneity. Beyond this appearance it is not possible for the observer to go, except to say that however spontaneous in feeling the letters are, it is likely that attacks on the Sabbath would go unobserved by many without the Society's activities. From the other side, despite the printing of postcards by the Sunday Freedom Association, hardly any correspondence was received by M.P.s.

Correspondence is effective when the M.P. has no other guide or control. However little it means, it means something—particularly on a subject on which the M.P. has no opinion. Certainly it enforces attendance. A vote of 338 members on a private members' bill on a Friday is extremely high. It may be that in their votes on this occasion they expressed their own views, but in their presence they expressed a reaction to pressure, for on many other issues they would be content to leave the decision to a few of their colleagues.

The Society deserves credit for having realized that a free vote can be made essentially a question of lobbying. This tactical insight is an example to other groups and a warning against the free vote. But the Society has one great advantage. It defends an entrenched position, where many groups which pursue active parliamentary policies cannot even look forward to success in the future with any certainty.

[1] *Joy and Light*, Apr.–June 1953, pp. 78–79.

5

Many differing types of groups have difficulty in attaining the sort of consultation that will provide a solution for their needs. The groups so far discussed in this chapter have all been concerned in campaigns for and against new principles. Other groups find that lack of consultation presents them with very similar problems and drives them to active policies.

It may be that through a campaign they hope to force the government to recognize them. But until they are recognized such groups are committed to a policy of permanent campaigning. The Engineering Officers' (Telecommunications) Association was a case in point. It claimed recognition as a negotiating body from the Post Office, but the claim was opposed by the Post Office Engineering Union. Its claim being refused, the Association turned to the tactics of the campaign, and gained much support from the Conservative Opposition in 1950 and 1951. It hoped that the claim would be granted on the return of a Conservative Government, but this hope proved ill-founded. The history of this group was a storm-swept one, fading to hopelessness, as typified by an angry letter circulated to Conservative M.P.s saying that the Association's members were being jeered at for placing confidence in the Conservatives—a letter that was almost immediately withdrawn.

A group which is weak turns to active measures in circumstances where other groups would seek consultation. The National Federation of Off-Licence Holders' Associations of England and Wales is a group which does not represent an interest important enough to enjoy full consultation, although the general interests of the licensed trade are adequately represented in consultation by bodies of which the Federation is a member. But when an issue arises on which the interests of the Federation are not in harmony with the interests of other parts of the trade, the Federation has no effective way of representing its views to a government unwilling to intervene in internal trade quarrels. In such a situation the group is forced to adopt some of the tactics of the campaign as the only means of bringing its views before Parliament and the government.

Between 1950 and 1956 the Federation attempted to secure permission for off-licensees to sell spirits in quantities of less than half a bottle. The representatives of the on-licensees opposed this application, taking their stand upon a pledge given by the off-licensees (when they were granted permission to sell half-bottles) that they would not press for further concessions. The Federation held that this pledge was given over twenty years ago and could not be regarded as perpetually binding. The Government refused to take action on the matter unless and until agreement was reached between the two groups, and the Chancellor regularly declined to receive a deputation on the subject. As a routine the Federation came to adopt the tactic of promoting an amendment to the Finance Bill and encouraging local campaigns to bring it to the notice of M.P.s. Each year it wrote to individual traders to ask them to secure the support of their local M.P.s by means of personal letters. The Executive Council rejected the idea of a petition on the grounds of expense, 'having regard to the fact that such projects nowadays need to be overwhelmingly successful if they are to make any impression whatsoever'.[1] But each year it persevered with its little lobbying campaign. Sometimes the amendment was not even called. Sometimes the amendment was debated and support given, but until 1956 nothing was achieved. Then in that year the Government very surprisingly accepted the amendment.[2] The Federation's campaign, though never a very strong one, had had over the years the desired effect.

6

There are some groups whose activities are associated too closely with party attitudes for them to be classed with the groups so far considered. They can never hope to attain recognition in consultation: they are partisan, existing to fight a battle, and do not require it.

The National Television Council and Popular Television Association were called into existence in 1953 by what came to be virtually a party political dispute over commercial television. Admittedly the National Television Council laid great emphasis on its support by various prominent members of the Conservative Party, who were opposed to commercial television, such as Lord Waverley and Lord Halifax. Its tactic was pressure by prestige

[1] *National Federation of Off-Licence Holders' Association Yearbook*, 1953, p. 15.
[2] H.C. Deb. 555, cols. 295–304.

and position. It attempted to follow the example set by the National Council for Civil Liberties in the years before the Second World War and assemble a galaxy of influential supporters,[1] a policy which in the case of the National Television Council had greater hope of success because its supporters were in a better position to influence those in authority. The Popular Television Association shrewdly placed more emphasis on influencing public opinion, which was very confused on the issue. It regarded itself as responsible for the remarkable change in public attitude. But the activity of both groups was secondary to the political struggle.

There are groups like Aims of Industry and the Economic League, whose objects are more general. Aims of Industry (although not very active till 1946) was founded in 1942 by Mr. H. G. Stanley of Champion Sparking Plugs and has as its object the presentation of the case for private enterprise by a combination of various public relations methods. It arranges tours of meetings among bodies which would eschew the straight political speech, such as schools, churches, armed forces study groups, factories, and so on. Leaflets and mobile picture vans are also much used. In 1949 it claimed to have arranged press publicity worth more than £1,800,000. Feature stories are placed in local and national journals.[2]

Its influence on Parliament is through elections. It is hostile to the whole purpose of the Labour Party and it can only gain its aims through a Labour defeat. Aims of Industry believes that its activities are effective in influencing votes. This is a matter upon which it is difficult to make a judgement without more detailed analysis of the motives in voting, but it seems likely that the issues with which Aims of Industry deals are not those that have made an impact on the electorate in recent years. But it can be argued that its activities have had an indirect effect in that they have contributed to the public disillusion with nationalization, which has prevented the Labour Party using it as an electoral weapon.

[1] Limited by political necessity in the case of the N.C.C.L., but including E. M. Forster, Vernon Bartlett, A. P. Herbert, Ramsay Muir, Bertrand Russell, H. G. Wells, and Eleanor Rathbone. A similar technique was used in 1955 by the National Campaign for the Abolition of Capital Punishment. It organized a petition which was signed by about 2,500 people who were prominent in various fields of activity (*Observer*, 21 Oct. 1955.)

[2] H. H. Wilson, 'Techniques of Pressure', *Public Opinion Quarterly*, 1951, pp. 225–42.

Its relationship with the Conservative Party is not clear. In certain areas it appears to be closely associated with it. It is inevitable that it should come to be regarded as a satellite to a political party, however separate it keeps its organization. That is ensured by its aims.

A similar body is the Empire Industries Association and British Empire League. It exists primarily to support imperial preference and private enterprise. It is mainly engaged in publicizing these causes by pamphlets, research, and speeches. It has a Parliamentary Committee which in 1951 consisted of 143 members of the House of Lords and 250 of the House of Commons.[1] It cannot be considered of importance. That is because it is overwhelmed by the political party with which it is in sympathy. The groups which parallel these bodies on the other side of the House are probably more closely and avowedly associated with the Labour Party.

Some of the groups previously considered advocate views which one of the major political parties might come to adopt. That would transform the group from an independent body into a satellite—in practice, if not in theory.

7

The active groups include some groups which are recognized in consultation or should have no difficulty in obtaining such recognition.

The R.S.P.C.A. is recognized by all ministries as being in a position to speak with authority on animal welfare. Yet it adopts a very different strategy from other groups in a similar position. It takes into its own hands the task of bringing about necessary changes in the laws relating to animal welfare. Admittedly it is well-equipped to do so. It does not normally have to struggle with the problems created by party discipline. Parliamentary sentiment is at once upon its side. There is ready support from the Animal Welfare Group, which in 1953 had about fifty members coming from both Houses. In the country the Society plays a major part in the administration and the enforcement of the law and thus gains the information upon which its proposals for new legislation are based.

[1] *Empire Industries League and British Empire League Annual Report*, 1952.

It relies upon the use of private members' time to secure the enactment of its bills. So important does it consider these bills that in the 1947–8 session it supported a campaign for the restoration of private members' time. Its bills are prepared in advance. Upon the outbreak of war in 1939 and the consequent abandonment of private members' time ten draft bills had to be put into cold storage.[1] Not all its bills have the same priority and it is customary for it to select three or four to press in any particular session.

As a first step before the ballot for places for bills the Society often circularizes all M.P.s. In the 1953–4 parliamentary session a letter from the Chief Secretary began by asking M.P.s to enter their names for the ballot, and if successful to introduce an R.S.P.C.A. bill. Then followed brief descriptions of the Slaughter of Animals (Horses) Bill, the Protection of Animals (Amendment) Bill, the Protection of Animals (Penalties) Bill, and the Animals (Cruel Poisons) Bill. Attention was drawn to the facilities provided by the Society. Finally, a slip was enclosed which members willing to introduce a bill were asked to sign.

Not many M.P.s are willing to commit themselves in advance, but the document serves to draw attention to the R.S.P.C.A.'s bills which may be remembered later. For it is after an M.P.'s success in the ballot that the real efforts are made. There are a number of M.P.s who are interested in this question and this alone gives the R.S.P.C.A. a large enough number of contacts. Besides, the R.S.P.C.A.'s offer is an attractive one. Piloting a bill through the House is no easy matter. In the first place drafting a bill is a question for experts and experts may require payment. In the second place to get a bill through the House requires information, ordered and prepared to enable the M.P. to deal with all questions, amendments, and arguments with efficiency. This the R.S.P.C.A. provides. When it is remembered that the subjects in which an M.P. is interested are as likely as not unsuitable for legislation by private members' bills, the R.S.P.C.A.'s case gains weight. But there is a further point—if the member desires to get his bill passed, and that is one of the objects of the operation, then other things being equal, his best chance is with an R.S.P.C.A. bill. For it is likely to be fairly uncontroversial,

[1] *R.S.P.C.A. Annual Report*, 1940, p. 3.

gain ready sympathy, and as often as not have Home Office support.

Granted all this it is not surprising that the R.S.P.C.A. gets so many of its bills sponsored. Figures for the first five sessions after the war in which private members' time was allowed were as follows:

Session	*Sponsored*	*Passed*
1948–9	6	2
1950–1	2	1
1951–2	2	1
1952–3	2	–
1953–4	3	2

In the 1952–3 session one other bill was successfully introduced under the ten minutes rule.[1]

The extent to which the member sponsoring the bill himself conducts the business, including negotiation with the interests affected, varies. The Parliamentary Organizer of the R.S.P.C.A. adapts himself to the needs of the member and will co-operate in any way necessary. In 1951 he conducted Mr. Roland Russell, the sponsor of the Pet Animals' Bill, round various London pet shops in order to enable him to speak of the conditions from actual experience.[2] He can supply facts, figures, and general information. He can be at hand during the committee stage to provide expert advice. He can get amendments drafted to meet points raised in debate.

The number of bills actually passed by the R.S.P.C.A. may seem small in proportion to the amount of work done, especially when one considers that some of these were emasculated in the process of legislation. But there is a steady progress which is seen more clearly when the legislation in any one session is viewed as amendment to the great bulk of animal welfare legislation. Sometimes the purpose of a bill is fulfilled without actual enactment, as in 1949 when the Coal Mines (Protection of Animals) Bill came up for a second reading and the Minister of Fuel and Power undertook to draw up new regulations governing the employment of animals in the mines.[3]

The R.S.P.C.A. undoubtedly considers that these activities

[1] *R.S.P.C.A. Annual Reports*, 1948–54.
[2] *R.S.P.C.A. Annual Report*, 1951, p. 193.
[3] H.C. Deb. 462, col. 2532.

are valuable for, though the Parliamentary Department cost only £1,516 to maintain in 1954,[1] it places great weight upon the Department in its annual reports and in other descriptions of its work.

However, private members' bills cannot provide the basis for a satisfactory approach to the law of animal welfare. The legislation is piecemeal. One of the Acts is the Docking and Nicking of Horses Act (1949), another the Cockfighting Act (1952). Neither of these subjects merit a separate Act; they should merely be parts of a general Animals Act. But such they could not be. One reason is that there is little parliamentary time available for private members' bills which therefore need to be short if they are to pass into law. But there is another reason in the politics of the operation. The R.S.P.C.A. is a sensible body attuned to the limits of the possible. Witness its attitude on fox-hunting which was supremely practical. In 1951 it issued a statement: 'The R.S.P.C.A. cannot support any Parliamentary Bill designed to prohibit fox-hunting, because they have yet to find a satisfactory way of dealing with foxes.'[2] In view of this approach, it is not surprising that many of the bills it promotes are so cautious. Even an R.S.P.C.A. bill can be opposed. Parts of the Docking and Nicking of Horses Bill were opposed by some equestrian societies as were parts of the Cockfighting Bill by the Poultry Association which felt that certain of the provisions designed to make the detection of cockfighting easier would hinder legitimate activities. A more general bill unites opposition otherwise isolated. The Pet Animals Bill suffered in this way.

If it is agreed that the R.S.P.C.A.'s methods lead to piecemeal legislation, it may be said that this is a small price to pay for the benefit such legislation brings. Such an argument is based on the assumption that the Home Office would not itself initiate legislation. Certainly continuing habits have bred the idea that animal welfare is a private members' subject. It is perhaps felt that it is better for them to occupy themselves thus than on more controversial matters. But this should not stand in the way of a determined attack on the problem of animal legislation which the Home Office could launch after full consultation with the R.S.P.C.A. and all other interested bodies.

[1] *R.S.P.C.A. Annual Report*, 1954, Financial Statement.

[2] Ibid., 1951, p. 216.

The use of the parliamentary question is much favoured by the R.S.P.C.A. and it also intervenes on government bills, but its main emphasis is on private members' legislation. In its attitude to this it is unique. There are other bodies which promote private members' bills, but only occasionally or as a climax to long years of propaganda. There are none which do so with such regularity and with such success.

8

Some of the groups representing the interests of pensioners are in a strong position as regards consultation and yet are active campaigners. On such questions the government is very responsive to the attitude of M.P.s. It is thought that on matters like this the M.P. serves as a good guide to opinion. It may be regretted that, whereas on other matters the government accepts the arguments put forward in consultation, here it is influenced by emotion and clamour. There is nothing inherent in these groups that leads them to active policies. Rather it is that they represent one of the major sections of discontent remaining in society. It is possible that pensions could be put on a more acceptable basis and tied to the cost of living. In these circumstances the groups concerned might be more willing to rely on consultation alone.

The British Legion has achieved a very close relationship with the Ministry of Pensions and National Insurance. It is based on the relationship with the former Ministry of Pensions which was so close that the Legion was very suspicious about the amalgamation of the Ministries, fearing to lose established contacts.[1] The Committee on Intermediaries has commented on the closeness of this relationship. Yet alongside this consultation the group campaigns. Until 1951 its campaign was for a select committee to investigate pensions policy for the war disabled. In 1951, as a result of a motion of urgency introduced by the National Executive Committee at the annual conference, the Legion became committed to a direct campaign to double the basic rate of the war disability pension.[2] This demand, which had underlain the previous campaign, came to be known as the 90*s.* pension. It never stood any chance of being met. In 1957, after two increases, the basic rate stood at 67*s.* 6*d.* a week. The

[1] *British Legion Journal*, Apr. 1953, pp. 1–2. [2] Ibid., June 1951, p. 86.

90*s*. pension was not so much a realistic demand, but a declaration of a permanent campaign.

Once the policy had been adopted, the preparations for a campaign went ahead, though at a more leisurely pace than is allowed by a campaign to oppose a government bill. The Legion first endeavoured to secure, not merely the support of the annual conference, but also of individual branches, which were asked to declare publicly their approval of the policy.

The campaign was launched at a meeting between the President, the Chairman, and twenty representatives of newspapers, press agencies, and the B.B.C. The Legion was well satisfied with the result:

> We bided our time before striking, but our striking was timely. Its impact has been immediate and the pressure will be sustained if the whole weight of the Movement is placed behind the Chairman. This, as he impressed the Press in saying, is an effort to rouse the interest and support of the nation. We are not relying on deputations to Parliament, processions in Whitehall and the like, though our sights are all the time trained on Parliament. It is our job to rally public opinion to our cause, knowing that all Parliaments are susceptible to public opinion.[1]

The campaign gained in force after the Government's announcement of a mere 10*s*. a week increase in the basic rate of the disability pension. Rather unfortunately 22 March 1952 was named a Day of Demand. 'Peterborough' in the *Daily Telegraph* described it as 'certainly one of the most concentrated exercises in political pressure ever organised by a national institution. Whether it is an equally good exercise for democratic methods is questionable. In America pressure groups have reached the point of threatening political stability.' This was a strange outburst in which to describe a not very unusual form of activity. The Legion's *Journal* itself said: 'Better by far to make courteous requests to Members of Parliament than to create other more melodramatic forms of "pressure" which the Legion would object to as strongly as Peterborough.' For the Day of Demand's main activity was local branches seeing their M.P.s and putting their case before them.[2]

[1] Ibid., Dec. 1951, p. 177.

[2] Ibid., May 1952, p. 2. The majority of M.P.s were seen and a majority of them felt some further increase was necessary.

The campaign has gone on with varying degrees of success and of fervour for nearly seven years and in 1957 it is still going on. Great emphasis has been laid on the importance of public opinion:

> *You* are public opinion. All at Westminster will respond to it. Let it be known the casualties and bereaved of Britain's wars are *your* priority. . . . Let your M.P. know this is a matter for his urgent attention; make this case known in any voluntary organisation you belong to; support your local British Legion in its efforts to arouse public feeling on the issue.[1]

It is doubtful whether anything was gained by these tactics, but the British Legion may have adopted them because it did not have as much support among its own members as most other campaigning groups. The majority of its members are not directly concerned in the issue of disability pensions.

This campaign has gone on alongside consultation. It is the strength of the Legion's position that it has been able to combine the two. The National Federation of Old Age Pensions Associations has not been able to achieve this combination. It is regarded by too many people as not being a responsible representative body. This is unfortunate for itself, but also for the government, which has no real sounding board for its proposals on old age pensions and no channel through which it can readily learn of grievances.

The Federation has grown too rapidly to settle down. It was founded in 1940 and its membership has grown quickly. In 1944 it had 500 affiliated branches and in 1951 there were over 1,000.[2] Its headquarters are still in Blackburn; it is possibly the only important English pressure group not to have offices in London. It has not laid enough importance on establishing a background of factual and case knowledge which would entitle it to automatic respect. Financial difficulties may be the explanation of these failings.

It regards its purpose as a fight. There is a campaign and nothing but a campaign. Four petitions have been organized. The annual conference is a battlefield of complaints. Parliamentary action is regarded as invaluable:

> A recent occasion was when the Chancellor of the Exchequer

[1] *British Legion Journal*, Feb. 1953, p. 1. Quotation from a Legion campaign pamphlet. [2] E. Melling, *Pensioners' Progress* (undated), p. 11.

made his statement in the House of Commons, in which the claims of the pensioners were totally ignored; within 48 hours a strong letter of protest had been sent to the Chancellor, the newspapers were written to twice and every branch was supplied with a 'Call to Action' leaflet asking them to call immediately special meetings of their branches and to send to their M.P.s and all Cabinet Ministers a resolution in strong terms.[1]

In 1955 the old-age pensioners were given an increase. Whether that increase was great enough for it to be regarded as a success for the pensioners is dubious. Few pensioners can regard it as such. The Federation must alter its organization if it is to realize its potential. Its campaigns can never be really successful until it gains fuller recognition from the government. Yet as the Federation's strength builds up it is hard to see how that fuller recognition can be denied it if it aims to achieve it.

9

It can be seen that various factors influence groups to adopt active parliamentary policies. Part of the reason lies in the House of Commons itself. On certain questions free votes are taken and they create situations which demand from the group concerned active parliamentary policies, since on those occasions the point of decision is the House of Commons and the means of influencing the decision is by influencing the individual member. The same remarks apply to a less extent to questions which have been held to be matters of conscience, where though a free vote may not be the official rule, the Labour Party by its standing orders and the Conservative Party by tradition will look benevolently on minor defections from the party line. In addition on such questions as animal welfare and possibly pensions policy, party discipline is often light.

The private members' bill attracts many groups. The possibility of securing legislation directly and suddenly is a tempting one. The private members' bill offers even the weakest group a chance for action provided some support can be obtained in the House of Commons. This is the attraction the House of Commons exerts on many groups. It brings the group nearer to the centre of achievement.

[1] Ibid., p. 10.

One other factor is the attitude of M.P.s themselves. For the M.P. loves a 'good cause' as well as any old maiden lady. Indeed, it hardly needs to be a 'good cause'. At times it seems there is no idea, scheme, or purpose known to man which, sponsored by a society, could not gain the support of some M.P.—perhaps of many. Was not the Simplified Spelling Bill passed upon the second reading?[1] Anti-vivisection, anti-vaccination, vegetarianism, and a decimal currency all had advocates in the 1951–5 Parliament.[2] But it is the 'good causes' that bring the whole House in support. The 'good cause' is concerned with one of the basic principles which are part of the sentiment of the nation. What M.P. is there who does not love children, is not kind to animals, does not like country walking, or revere our architecture? Few at any rate who would say so.

In 1947 the Agriculture Bill was going through its committee stage in the House of Commons. The Standing Committee to which it was referred was naturally largely composed of those sympathetic to the farmers' viewpoint—many members being farmers themselves. Included in the Bill was a provision to allow the continued use of gin-traps to catch rabbits. This proposal was opposed by all the animal welfare societies, but it can hardly have been the vigour of this campaign that swayed members from agricultural constituencies into voting against a clause supported by farmers. Every member of the Committee present except the Minister of Agriculture, his Parliamentary Private Secretary, the Parliamentary Secretary, and one other member, voted against the clause.[3] House of Commons sentiment was at work.

10

But there are other factors leading some groups to active parliamentary policies. A group fighting for a new principle is likely to be forced into active policies by the necessity of securing the support of opinion. A group which is seeking to create a new framework of legislation has to show reason in opinion for its case, even when other arguments aid it. Since opinion in

[1] H.C. Deb. 511, cols. 2417–500.

[2] Examples of each were Messrs. James Harrison, S. P. Viant, Peter Freeman, and Mont Follick, respectively.

[3] Standing Committee Debates, Standing Committee A, 16 Apr. 1947, cols. 937–8.

politics is often judged by its effect on M.P.s, the group adopts active parliamentary policies.

Important, too, is the attitude of the members of the group. A major cause of discontent may not be worked out in a single campaign, but lead to a demand for a permanent campaign. Some such factor is at work in the National Federation of Old Age Pensions Associations.

Most important is the position of the group in consultation. This point need not be laboured. It has been illustrated and discussed enough already. A group which cannot take part in consultation must seek other methods.

CHAPTER VIII

Group Representation

Part I

1

GROUP representation through M.P.s provides the means for the routine use of parliamentary activities as a way of supplementing consultation. That is its main point. Though a group will find close contact with individual M.P.s of great use in a campaign, it is usual for a campaign to be directed at influencing the whole body of M.P.s. But the limited support a group obtains through its relationship with individual M.P.s is sufficient for the purposes of routine pressure. It enables the group to get questions asked and amendments tabled. It secures that the group's interests are represented in the formation of parliamentary opinion. It brings to the group useful advice on political matters.

2

Few pressure groups—trade unions apart—have created formal machinery to achieve representation in the House of Commons. Many do not need to. They already have M.P.s as elected members of their executives or as members of their permanent staff. Executive membership is the more common, for while it is unlikely that an M.P. will be appointed to a permanent staff position, it is likely that an M.P. will have a greater chance of being elected to a position on a group's executive than will an ordinary member of the group. A group likes to have an M.P. on its executive. Its members vote for him with a feeling that he will be useful to the group. However, many M.P.s have achieved positions in groups without the boost given by the letters after their names. They are naturally inclined to work in pressure groups, for their outlook leads them in that direction. They realize the importance of these groups. They appreciate the help a group can give them in their parliamentary work. But above all they are politicians whose pleasure it is to move in organizations and committees. If they are tanners by business it is as natural for them to be active in the United Tanners' Federation as for a political miner to be active in the National Union of Mineworkers. This is representation by chance, but in certain organizations it is a sufficiently good chance to obviate the need for any other arrangements. The National Union of Manufacturers and the County Councils' Association have rarely been lacking in representation achieved in this way.

A group may achieve representation by the election to Parliament of a permanent salaried official. Such a situation is not always satisfactory for the group. His parliamentary work is not likely to leave the official much time for his normal duties. If the group considers that the value of an official being an M.P. is great, it may be possible for arrangements to be made to relieve him of some of his more burdensome tasks in the group. Sir Jonah Walker-Smith was both an M.P. and Director of the National Federation of Building Trade Employers from 1931 to 1945.[1] Sir Herbert Williams was for most of his parliamentary career either Secretary and Manager of the Machine Tool Trades Association or Executive Director of the Incorporated Association of Electric Power Companies.[2] It may be argued that parliamentary business has become more absorbing, and the resignation of Dr. Charles Hill from the Secretaryship of the British Medical Association in 1950 and of Mr. Gresham Cooke as Director of the Society of Motor Manufacturers and Traders in 1955 upon their election to Parliament can be quoted in support of that view. But in 1954 Mr. W. J. Owen did not resign his position as General Secretary of the Master Ladies Tailors' Organization upon his election to Parliament and a glance at Appendix B will show a number of permanent officials who were M.P.s in 1951.

The group may take measures to encourage members of its executive or members of its staff to enter Parliament, but for the most part it remains representation by chance, dependent as it is upon the impulses of individuals and the actions of constituency parties. Groups which do not achieve representation

[1] *National Builder*, Mar. 1945, p. 171.
[2] *Who's Who*, 1954.

by these means or wish to supplement it have devised other methods of securing representation. One quite frequently used is the appointment of M.P.s to honorary positions within the group. Some of the English local government associations rely upon this method. They appoint M.P.s of both parties to the position of honorary vice-president, a position that carries with it, at least in certain cases, the right to attend the meetings of their executive bodies—a right rarely exercised. In 1954 the Association of Municipal Corporations had more than ten M.P.s in this position, as had both the Urban and the Rural District Councils' Associations. The National Association of Parish Councils had only two.[1] There is little difficulty in making the initial contact. There are sufficient M.P.s with a background of work with the various local authorities. Besides, most M.P.s feel it a duty to represent the views of the particular type or types of local authority which exist in their constituencies.

The Poultry Association of Great Britain also appoints M.P.s as vice-presidents and in addition its president is usually an M.P. In 1953 there were seven M.P.s from three parties associated with it.[2] One of these was Mr. Tom Williams, the former Minister of Agriculture. In his position, as the Opposition spokesman on agriculture, he lacked the freedom of action to help the Association which a back-bench member possesses, without being likely to be influenced by this connexion in the determination of party policy. In his case, and perhaps in others, the title was given solely as an honour for services to agriculture.

The Building Societies' Association has vice-presidents in both parties and with varying degrees of parliamentary prominence.[3] These vice-presidencies are given as a recognition of an interest shown and a concern in the affairs of building societies. A vice-president is a friend in the House, whom the Association is able to contact on an informal basis.

The National Chamber of Trade in 1954 had forty M.P.s among its honorary vice-presidents. Many of the other twenty-one honorary vice-presidents were former M.P.s, who had been

[1] B. Keith-Lucas gives these figures for 1954: A.M.C. 11; R.D.C.A. 19; U.D.C.A. 16; N.A.P.C. 2. 'Local Government and Parliament', *Public Administration*, vol. xxxiii, p. 207.

[2] *P.A.G.B. Yearbook*, 1953, p. 5.

[3] See *Building Societies' Yearbooks*.

given the position during their period in the House. All these M.P.s were Conservative and represented, for the most part, borough constituencies. These vice-presidents are generally nominated for that position by the local Chamber of Trade, which is regarded by most Conservative M.P.s as an influential element in the constituency.[1]

A variant is provided by the Association of British Chambers of Commerce. The position to which it appoints M.P.s is not vice-president or president, but honorary secretary to the Association or honorary adviser to one of the committees of the Association. Until 1945 there were generally two M.P.s as honorary secretaries, but since then there has been an M.P. and a peer. The position of honorary adviser has been given to M.P.s only since 1950, previously being held only by technical experts. Those M.P.s who have held this position have included men like Mr. Reginald Maudling or Mr. G. P. Stevens, themselves experts on the questions of finance or economics with which the committees are concerned.[2]

Some groups choose, in preference to giving M.P.s honorary positions within their organization, to constitute a parliamentary panel. It is a method used by many trade associations. To be on the parliamentary panel of a group is merely to agree to help the group if possible. The relationship is informal. It may mean no more than an invitation to the annual dinner of the group and the asking of an occasional question in the House. Even the term 'parliamentary panel' gives the relationship more formality than it sometimes possesses. It is merely the recognition by agreement of a more permanent relationship than that which may exist between any group and any M.P. on specific issues. The term 'parliamentary panel' is a convenient fiction.

The nature of the relationship between the group and the panel can vary greatly. N.A.L.G.O. places weight upon it. It normally has two M.P.s of different parties associated with it. They speak at the annual conference and their work is fully reported on in the annual report. They arrange deputations and the tabling of amendments.[3] At the other extreme is the National Association of Master Bakers, Confectioners, and

[1] *N.C.T. Annual Report*, 1953–4, pp. 3 and 8.
[2] *A.B.C.C. Annual Reports*, 1945–55.
[3] *N.A.L.G.O. Annual Reports*, 1945–55.

Caterers. As a result of the difficulties encountered in its campaign on the bread subsidy, it formed a sort of parliamentary panel—perhaps even that is too strong a term. It was merely a list of 150 M.P.s to whom the Association, on the basis of advice from regional federations and local branches, felt that communications could usefully be sent. Such a panel is probably too large and it is perhaps significant that in the first year no communications were sent.[1]

Normally work for the group lies lightly on the members of a parliamentary panel. It is a position in which there is little difficulty in finding M.P.s to serve. Like the position of vice-president it brings few responsibilities but considerable advantages. The M.P. needs to be informed and he often lacks sources of information. He has his own personal background and his constituency to draw upon. He reads the press, he can consult the House of Commons library, but unless he is well briefed he is unlikely to be able to speak with authority upon any of the intricate sectional problems which take up much parliamentary time. Some M.P.s obtain their briefs from the party. Others prefer to relieve the monotony. The pressure group is an informed body. In the field with which it is concerned, it needs to be well-informed if it is to convince the government in consultation. Indeed, if it is not well informed is it unlikely to be fully consulted by the government. Information supplied by a pressure group is of great value to an M.P. It gives him a chance to aspire to a specialist's knowledge and an expert's authority. A relationship with a pressure group is to the advantage of both group and M.P.

However valuable this may be as a statement of abstract principle, it does not explain how the group makes contact with the M.P. For an M.P. is no more likely to welcome a blunt approach than a man walking down a street likes being greeted by a stranger with the words 'Let's be friends', however much that man is in favour of making friends as an abstract principle.

The quality of duration introduced by any relationship of this kind is likely to be based upon aid given on one particular occasion. The M.P. may have been approached by the group in his constituency as part of a general campaign and, having helped it, been invited to interest himself in the affairs of the group in the future. The constituency provides the basis for the

[1] *N.A.M.B.C.C. Report to Annual Conference,* 1953, p. 30.

contact in other cases, as when the particular interest is represented in his constituency or when some prominent individual in the group resides in his constituency. In other cases the contact may arise out of the M.P.'s personal background. Another means of contact is provided by M.P.s already connected with the group. In 1945, after the defeat of Mr. Geoffrey Hutchinson, Mr. T. W. Burden found himself the only M.P. associated with N.A.L.G.O. in the House of Commons. At the annual conference in the following year he said 'he was looking anxiously for a successor',[1] and in 1947 Mr. D. C. Walker-Smith joined him on the platform.

Though the informality of this method of attaining representation provides its main attraction, that informality can destroy some of its value. Unless he is asked to serve on the executive of the group, the M.P. is likely to remain an outsider, called in to help occasionally, but unable to give the group the full benefit of his advice because he has been approached only after decisions have been made. He can, it is true, be invited to join special committees, but that is no substitute for his presence on the main committees where he could appreciate the real atmosphere of the group and the group executive learn from him how an M.P. can be of help to it. Interest may wane if an M.P. remains an outsider. In some cases the personality of the M.P. or his knowledge of the field and interest in it, overcomes these difficulties.

A typical relationship was that between Mr. D. L. Lipson, the Independent M.P. for Cheltenham, and the United Commercial Travellers' Association. Mr. Lipson was President of the Cheltenham Branch of the Association:

> Mr. Lipson is available at any time that I like to get in touch with him either by letter or by phone, and he always listens respectfully to what I have to say to him, and he also pays me the compliment that whenever I want a question put in the House he asks me actually to draft the question. I cannot expect more than that from a Member of Parliament.[2]

A number of other M.P.s were also vice-presidents of local branches. They came from all parties, although in 1949 the

[1] *Local Government Service*, July–Aug. 1946, p. 128.
[2] *U.C.T.A. Annual Conference Report*, 1949, p. 97.

Honorary Parliamentary Agent of the Association said that there was a need to establish some more contacts on the Labour side of the House.

To achieve representation the group may not need to go to even this degree of formality. It may prefer to rely on the *ad hoc* contact or the unstated understanding. These are easy to achieve in two cases. The first is where the interests represented by the group are geographically concentrated. The cotton and fishery industries achieve ready representation in the House because they are economically dominant in certain constituencies. While an M.P. would not be regarded as failing in his duty if he did not express himself on bolt manufacture in an appropriate debate, although he had a bolt factory in his constituency, an M.P. for Yarmouth or Grimsby who refused to defend the fishery industry would stand condemned for failing in his duty to his constituency. Debates on these issues are almost monopolized by representatives of the interested constituencies, and it is held to be proper in a way that other group representation is not.[1] There is a tendency to look down upon groups which, finding this means of representation difficult, resort to others. One M.P. states proudly his concern in his constituency's affairs, another confesses an 'interest'.

A group may rely on *ad hoc* contacts with members of the House of Commons who share its interests or even belong to it. The accountancy societies maintain contact with accountants in the House.[2] Trade associations can make representations through directors of member firms. In certain circumstances they may join forces with a trade union representative. In 1940 Mr. George Isaacs, then General Secretary of the National Society of Operative Printers and Assistants, led the campaign in the House of Commons against the imposition of purchase tax on books, newspapers, and other printed articles for both sides of the printing trade.[3]

[1] e.g. Debate on White Fish and Herring Industries Bill, 2nd Reading in 1953, when out of fifteen back-bench speeches, there spoke the M.P.s for Lowestoft, Aberdeen (N.), Aberdeenshire (E.), Hull (Central), Hull (Haltemprice), Orkney and Shetland, Banff, Pembroke, Caithness and Sutherland, and St. Ives; see especially speech by Mr. E. Evans, M.P. for Lowestoft: 'we have to look after our own interests' (H.C. Deb. 510, col. 93).

[2] See amendment moved by Mr. G. P. Stevens, C.A., on Iron and Steel Bill in 1953, H.C. Deb. 511, cols. 1289–91.

[3] Ellic Howe, *British Federation of Master Printers, 1900–1950* (1950), p. 156.

3

Group representation through individual M.P.s gives to the group a means of tabling questions and amendments and of making its views known. It gives the group a foothold in the House. This is a limited function, though at times and in some groups a useful one. If a group seeks to influence parliamentary opinion and thus the formation of policy, something more is needed. Not enough support can be obtained through these methods, nor is the support necessarily influential at the important points within the political system. The party committee is probably the point for the group to aim at in Parliament. It is true that individual representation may give the group an opportunity to put its views before the appropriate party committee, but that is not necessarily enough.

Since 1944 the National Farmers' Union has placed the whole emphasis of its parliamentary work on building up close relations with the appropriate party committees (or party groups) of both the Labour and Conservative Parties. It has turned away from the system of sponsored M.P.s as, previously, it had turned away from the system of contact with an all-party agricultural committee which it itself took the initiative in forming.[1] If the Union succeeds in having good relations with the party committees other means of contact are unnecessary. It is not so much that favourable relations with these committees give the group a means of promoting amendments, but that an opportunity is obtained to establish good relations with those who are influential in the formation of party policy on agriculture. The attitude of the party committee to a group is a factor that even a minister must take into account *before* he makes decisions on its representations. It is the party, not the all-party, committee that is important, as the National Farmers' Union has realized, for that is a form of machinery which has not been created by the group but by the party, and therefore the party is attentive to it. It contains all within the party interested in the question. If that committee is won over to a group's point of view, then that group's influence in consultation becomes greater. Close contact has been effected by the Union. It has ready access to the party committees and is

[1] *N.F.U. Yearbook*, 1923, p. 197.

frequently consulted by them. Its permanent officials are in close touch with the committees' secretaries:

> Throughout the year the closest contact was maintained with the Parliamentary Agricultural Committees of the main political parties. The principal officers and staff of the Union went to the Houses of Parliament on a number of occasions to address these committees on such important subjects as housing, the Geneva Trade Agreement and opencast coal mining, and upon individual Bills to which the Union wished to secure amendments. In addition, personal contacts with members of both Houses of Parliament were maintained and improved—the benefits from which were reflected when farming affairs were debated in either House.[1]

Other groups often have close relationships with the committees of one of the parties, but rarely with both. Trade associations tend to have close contacts with one side of the House and trade unions with the other. However, recently there have been signs of a desire—more particularly on the part of trade associations—to escape from the limitations of this attitude. Trade unions are too tied to the system of sponsored M.P.s and too involved with the Labour Party to have gone as far as trade associations. But even here circumstances can force a change, and in March 1955 representatives of the United Textile Factory Workers' Association met the Conservative group of Lancashire M.P.s who were considering the cotton industry's problems.[2]

Political difficulties may prevent these contacts growing in certain cases. The Road Haulage Association's campaign against the nationalization of road transport has raised a barrier between it and Labour M.P.s. There is a lasting prejudice in certain sections of the Labour Party against the Brewers' Society and its associated organizations. Other groups such as the Association of British Chambers of Commerce are prevented by nothing save force of habit from making regular approaches to the Labour Party's parliamentary committees. In the future more groups are likely to follow the example of the N.F.U. and use contacts with the parliamentary committees of both parties as the basis for permanent relationships.

Some groups have chosen to make contact with all-party committees, perhaps of their own forming. Part of the impulse

[1] *N.F.U. Yearbook*, 1949, p. 102. [2] *Manchester Guardian*, 17 Mar. 1955.

may come from a desire to avoid contact with the party machinery. The phrases 'non-partisan' or 'non-political' occur frequently in groups' descriptions of themselves, and a group may hope to preserve its political chastity in this way. But a group cannot avoid the party where the party is involved in the issues with which it is concerned.

The all-party committee is a more natural development for groups which are concerned with matters upon which party discipline is light. The Animal Welfare Group has a very close relationship with the R.S.P.C.A. It is a Group which is open to members of all parties and of both Houses. It had a membership of about fifty in 1953. Contact between the Group and the Society is maintained by the Parliamentary Organizer of the Society who acts as secretary to the Group. Before the Second World War the Amenities Group in Parliament had a very similar relationship to the Council for the Preservation of Rural England.[1]

These parliamentary committees have an existence independent of the group outside. Certain committees are more openly attached to the outside body in that the outside group takes the initiative in forming them and membership of the committee implies support of the group's policy in principle if not in detail.

Just before the general election of 1945 the Howard League for Penal Reform issued a statement of policy which stressed the need for a new Criminal Justice Act and in particular pressed for certain provisions to be included in it. Members of the League were asked to bring this statement to the notice of candidates. In October 1945 the League circularized all members of the new House asking them to join an all-party Penal Reform Group to be formed on the basis of this policy, even though they might feel the need to make some reservations. One hundred and eight M.P.'s joined—the majority without any reservations—and this represented a great increase in the membership of the 25-year-old Group.[2] After the passing of the Criminal Justice Act in 1948 interest declined and the group formed after the 1950 election had a membership of only

[1] e.g. see *C.P.R.E. Monthly Report*, June 1934, p. 9, a meeting of House of Commons Amenities Group with representatives of C.P.R.E. present by invitation.

[2] *H.L. Annual Report*, 1944–5, pp. 3–4.

fifty-five.[1] The Temperance Group is formed in the same way, on the basis of policy statements sent out during elections.[2]

The British Legion has a House of Commons Branch. It was originally formed in 1922 shortly after the creation of the Legion itself,[3] and has had a continuous existence since then, although it met only a few times during the Second World War. Even today it does not meet very frequently. When it does it is in order to give officials a chance to address it on Legion policy. 'It is a centre for spreading goodwill and information.'[4] Its membership is drawn from all parties (its officers rotate among the parties), many of them being honorary officials in the local branches. The British Limbless Ex-Service Men's Association also has the All-Party Committee of supporters in the House, which is active on its behalf.[5]

Members of the professions tend to form groups in the House of Commons, and the professional organizations outside naturally maintain contact with them. In 1950 Mr. Sydney Silverman described one of the groups in these terms: 'there are a number of hon. Members on both sides who are solicitors, and who on professional points like to consult one another from time to time.'[6] The Law Society keeps in touch with this informal group and occasionally circularizes its members on points it wishes to have raised. The British Medical Association keeps in touch with the all-party Medical Group (a group not confined to doctors).

The Trustee Savings Banks' Association has a Parliamentary Committee with members from all parties. In 1955 it had twenty members.[7] The function of this committee, despite its formal constitution, probably resembles that of the parliamentary panel with special responsibilities falling on the Chairman and the Secretary. It is doubtful if trustee savings banks' affairs will require many meetings of the Committee.

[1] *H.L. Annual Report*, 1949–50, p. 7.

[2] *National Temperance Federation Annual Reports.*

[3] Graham Wootton, *The Official History of the British Legion* (1956), p. 44.

[4] *British Legion Journal*, Jan. 1950, p. 4.

[5] e.g. in 1954–5 this Committee met the Minister of Pensions and National Insurance to urge B.L.E.S.M.A.'s case on pensions. Mr. Leslie Lever, M.P., the Secretary to the Committee, helped to secure 324 signatures for a motion tabled by Mr. C. J. Simmons calling for special consideration for the severely disabled. *B.L.E.S.M.A. Annual Conference Report*, 1955, p. 5.

[6] H.C. Deb. 480, col. 990.

[7] *Trustee Savings Banks' Year Book*, 1955, pp. 12–13.

The Glass Manufacturers' Federation has a Parliamentary Group with members from both sides of the House. It works in association with the Federation's Executive Committee and it is claimed that the Group's activities secured a reduction in purchase tax on cut glassware.[1]

An all-party committee is of most value when, with fairly frequent meetings, it becomes a body of M.P.s working together. It is rare for this to happen upon matters likely to be affected by party discipline. In that case, the committee will be and will remain an artificial creation, giving the group little that could not be obtained by less formal machinery.

A group may achieve representation by means of a special meeting held in a committee room of the House to consider group representations. This meeting must be arranged with the help of an M.P. who will sponsor it and either take the chair himself or make arrangements for another member to take it.

The meeting will probably be called to deal with a specific issue. Invitations may be general, or restricted to those likely to be interested in the issue or favourable to the group. A meeting called by the Theatre Entertainments Tax Committee in 1955 was a general invitation since it was desired to obtain wide support.[2] A meeting called by the Scottish Housewives Association in 1950, at which Captain (now Sir) James Duncan took the chair, was of interest only to Scottish M.P.s.[3] A meeting called by various professional organizations in the national health service in order to protest against the Health Service Superannuation Regulations (1950) appears to have been restricted, although some members from all parties were invited.[4] Presumably it was desired to explain the groups' case to potential supporters only.

These meetings normally proceed by means of statements and questions. They are popular with M.P.s in the sense that most secure a fair attendance. Many M.P.s, however, tend to be but birds of passage, staying for a short while only. The meetings fulfil a useful function in giving groups a chance to explain their viewpoint to those M.P.s likely to be interested. The calling of

[1] Political and Economic Planning, *Industrial Trade Associations* (1957), p. 88.
[2] *Stage*, 24 Mar. 1955.
[3] *Scottish Housewives' Association Bulletins*, 1950.
[4] H.C. Deb. 473, col. 696.

the meeting does not depend upon the procedures of a party committee, reluctant to be overwhelmed by group representation, but upon the initiative of the group and the support of an M.P. However, these meetings only provide the group with representation on specific issues, and are not a basis for permanent representation.

4

There is another method of achieving representation, which differs greatly from those previously considered. This is through an outside individual who is employed by the group on the basis of his contacts with M.P.s. Quite a number of groups employ an official, one of whose functions is to maintain contact with M.P.s and generally to conduct the parliamentary business of the group. The Association of British Chambers of Commerce employs a Parliamentary Officer, the R.S.P.C.A. a Parliamentary Organizer, and the National Conference of Friendly Societies a Parliamentary Liaison Officer. A number of organizations tend to use the word 'Parliamentary' rather loosely. For example, the Parliamentary Secretary of the National Council of Women is in fact the secretary, with very much the normal duties of that position.

But what is meant here is rather a person employed by a number of groups on specific issues and problems. The parliamentary agent proper is rarely used in this way. His work is primarily on private bills[1] and it is regarded as improper for anyone engaged in such work to take advantage of his position in order to devote much attention to the routines of pressure-group activity. That is not to say that there is anything improper in the agent drafting amendments to bills or advising the group on the nature of the business to be brought before the House. The Parliamentary Agent for the Building Societies' Association sends it reports on all impending bills and regulations with regard to their effect on building societies.[2] Nor is it improper for an agent occasionally to arrange for an amendment to be tabled. What would be improper is lobbying on a large scale.

[1] See p. 86.

[2] 'The Association's Parliamentary Agent Sir Harry Pritchard reports daily on all business arising in either House which is likely to concern building societies' (*B.S.A. Annual Report*, 1945–6, p. 8).

There is, however, a different type of agent of whom there has been at least one example in Britain. Lieutenant-Commander Christopher Powell, the Administrative Secretary of the Parliamentary and Scientific Committee (an unofficial group of members of both Houses and representatives of scientific and technical institutions), has acted as a 'consultant' for a number of groups to assist them in their parliamentary work. These have included the Theatrical Managers' Association and the British Road Federation. He has advised these associations on parliamentary matters and lobbied M.P.s. In 1949 it was reported in the House that he had been endeavouring to dissuade Professor D. L. Savory from entering the Standing Committee on the Censorship of Plays Bill in order to prevent a quorum.[1] Most associations do not require a 'consultant', being able to rely on their own contacts.

5

One other important method of obtaining representation remains to be considered. The group can itself actively promote the candidature of one of its own members for the House of Commons and if successful support his membership there. Very occasionally the group will seek to do this directly, itself playing the role of the political party. In 1918 the National Federation of Discharged Sailors and Soldiers promoted several candidates for Parliament of whom one was successful.[2] The N.F.U. has on at least one occasion promoted independent agricultural candidates.[3] In 1935 Miss Florence White stood in a by-election on behalf of the National Spinsters' Pensions Association. The case for prohibition and that for world government have both been put directly to the electorate. In 1952 the General Secretary of the National Anti-Vivisection Society suggested that the movement should promote candidates. In 1951 an *ad hoc* group of members of the Peace Pledge Union discussed ways of giving significance to their dissent from the foreign policies of all parties, which left these particular members unable to vote in elections. This group later sent representatives to a meeting to discuss the possibility of founding a new party.[4] The Co-operative Party might appear to be the most important example of

[1] H.C. Deb. 470, cols. 1150–2 and 1535–8.
[2] R. H. Barker, M.P. for Sowerby 1918–22.
[3] See p. 173.
[4] *Peace Pledge Union Annual Report*, 1951, p. 5.

a group directly promoting candidates, and in its first years perhaps it was,[1] but since then it can hardly be considered separately from the Labour Party.

Most groups have sought to promote candidates through the machinery of the existing parties. There are means by which this can be done at an unofficial level. Since 1945 the N.F.U. has attempted to secure the selection of a number of its supporters as candidates in agricultural constituencies by encouraging N.F.U. members to take an active part in the selection of party candidates. There are few active group members who would not look with favour on the selection of another member of their group by their party.

This method does not provide an official connexion between the group and the member in his capacity as a candidate or later as an M.P. In order to achieve this it is normally necessary for the group to have something to give to the candidate and the constituency, and this is generally financial support. This financial support provides the binding link between group and candidate. The resultant relationship can be described, in the language of the Labour Party, as 'sponsorship' of a candidate by a group.

The system has been highly developed by the trade unions affiliated to the Labour Party. In 1951 they sponsored 139 candidates. This system of sponsorship is officially recognized by the Labour Party, which lays down the conditions on which it takes place. For example, the amount which a sponsoring body, or indeed any candidate, can contribute towards organizational expenses is not more than £350 a year in a borough and not more than £420 in a county constituency. At a parliamentary election up to 80 per cent. of the expenses involved may be paid.

The Conservative Party does not admit this kind of organization into membership and does not therefore provide for a system of sponsoring candidates. In addition, the party rule which lays down that a constituency must itself provide all the funds for election expenses, must restrict any large-scale development of the system of sponsoring.

There are legal restrictions placed by the Trade Union Act (1913) upon the right of trade unions to promote candidates.

[1] See G. D. H. Cole, *Century of Co-operation* (1946), chap. xiv.

Expenditure by a trade union on the promotion of candidates can only take place after a ballot of its members has been held on whether or not the union should adopt 'political objects'. In addition, a separate fund must be set up, the rules for which must be approved by the Registrar of Friendly Societies and must provide for members to contract out of the fund without losing any of their rights in the union.

The political objects which fall under the Act are the expenditure of money:

(*a*) on the payment of any expenses incurred either directly or indirectly by a candidate or prospective candidate for election to Parliament or to any public office, before, during, or after the election in connexion with his candidature or election; or

(*b*) on the holding of any meeting or the distribution of any literature or documents in support of any such candidate or prospective candidate; or

(*c*) on the maintenance of any person who is a Member of Parliament or who holds a public office; or

(*d*) in connection with the registration of electors or the selection of a candidate for Parliament or any public office; or

(*e*) on the holding of political meetings of any kind or on the distribution of political literature or political documents of any kind unless the main purpose of the meeting or of the distribution of the literature or documents is the furtherance of statutory objects within the meaning of this Act.[1]

On 31 December 1953 there were 116 registered and 16 unregistered trade unions which had power under their rules to collect contributions from their members for expenditure on political objects. Included in this list were certain employers' organizations such as the National Farmers' Union, the Cinematograph Exhibitors' Association, the National Union of Small Shopkeepers, the News and Specialized Theatre Association, and the National Federation of Retail Newsagents, Booksellers, and Stationers. But the majority were trade unions not only in the legal sense, but also according to common usage. The number is inflated by the fact that the areas of the National Union of Mineworkers were registered separately, as were various local textile workers' associations which attain representation through the United Textile Factory Workers' Association.[2]

[1] 2 and 3 Geo. V, c. 30, s. 3 (3).

[2] *Report of Chief Registrar of Friendly Societies*, 1953, Part 4, pp. 12–13.

Neither the fact that a union has power to pursue political objects nor even the existence of a political fund should necessarily be taken to imply that the union actually sponsors candidates. The power may never be used, or the power if once used may now be neglected.[1] On the other hand, the fund may be used for purposes which appear to fall under section (*e*) of the clause quoted above. The Association of Scientific Workers has stated that it uses its political fund for:

(*a*) Expenses involved in preparing and circulating memoranda amongst M.P.s on matters of direct concern to science and scientists, such as: the provision of equitable income tax reliefs; a policy for higher technological education; the purpose and method of setting up a British Science Centre.
(*b*) Expenses involved in arranging meetings of groups of M.P.s to discuss such matters as above.
(*c*) Contributions towards the cost of pamphlets and conferences having the purpose of preparing the ground for legislation on matters of scientific interest.
(*d*) The cost of affiliation to the Parliamentary and Scientific Committee.[2]

It seems unnecessary for the Association to have a political fund for these purposes. Mr. N. A. Citrine in his work on trade union law has written:

> In examining the purpose of a meeting or the distribution of literature or documents within this paragraph, the first test to be applied is 'How much of this is within the statutory objects of a trade union, i.e. how much of it concerns the regulation of the relations between workmen and masters or workmen and workmen or between masters and masters, or the imposing of restrictive conditions on the conduct of a trade or business, or the provision of benefits to members.' In applying this it is important to remember that if the matter is within the statutory objects of a trade union it is excluded from the ambit of the term 'political' even though it happens to have been taken up by a political party as part of its programme.[3]

It seems clear on this interpretation that it is unnecessary

[1] In some cases, such as the Musicians' Union or the National League of the Blind, the main purpose for which the fund is used is to pay affiliation fees to the Labour Party.

[2] Statement issued by the Association of Scientific Workers.

[3] N. A. Citrine, *Trade Union Law* (1950), p. 336.

for the Association of Scientific Workers to have a political fund for the purposes it stated. Most other unions use their ordinary funds for such purposes. After all, how could the N.F.U. have preserved its fund intact since 1945 if it had interpreted the Trade Union Act (1913) in that way?

A group can sponsor a candidate either as a means of achieving representation in the House of Commons or as a means of achieving greater control over its representatives. The large-scale development of the system by trade unions was due to the fact that for many years it was their only means of securing representation in the House and such representation was the only means of bringing attention to their grievances. Trade union representation in the House was one of the means used to establish the present position of trade unions in relation to the process of government.

Most groups can now achieve representation in the House without sponsoring candidates. Trade unions lacking sponsored M.P.s do not lack representation. Mr. Austen Albu has on several occasions put the National Union of Furniture Trade Operatives' viewpoint in the House.[1] Yet in groups considering the problem the argument is often put forward that by sponsoring candidates the group will secure representation, as though no other method were possible.

When the British Dental Association's Council considered this question in 1945, faced as it then was with the major political problems raised by the proposals for a new health service, Mr. E. E. Wookey moved that the Association sponsor candidates, paying successful ones £500 a year while they remained M.P.s. He argued that in the past the Association had been inadequately represented by lay M.P.s and that this was a proper and legitimate way to secure better representation. It was to be supposed that any dentist elected would have sufficient loyalty to the profession to present its case.[2]

Arguments in favour of a group adopting the system of sponsored M.P.s may draw attention to the special experience such M.P.s would have, experience which others representing the group do not always possess. In 1952 the General Secretary of the National Union of Furniture Trade Operatives, while praising Mr. Albu's work in Parliament in relation to the

[1] e.g. see pp. 70–71.

[2] *British Dental Journal*, 1945 (2), p. 59.

D scheme, stated that he felt that the Union should 'have had a Member available with Trade knowledge to back his effort'.[1]

In 1949 Mr. W. E. Leftly, the President of the Civil Service Clerical Association putting the case of those who advocated that the union should adopt political objects said:

> They argue, moreover, that critics of the Civil Service, many of them unfair and ill-informed are present in large numbers in Parliament and that some of the misrepresentations about the Civil Service would be discouraged and certainly answered if there were more M.P.s who are familiar with the true facts about the Service.[2]

It is true that some of the groups' representatives in the House of Commons do not have that intimate knowledge of their affairs which comes from a close connexion with the groups. If parliamentary debate were crucial this might matter, but it is doubtful whether the importance of the House of Commons to a group is great enough to make this factor of much weight. A tendency to exaggerate the importance of action in Parliament is a feature of trade union statements on the subject, perhaps inevitable in view of the sums expended on sponsoring candidates.

In 1954 the *Transport Salaried Staff Journal* printed an article discussing the role of the Association in politics. It discussed the value of the Association's affiliation to the Labour Party and of trade union representation in the House. The two issues were linked in the article, as they are by most unions, although there is no necessary connexion between them:

> We are not intending here and now to put the full case for trade union participation in politics, but only to remind T.S.A. members, whether contributors to the Political Fund or not, of some of the benefits which they would not be enjoying to-day if the Association had remained aloof from political activities, and of the valuable work done by the Labour Party and the Association's M.P.s in protecting and promoting the interests of members in relation to their very conditions of service which are the primary business of the Association.

There later follow a list of occasions on which the Association's M.P.s have helped it. For example:

> 1946/7: On committee stage of National Insurance Bill action taken regarding modified pensions, reorganisation of Superan-

[1] *N.U.F.T.O. Record*, June 1952, p. 3.

[2] *Red Tape*, Oct. 1949, pp. 5–6.

nuation Funds and other matters. Important assurances secured from Minister. 1947/53. . . . Association's M.P.s moved amendments during passage of [Transport] Bill through Parliament.

Further intervention by our M.P.s during the debate on Pensions (Increase) Bill 1947 respecting position of railway superannuitants.[1]

That these actions took place cannot be doubted, but that they need have been anything more than a subordinate part of the process of consultation seems unlikely. Nor do they seem actions for which the presence of sponsored M.P.s was necessary. Harmless amendments on railway superannuitants will never lack supporters.

It may be argued that the sponsoring of M.P.s by a group gives it greater control over its representatives. Control is only valuable if parliamentary action is likely to be important for a group. In any case it is likely to involve the group in more problems than it solves. Mr. McFarlane felt this in opposing the resolution at the British Dental Association's Council, mentioned above. 'He did not like the idea of the Association saying to a Member of Parliament, "We will give you £500 as long as you support us but not when you do not support us".' He thought that amounted to coercion. He saw, too, that an M.P.'s loyalty to his party would come before that to his group should the two clash.[2]

These are difficulties which might be worth struggling with if there was something important to be gained, but as the balance of the political system stands, a group has no great incentive to attempt to exert a very uncertain control.

6

It is not surprising that the sponsoring of candidates and M.P.s has not been developed to any great extent by groups other than those trade unions affiliated to the Labour Party, or that where funds have been collected they have often proved to be of little importance in practice.

The British Medical Association in 1919 established a Medical Representation in Parliament Fund with its main object the provision of financial assistance to such prospective candidates as were judged likely to prove effective in putting the profes-

[1] *Transport Salaried Staff Journal*, Apr. 1945, pp. 152–3.

[2] *British Dental Journal*, 1945 (2), p. 60.

sion's point of view in Parliament. The fund was not widely supported and was finally wound up. However, at the 1945 election a number of doctors came forward as candidates and appealed to the Association for financial aid towards their election expenses. It was legally impossible for the Association (owing to its definition of objects) to use its own fund for this purpose, but it was decided to set up a new fund and to invite voluntary subscriptions. The Council, rather surprisingly, believed that doctors were more alive then to the need for such a fund than they had been before the war and that the appeal would be successful. A Parliamentary Elections Committee was set up to manage the fund.[1] The fund has not been a striking success, and is rarely mentioned by the Association. The reason for its failure has probably been, not lack of support, but rather that little use could be made of it owing to the lack of suitable candidates requiring aid. Most doctor M.P.'s do not want to use the fund.

The Pharmaceutical Society's fund has been in existence since 1926, though its basis was altered in 1943 when it ceased to be a fund under the joint control of various pharmaceutical bodies and came under the sole control of the Society. It has appointed a Parliamentary Fund Committee, which invites those members of the Society who contemplate offering themselves as candidates to get in touch with it. They are later met by the Committee in order to discuss their plans and to give it the opportunity to judge their prospects, for the Society does not want to spend money on the support of unsuccessful candidates. The rules of the fund permit it to be used, not merely to pay election expenses, but also to grant an allowance to successful candidates.[2] However, while £1,220 was spent at the 1950 election and £600 at the 1951 election, no money was spent on allowances.[3] The fund, which stood in 1953 at over £3,000, cannot be regarded as moribund, but it does not play an important part in the affairs of the Society.

In 1917 the United Kingdom Commercial Travellers' Association authorized the establishment of a parliamentary fund of £250. Previously it had conducted its parliamentary business

[1] *British Medical Journal*, 23 June 1945 (Supplement), p. 121.

[2] *Calendar of the Pharmaceutical Society of Gt. Britain*, 1954–5, pp. 88–90.

[3] *Pharmaceutical Journal*, 10 May 1952, p. 328.

through a paid official known as the Parliamentary Agent, who established his own contacts in the House of Commons. The decision to start a parliamentary fund aroused considerable hostility in the Association, largely because of the party questions involved. For the main purpose of the fund was to secure the election of the General Secretary, Mr. F. L. Coysh, a Liberal.[1] Following his failure to secure election, and with increasing bitterness over the party issue, the fund was suspended in 1924.[2]

The National Farmers' Union has a political fund which at the end of 1952 stood at £78,026.[3] There have been no subscriptions to the fund since 1927, at the end of which year the fund stood at £52,649.[4] Since then, the increase has been due to accumulated interest. This fund was formed as a result of a ballot held in 1921 under the Trade Union Act of 1913. This was necessary because of a reorganization of the Union in the previous year, and, in fact, the fund had been initiated in 1909, although no candidates were sponsored until 1918.[5]

The policy under which the fund was to operate was stated in the following terms:

> The politics of agriculture remain the only politics known to the organisation. The union has not been, is not, and will not be attached to any political party. It is not proposed to establish an independent 'N.F.U. party' in the House of Commons, but efforts will be made to secure the return of a few practical working farmers to it by securing their adoption as prospective candidates wherever the opportunity occurs, the union being firmly convinced that the absence of such representatives from the agricultural councils of the House has militated severely against the interests of the farming community and the nation's premier key industry.[6]

In 1922 seven candidates were supported, four being successful;[7] all the successful candidates were Conservative, the three unsuccessful candidates all being described as Agricultural.[8] £4,891 was spent on election expenses. In 1929 the policy changed:

[1] United Commercial Travellers' Association, *Seventy Years* (1953), p. 54.
[2] Ibid., p. 60.
[3] *N.F.U. Yearbook*, 1953, p. 195.
[4] Ibid., 1928, p. 328.
[5] Ibid., 1922, pp. 99–100.
[6] Ibid., pp. 201–2.
[7] Ibid., 1923, p. 197.
[8] *Dod's Parliamentary Companion*, 1923.

In point of fact no expenditure was incurred in connection with the general election, the results of which fully confirmed the wisdom of conserving the resources represented by the Political Fund so that the Union may be in a position to take full advantage of circumstances, whenever they may arise, which make it necessary to support candidates to promote the best interests of farmers in relation to any question of agricultural policy.[1]

A similar policy was followed in 1931,[2] but in 1935 the Union endorsed the candidatures of Major R. H. Dorman-Smith and Sir Joseph Lamb, both of whom were elected as Conservative M.P.s,[3] £1,300 being spent out of the fund in this year.[4] In 1943 the candidature of Mr. Thomas Peacock as a Conservative was endorsed in a by-election.[5] The fund was used for the last time in 1945.[6] Since, during the period 1935–9, the Union spent about £500 a year on political organization, whereas in the period immediately before the election, nothing was spent,[7] it can be seen that the sponsoring of candidates involved the Union in commitments continuing beyond the election period.

In 1955 the fund was still administered by a Political Fund Committee, whose membership was identical with the Union's Parliamentary Committee. There has been no indication that the Union has any intention of using this fund in the foreseeable future.

In 1929 the National Federation of Retail Newsagents, Booksellers, and Stationers held a ballot of members on the adoption of political objects, but it was not till 1939 that the General Secretary was nominated as the Federation's first candidate. He did not succeed in getting into Parliament.[8] In 1954 the political fund stood at £6,667 and was being used for parliamentary and office expenses. The only income was from interest.[9]

The Educational Institute of Scotland had a sponsored M.P. from 1918 till 1945. It had virtual control of one of the Scottish Universities seats. Dr. G. A. Morrison, at first a Liberal and then a Liberal National, was its M.P. during

[1] *N.F.U. Yearbook*, 1930, p. 432.
[2] Ibid., 1932, p. 436.
[3] Ibid., 1936, p. 360.
[4] Ibid., p. 388.
[5] *Farmers' Weekly*, 26 Feb. 1943, p. 15.
[6] *N.F.U. Yearbook*, 1946, p. 128. In 1945 political organization expenditure was £1,604.
[7] *N.F.U. Yearbooks*, 1931–9.
[8] *N.F.R.N.B.S. Yearbook*, 1955, pp. 164–6.
[9] *N.F.R.N.B.S. Annual Report*, 1953–4, para. 27.

the latter part of the period. 'Owing to a split in the unity of the teaching profession the seat was lost to the Institute' on the retirement of Dr. Morrison.[1] It is unlikely that, with the abolition of the University seats, the Institute will ever again sponsor candidates.

In 1925 the British Undertakers' Association appointed T. Groves, M.P., as its 'Parliamentary Agent' and it is recorded in its annual report for that year that he was active on its behalf.[2] In the following year it is recorded that the Association was unable to appoint a parliamentary representative 'on account of finance'.[3] After this, the Association seems to have abandoned the idea of being represented in the House of Commons by these means.

The Country Landowners' Association has amongst its objects: 'to secure that (so far as possible) agricultural constituencies shall be represented in Parliament by persons conversant with and in sympathy with the wants of the rural community. . .'[4] But, in the 1950 election at least, this seems to have been interpreted as requiring no more than a little judicious interrogation of the candidates.[5]

The wine and spirit trade has a Defence Fund associated with the Wines and Spirit Association, and run by its Trade Defence Committee. Among its objects is 'to secure, regardless of party politics, the return to the House of Commons and other elected bodies, of candidates favourable to trade interests'.[6] The National Trade Defence Association, whose purpose is 'to protect at all times the general interests of the Licensed Trade as a whole in and out of Parliament', is supported by all the main groups of the licensed trade and also by individual subscribers. Amongst those who are entitled to sit *ex officio* on the Council are M.P.s whose firms subscribe to its funds.[7] It is impossible to say anything of the workings of either of these funds from published material, but in view of the comparatively slight representation of the licensed trade in the House of Commons from 1945 to 1955, it is unlikely they were much used in sponsoring candidates.

[1] A. J. Belford, *Centenary Handbook of the Educational Institute of Scotland* (1946), p. 409.
[2] British Undertakers' Association, *Annual Report*, 1925.
[3] Ibid., 1926.
[4] *C.L.A. rules*, Rule 2 (F).
[5] *C.L.A. 43rd Annual Report*, 1950, pp. 15–16.
[6] *Brewers' Almanack*, 1953, p. 811.
[7] Ibid., p. 815.

The National Union of Teachers is probably the only group, other than trade unions affiliated to the Labour Party, which places any great weight on sponsored candidates. The Union is scrupulously non-partisan. Its principle is to distribute support equally between the Labour, Liberal, and Conservative Parties. Up to four candidates from each of these parties can be sponsored provided they have a reasonable chance of success. In practice there has been a lack of Conservative applicants and of Liberal applicants fulfilling the necessary conditions. The result was that in the 1945 Parliament the Union was represented only by Labour M.P.s although before then there was one Conservative,[1] and in 1955 two Conservative M.P.s.[2] All sponsored candidates receive grants of 50 per cent. of their expenses up to a maximum of £400, and if elected can receive an allowance.

All applicants, who must have been members of the Union for the seven preceding years must agree:

(1) to make themselves acquainted at all times with Union policy,
(2) within the bounds of Parliamentary Privilege to have regard to such policy, and
(3) to assist the Union in Parliamentary matters wherever possible.[3]

However, an additional provision was made in 1952 for a system of assisted candidates who shall be chosen from elected members in such a way that 'the total number of Supported and Assisted M.P.'s shall not exceed 12, providing that not more than four are drawn from any one political party'.[4] The object was to redress the balance in party representation. The scheme was to operate after the next general election. The reorganization of the system is a clear reaffirmation of faith in it by the Union. It is a rare phenomenon.

This is not a complete list of the bodies sponsoring candidates[5] but it is sufficient to give a fair indication of the attitude to such funds outside the trade unions.

[1] Mr. R. H. Morgan, see *Schoolmaster*, 2 Aug. 1945, p. 86.
[2] Mr. J. C. Jennings and Mr. I. J. Pitman.
[3] Statement issued by the National Union of Teachers.
[4] Ibid.
[5] For the National Federation of Meat Traders' Associations' fund see p. 187.

7

Those trade unions which are affiliated to the Labour Party show no sign of a desire to abandon the system of sponsored candidates. The number promoted at the 1951 election was exactly the same as at the 1929 election. The reasons for this do not lie in the narrower needs of the pressure group, the need to promote amendments, ask questions, and so on—sponsored M.P.s are not necessary for that. It is true that time and habit create their own reasons, and trade unions have grown accustomed to sponsored M.P.s. Their techniques of pressure have accepted the existence of sponsored M.P.s as a basic premiss. For this reason they sometimes use parliamentary routines more often than the system of consultation renders necessary.

But inertia is not sufficient to account for the continuance of the system. To the trade unions, sponsored M.P.s are associated with affiliation to the Labour Party and both with the achievement of their present position in society. Today that position has more powerful bulwarks in the economic strength and voting power of their members, but it is not likely that the unions will discard a system associated with past successes until it becomes a positive hindrance.

It is true that the trade unions could continue their affiliation to the Labour Party without sponsored M.P.s, but the number of trade unionists among Labour M.P.s would be drastically reduced and the Parliamentary Party virtually monopolized by lawyers, teachers, journalists, and free-lances. The trade unions do not fancy losing all control of the Parliamentary Labour Party.

There can be no doubt that confidence is still felt in sponsored M.P.s and that the unions feel that without them their position would be weaker. It is their status they fear for, not the loss of opportunities for group representation.

The importance given in the past to representation by different groups is reflected in the present distribution of candidates between the main sponsoring unions, as the table on p. 178 shows. The only significant changes that these figures for candidates promoted show compared with the figures for the pre-war period are in the U.T.F.W.A. which in 1929 sponsored 6 candidates and had 4 elected and in the A.E.U. which in 1929 only sponsored 3 candidates of whom 2 were elected. The A.E.U.'s increase was possibly the result of a war-time drive to increase the affiliated membership.[1]

Union	*No. of candidates, 1951**	*No. of affiliated members per candidate*	*No. of members per candidate*
National Union of Mineworkers	37 (36)	17,827	16,571
Transport and General Workers' Union	17 (15)	49,118	75,600
Amalgamated Engineering Union	12 (6)	48,854	63,012
National Union of Railwaymen	11 (9)	28,809	36,024
Transport Salaried Staffs' Association	11 (7)	6,921	8,099
Union of Shop, Distributive, and Allied Workers	10 (8)	31,700	34,773
National Union of General and Municipal Workers	5 (4)	80,000	161,706
Union of Post Office Workers	4 (2)	36,739	38,900
Associated Society of Locomotive Engineers and Firemen	3 (2)	12,560	23,043
Amalgamated Society of Woodworkers	3 (3)	43,085	65,400
Electrical Trades Union	3 (1)	40,000	65,969
United Textile Factory Workers' Association	3 (1)	47,932	..
National Union of Public Employees	2 (2)	22,500	87,500
British Iron, Steel, and Kindred Trades Association	2 (2)	42,191	51,223
National Union of Agricultural Workers	2 (1)	35,400	67,500

* Number of successful candidates in brackets.

Since historical factors are at the back of the system of sponsored M.P.s, it is not surprising that for the most part trade union representation has altered little. The very strong representation of the T.S.S.A. in the House as opposed to, say, the N.U.G.M.W., can best be explained by the past importance of parliamentary action to the former, rather than by present circumstances in which legislation concerns both groups. In the inter-war period the T.S.S.A. along with the other railway unions developed the technique of opposing private bills promoted by the railway companies in order to secure concessions from them on industrial matters.[2] This past importance of parliamentary action is reflected in their representation today. In the

[1] J. B. Jefferys, *The Story of the Engineers* (1946), p. 251.

[2] '1942 Blocking of Railway Bill resulted in recognition of Association by Messrs. Pickfords'; '1938 L.N.E. Railway Bill opposed in order to secure negotiations on new Superannuation Fund' (*T.S.S. Journal*, Apr. 1945, p. 153).

same way the miners and the shopworkers have in the past secured many of their aims by legislation and to this end developed parliamentary representation. Geographical concentration aided the miners by enabling them to dominate a large number of constituencies.

8

In assessing the role of the sponsored M.P., his liaison with the union is crucial. How does the union keep in touch with him? Those unions which have only one or two members do not find this much of a problem. It is easy to maintain contact with one M.P. without formalizing the machinery. It was said of Sir Joseph Lamb that he used to go to the National Farmers' Union headquarters every day 'to report upon the previous day's sittings and to discuss the attitude he should take on future business'.[1] His case was exceptional. The usual contact is more casual, depending upon some question having arisen upon which either side desires consultation. This sort of contact can be formalized if necessary. In 1947 the Electrical Trades Union had only one sponsored M.P., Mr. T. F. Cook. When the Bill to nationalize electricity undertakings came before the House, Mr. Cook was co-opted to a special committee of the Executive Council of the Union which had been appointed to examine the Bill.[2] The British Iron, Steel, and Kindred Trades Association adopted a more unusual method. Its sponsored M.P.s were *ex-officio* members of the Executive Committee.[3] This method is most likely to lead to an effective use of the sponsored M.P., since it enables the M.P. to assess the needs of the executive, and the executive to assess the uses of the M.P. and for these two assessments to be correlated. There is, however, an understandable resistance in most unions to bringing on to their executives, even in an advisory capacity, men who are not under the same conditions of service as their other members.

In certain unions the problem is avoided because the M.P. holds a position in the union. The position of president of a union was held by a number of M.P.s for the whole or part of the period from 1945 to 1955. These included Mr. E. G. Gooch

[1] *British Farmer*, 31 Dec. 1949, p. 10.
[2] *Story of the E.T.U.* (1953), p. 220.
[3] V. L. Allen, *Power in Trade Unions* (1954), p. 152.

of the National Union of Agricultural Workers, Mr. Walter Padley of the Union of Shop, Distributive, and Allied Workers, Mr. Ellis Smith of the United Patternmakers' Association, and Mr. Percy Morris of the Transport Salaried Staffs' Association. The position of president is one that an M.P. can easily manage, since its duties are generally part-time.

Difficulties arise in the case of full-time paid officials. In 1956 there was no general secretary of a union who was also a sponsored M.P. for that union. Mr. R. Edwards, General Secretary of the Chemical Workers' Union, was sponsored by the Co-operative Party, while Sir Tom O'Brien, General Secretary of the National Association of Theatrical and Kine Employees, and Mr. Douglas Houghton, General Secretary of the Inland Revenue Staff Federation, were not sponsored by any group. These three unions are comparatively small. The last general secretary of a large union to be an M.P. was Mr. (now Sir) Tom Williamson, of the National Union of General and Municipal Workers, who resigned in 1947 as a result of a pledge given upon his election to his Union post.[1] On the other hand, between 1945 and 1950 Mr. Percy Collick and Mr. W. R. Williams combined being sponsored M.P.s with being Assistant General Secretaries of the Associated Society of Locomotive Engineers and Firemen and the Union of Post Office Workers respectively. In most unions officials are either not allowed to stand for Parliament or, having stood and succeeded, are required to abandon their other functions. The reason is clear. It is merely the difficulty of combining efficiently and effectively two demanding jobs. The Labour Party has been disturbed at this tendency. In 1942 affiliated organizations were circularized on the failure of trade unions to put forward their more prominent members as parliamentary candidates: 'it excludes from Parliamentary discussions Trade Unionism's most authoritative representatives, and reduces the status of Trade Union M.P.s to a secondary position in industry.'[2] But it was of no avail. Trade unions know where they need their ablest men, and they want them there all the time.

The problems of liaison are most serious in those unions with a large membership in the House, because they also have the problem of co-ordination between the members. This latter

[1] H. A. Clegg, *General Union* (1954), pp. 309–10. [2] Ibid., p. 309.

problem is generally solved by the formation of a group or committee of these members. The problem of liaison becomes the problem of liaison between the House of Commons group and the Union's headquarters.

The National Union of Mineworkers has nearly three times as many sponsored M.P.s as any other union. There is an officially constituted Miners' Group in the House of Commons which comprises all the N.U.M. M.P.s, all of whom are, in fact, sponsored. It elects a Secretary who attends the monthly Executive meeting of the Union to report and answer questions. He sits in an advisory capacity only. The officials of the Union attend the Miners' Group as they require or as they are requested. This provides sufficient liaison for the normal activities of the Union, but when a bill which deals with mining is brought forward and is of sufficient importance, a joint working party from both sides is set up, as for the Mines and Quarries Bill in 1954. An added contact has been provided by the fact that a sponsored M.P., Mr. R. W. Williams, is also the Honorary Legal Adviser of the Union and therefore concerned with the drafting of amendments; he is normally a member of all deputations relating to amendments as well as acting as the miners' solicitor-general in standing committees.

The Transport and General Workers' Union's main point of contact is through the Political Secretary, a permanent official of the Union who also acts as Secretary of the Parliamentary Group. This Group consists of all the M.P.s who are sponsored by the Union though not the considerable number of members of the Union in the House who are not sponsored. At its meetings the Political Secretary reports on Union activities, gives its views on matters likely to come before Parliament and details the matters upon which it needs help. This is not the only contact. The Chairman of the Group attends the National Executive Committee of the Union to report and advise, although it is always made clear to the Executive that the M.P.s retain their freedom of action.

The Parliamentary Group of the Union of Shop, Distributive, and Allied Workers meets regularly once every four months although it may receive special statements from Union officials on other occasions. Mr. Walter Padley, the President, has been the main point of contact since 1950 when he was elected to

Parliament. The Union procedure requires that an M.P. should be present at all deputations to ministers. Mr. Padley has in fact been present at most of these deputations.

In the National Union of Railwaymen contact is maintained by regular meetings of the Group (usually quarterly) and the Political Sub-Committee of the Executive Committee, by the submission by the Group of a quarterly report on the work of Parliament, and by general correspondence between the Group and the Union Secretaries.

These systems all follow a similar pattern. However, there is bound to be far more to the relationship than can be expressed in formal machinery. There is, inevitably in such a relationship, far more of mutual sympathy than of committees and minutes.

The Co-operative Party M.P. is in a very similar position to a trade union M.P., though the relationship is more complex owing to the fact that the Co-operative Party does not merely sponsor M.P.s, but has a wider purpose. The Assistant Secretary has pointed out that it has three objects:

(1) to defend the Co-operative movement;
(2) to represent and promote consumers' interests;
(3) to ensure that the experience of the Co-operative Movement and the principles of Co-operation are widely used in the building of the New Society.[1]

But the importance of the Co-operative M.P.s is undoubtedly as representatives of a pressure group. The Party originated in 1917, partly as a protest against the abuses of food control and the injustices of the excess profits tax,[2] and its representatives have continued to seek to defend co-operative interests in the House of Commons.[3]

[1] *The Organisation of the Co-operative Party* (1953), p. 1.

[2] G. D. H. Cole, *A Century of Co-operation* (1946), pp. 315–16.

[3] 'The Co-operative Parliamentary Group has often been called upon in the past to oppose legislation which would retard the Movement's growth or limit its opportunities of expansion. The Joint Parliamentary Committee from its inception has scrutinised legislation, Orders and Regulations to protect the rights of the consumer. It has made representations to Government Departments, Ministers, and Members of Parliament whenever the need has arisen.

The function of the Co-operative M.P.s has been to bring these representations to the notice of Parliament and to take action on the floor of the House of Commons if

The Co-operative Party is not the representative body of the Co-operative movement. Its concern is with the more general political issues and with the political organization required by a political party. In many ways this organization is similar to that required by a trade union for its political purposes. Local Co-operative Parties are affiliated to Constituency Labour Parties and have the same rights in the nomination and selection of parliamentary and local government candidates as other affiliated bodies. The National Committee of the Party forms from local nominations a parliamentary panel and will, when a candidate is adopted, provide £120 a year, unless there is a full-time agent, when the sum is increased to £200 a year. The local Co-operative Party can make it up to the maximum permitted by the Labour Party. At election time the National Committee will provide two-thirds of the amount the Labour Party permits a sponsoring organization to pay.[1]

The candidate undertakes, if he is elected, to join the Parliamentary Labour Party and runs as a Co-operative and Labour candidate.[2] If returned he is primarily a Labour M.P. His main function in relation to the Co-operative movement is similar to that of a sponsored M.P. in relation to his trade union. He is a member of the Co-operative Parliamentary Group, which mainly concerns itself with matters of special co-operative and consumer interest which need to be dealt with on the parliamentary level. It is attended by all the Co-operative M.P.s and by some peers, also by the Secretary, Assistant Secretary, and Research Officer of the Co-operative Party, the Editor of *Reynolds News*, the London Representative of the *Co-operative News*, and the Secretary of the Parliamentary Committee of the Co-operative Union.[3]

The agenda of the Group provides for three types of items. These are matters raised by the Party, by M.P.s, and by the Parliamentary Committee. This Committee is a sub-committee of the Central Board of the Co-operative Union charged with the control of the Union's consultations with the government. To the Parliamentary Group it brings mainly matters arising

necessary. Whatever Government is in power, the voice of the organised consumers must be heard' (Co-operative Union, *Report of the Central Board to the 77th Congress* (1946), p. 102).

[1] *The Organisation of the Co-operative Party* (1953), pp. 44-45.

[2] Ibid.

[3] Ibid., pp. 25-26.

from an examination of bills and orders.[1] In 1947 the Joint Parliamentary Committee (as it was called before the reorganization of the Co-operative Union in 1950) urged local societies to bring their problems to it rather than to their local M.P.s, so that if necessary the Co-operative M.P.s could deal with them.[2] 'The Joint Parliamentary Committee obtains the services and influence of the Parliamentary group whenever it requires a deputation to ministers.'[3]

Besides the Parliamentary Group there is a steering committee set up to ensure prompt action. It consists of seven of the M.P.s and meets weekly.[4]

Liaison is improved by a system of interlocking membership. The Parliamentary Group sends its Chairman and two representatives to attend the National Committee of the Party and one representative to attend the Parliamentary Committee. It appoints four members to attend the Annual Congress of the Co-operative Union and six to the Party Conference. This system of interlocking membership is used throughout the organization of the Co-operative Union.[5]

The need for formal procedures to maintain contact arises from the more formal nature of the relationship between groups and sponsored M.P.s. It is a relationship which has its rules and a set pattern. Apart from this it does not differ greatly from the other relationships examined.

Part II

I

The relationship between an M.P. and a group is not always an easy one. The group cannot expect from the M.P. a wholehearted loyalty. However close an M.P.'s ties are to a group, he has also many other ties, possibly even to other groups but in particular to his party and his constituency. These ties may prevent perfect harmony since they may lead the M.P. to do something of which the group does not approve or fail to do

[1] *The Organisation of the Co-operative Party* (1953), pp. 25–26.
[2] Co-operative Union, *Report of the Central Board to the 79th Congress* (1948), p. 128.
[3] *Co-operative Party Conference*, 1947, p. 11.
[4] *The Organisation of the Co-operative Party* (1953), p. 26.
[5] Co-operative Union, *Reports of the Central Board.*

something which it desires.[1] The group may find the position hard to understand. That an M.P. should not be willing to do what the group wants him to do although he may, in some sense, be anxious to do it, is a difficult conception to appreciate. That an M.P. who has voluntarily accepted a relationship with an association should not be ready to accept the views which that association has reached is a claim to a special position which some members of the association find hard to concede. Yet it must be conceded if the relationship is to be continued, for that is the only basis upon which the relationship can exist. The group enters into a relationship with an M.P. knowing that the M.P. is sympathetic with it, but knowing too that that sympathy may be overridden by other factors.

In 1947 the Rural District Councils' Association was aggrieved at the proposal contained in the Town and Country Planning Bill that planning powers should be removed from rural district councils. Having failed to convince the Government of its point of view in consultations prior to the introduction of the Bill, the Association sought the aid of its honorary Vice-Presidents among whom were members from both sides of the House. It asked them to oppose the second reading of the Bill on the grounds that it took planning powers away from rural district councils.[2] The Labour Vice-Presidents did not carry out this request. The Conservative Vice-Presidents did vote against the second reading, but almost certainly because they were in the Opposition and not because they were Vice-Presidents of the Association. It was one of the Vice-Presidents of the Association who moved the main Opposition amendment on the second reading.[3] But the grounds he took were very much wider than those taken by the Association, and he gave comparatively little attention to its main points. He was later to move some of its amendments in the Standing Committee,[4] but by this time its point of view had been modified and these amendments merely sought that the rural district councils should be given some

[1] The solution found by Sir Joseph Lamb is not likely to be repeated. He accepted the Conservative whip on all save agricultural questions (*British Farmer*, 31 Dec. 1949, p. 10).

[2] *R.D.C.A. Circular*, Council Meeting, 23 Apr. 1947.

[3] Mr. (now Sir) Reginald Manningham-Buller, H.C. Deb. 432, col. 1129.

[4] Standing Committee Debates, Standing Committee D, 25 Feb. 1947, cols. 119–23.

opportunities by delegation of powers in the field of planning, rather than that the *status quo* should be preserved.

Yet the lack of support obtained by the Association, particularly from its Labour Vice-Presidents, did not lead to any alteration in the relationship between it and these M.P.s. The Association realized that it could not enforce conformity to its views and that the best it could hope for was that M.P.s sympathetic to its point of view would do their best for it within the limitations of their political position.

Nevertheless, such a position may lead to criticism within the body concerned. It is only too easily misunderstood. In the British Legion in 1952 there was some criticism of the attitude of the President, Sir Ian Fraser, to the Government's decision to increase the basic rate of disability pension from 45*s*. to 55*s*. a week. Since the Legion's official policy was to demand a 90*s*. pension, it was held by some members that he was wrong to have thanked the Government in the House of Commons for this increase and should rather have criticized it as totally inadequate. Sir Ian defended himself at the annual conference by explaining the nature of his position: 'If every group were to press its claims by undue pressure and if Members yielded to this there would be a breakdown of Government.' Sir Ian recalled that in the last Parliament Brigadier Antony Head, having won a place in the ballot for private members' motions, chose war pensions as his subject and asked Sir Ian to wind up the debate:

> He and Brig. Head decided at the time not to put down a motion demanding 90*s*., because the Government had a majority of six and might have been beaten in the vote.
>
> They tabled a moderate motion, a Labour member seconded it and the debate was non-party.
>
> 'It would be an excessive use of political power to try and bring down a Government on an issue affecting a minority of the citizens . . . unless on an issue affecting the constitution or a matter of conscience or protest arising from prolonged negligence by Government'.[1]

If a group ignores the limitations of politics it cannot hope to maintain a satisfactory relationship with active politicians.[2]

[1] *British Legion Journal*, July 1952, pp. 1–2. A vote of censure at the annual conference was defeated by 650 votes to 5 votes.

[2] Cf. John H. Millett, 'The Role of an Interest Group Leader in the House of

Disagreement can arise from a genuine difference of opinion between the group and the M.P. upon some political issue. If the disagreement is serious enough it is likely to lead to the termination of the relationship by one party or both. Dr. Hyacinth Morgan was a member of the Council of the British Medical Association in 1946 when it was considering the Labour Government's proposals for a national health service. Since he supported these proposals while other members of the Council opposed them, it was perhaps natural that he should leave the Council at the end of the year. Dr. Charles Hill, the Secretary of the Association, was careful to explain shortly after the publication of the Bill that Dr. Morgan 'had consistently given very wise and useful advice to the Council in the presentation of a point of view which he did not wholly share'.[1]

Mr. Charles Royle found himself in a similar situation when the Labour Party published its proposals for the nationalization of the importing and the wholesaling of meat. As Vice-President of the National Federation of Meat Traders' Associations he was placed in a very difficult position. At its annual meeting in 1949 a resolution was passed instructing the Executive to take early action to combat nationalization of the wholesale meat trade. After it had also been resolved that no money be granted from the Parliamentary and Defence Fund to any member or prospective member of the House of Commons who supported nationalization of the meat trade, Mr. Royle announced his resignation and 'said that his political party had declared itself in favour of nationalization of wholesale meat distribution and that the time had come when political issues could not be divided from the trade point of view'.[2]

2

A formal relationship contains more danger than an informal one. Any impression that the M.P. is bound to follow a group's viewpoint leads to difficulties, even though the group would be unable to enforce an agreement to that effect. Politically an M.P. can only be controlled by his party or constituents, and legally such an agreement would not be recognized by the

Commons', *Western Political Quarterly*, Dec. 1956, pp. 915–20, for a detailed discussion of Sir Ian's position.

[1] *British Medical Journal*, 30 Apr. 1946, p. 580. [2] *The Times*, 27 Sept. 1949.

courts. The group does not possess powers to bind an M.P., but it does possess means of influencing him. The fact that an M.P. receives from a group financial aid either directly or to assist in his electoral campaigns may influence an M.P. as may the presumption that the group will suspend it in the event of a disagreement between them. The power to terminate a relationship even when financial aid is involved must be allowed to a group in the same way that a member must be free to suspend such a relationship. If the group did not possess the power to terminate it, the relationship would have a peculiarly one-sided character. The fact that financial considerations are involved should not create a special relationship between M.P.s and groups. The principles upon which the termination of such relationships is judged should differ in no way from those upon which the termination of other relationships between groups and M.P.s. Freedom to enter and to terminate all relationships between M.P.s and groups is essential.

The freedom of action of the M.P. is widely recognized as important. Less often proclaimed is the case for the freedom of action of the group. The group has a place to play in society and in government. It has to consider the implications of association with M.P.s in the light of that role. It would be a severe handicap if it could not terminate a harmful association. This obvious conclusion would not need stating were it not possible to look at this situation from a different angle. The desire of a group to withdraw support from an M.P. can be regarded as an attempt to make him change his view which, when financial and other considerations are added, can be construed as 'improper pressure'. This is to ignore the nature of the relationship into which the M.P. has entered. Its justification is the sympathy existing between him and a group. He must recognize that the group cannot perpetuate that relationship when it no longer feels that sympathy.

3

This is the background against which the W. J. Brown case should be approached. This case, considered by the Committee of Privileges of the House of Commons, had a curtain-raiser in 1944. Mr. W. A. Robinson, the Labour M.P. for St. Helens, was until 1942 Political General Secretary of the National

Union of Distributive and Allied Workers and a member of the parliamentary panel of that Union (which meant that he was sponsored by the Union). Having reached retiring age he vacated the position and came off the panel, but the Union continued to give him £200 a year as a retaining allowance along with postal and secretarial assistance. However, in 1944, as a result of a deputation from the local Labour Party Executive, the Union called for Mr. Robinson's resignation from Parliament. The grounds for this request were alleged neglect of constituency matters and dissatisfaction with his conduct as an individual. Upon his refusing to resign the Union discontinued the allowance and the assistance. The matter was raised in the House and referred to the Committee of Privileges. They decided that:

> While the payment to, or receipt by, a Member of money or the offer or acceptance of other advantage for promoting or opposing a particular proceeding or measure, constitutes an undoubted breach of privilege, it has long been recognised that there are Members who receive financial assistance from associations of their constituents or from other bodies. A body which provides such assistance must normally be free and entitled to withdraw it. A statement that such support would be withdrawn unless certain action was taken in relation to the business of the House might come within the principles laid down in the precedents as a breach of privilege.[1]

Since the grounds for the action in this case were constituency matters and personal questions it was decided it was not necessary to take any decision on this wider problem.

In 1942 Mr. W. J. Brown, the General Secretary of the Civil Service Clerical Association, was elected as Independent M.P. for Rugby. His candidacy was not directly sponsored by that body, indeed, under the Trade Disputes and Trade Unions Act (1927)[2] it would have been illegal for it to do so, but in September 1943 the Association drew up an agreement to cover Mr. Brown's position. He was relieved of his post as General Secretary for such time as he should continue as an M.P. and given instead the new position of Parliamentary General Secretary. In

[1] H.C. 85 of 1943–4, p. 5.

[2] This Act, which was repealed in 1946, laid down that civil service unions must not include among their objects political objects 'and must not be associated with any political party or organisation'.

this new position he was to receive substantially the same remuneration as before, whilst retaining his pension rights and various office services.[1]

It is very difficult to say what were the duties and responsibilities attached to this new post. It was designed to retain the general services and advice of Mr. Brown. He had been the main influence in building up the strength of the Association and, despite some stormy periods in the 30's, still retained the confidence of the members. To many he was the Civil Service Clerical Association.

In view of this, it is perhaps surprising that it was thought necessary to have a formal agreement specifying his duties. The Agreement, however, appears to have been made in the interests of Mr. Brown himself in order to clarify and secure his position. Its contradictions and ambiguities arise from the fact that it had this negative and not a positive purpose. Clause 6 of the Agreement specified that he shall 'only represent' the Association on civil service matters whilst being entitled to engage in his political activities with complete freedom. Since this clause existed to protect Mr. Brown it is clearly of more value in interpreting the relationship on political matters than on civil service matters.

The real duties of Mr. Brown are laid down in another clause. He 'shall deal with all questions arising in the work of the Association which requires Parliamentary or political action and shall advise the Association from time to time on such matters'. He 'shall further confer and consult with the Association on all problems requiring his assistance and advice thereon if and when so required by the Association'. These clauses use neutral words avoiding any suggestion that Mr. Brown was bound to represent the views of the Association. They seem to express the purpose behind the agreement.[2]

The President and Vice-Presidents of the Association appearing before the Committee of Privileges did not accept this view and held that Mr. Brown was bound to represent the Association's view on civil service matters.[3] Mr. Brown himself appeared confused on the issue:

[1] H.C. 118 of 1946–7, pp. iii–iv.

[2] See Appendix C for the text of the Agreement.

[3] Q. 378. 'Was Mr. Brown bound to carry out the wishes of the Civil Service

Mr. Attorney-General: 199. If the Association had said: 'The line that you have taken in the Debate on Equal Pay for Civil Servants' or 'In regard to the question of the right of Civil Servants' organisations to affiliate to the T.U.C. is not the line which the Association takes; will you therefore agree to terminate the agreement between us' you would have said, would you not: 'That is a breach of Parliamentary Privilege'?—With respect, that is the third time that you have put that to me.

Mr. Churchill: 200. I should like an answer. I think you ought to give an answer to that. It is on the Civil Service side of it. It is nothing to do with general affairs?—The answer is that that is a hypothetical situation which did not in fact arise and to which I have given no consideration.[1]

His hesitancy seems genuine and was probably due to the fact he had never considered the formalities of the Agreement[2] and had difficulty in doing so now. The question of duties did not arise:

. . . I am denying that I was a mandated delegate, and I am saying that I only represented the interests of the Association in the same way as any miners' Member of Parliament, any railwaymen's Member of Parliament . . . or any one of a dozen types of Labour Members of Parliament in this House would have tried to do his best for the people he knew best . . . if I were asked to take action, as I not infrequently was, which I thought was not the right action, I would say; 'No that cannot be done' or 'It cannot be done in that way'.[3]

However, the Committee continued to press the question of disagreement on civil service matters:

I have said over and over again to my Association over the last 30 years 'If ever the time comes when I no longer reflect your views on Civil Service affairs I do not want to remain your leader against your will' and if the hypothetical event had eventuated, I think it might very probably have been resolved not by action on the Association's part, but by action on mine.[4]

The relationship was, according to Mr. Brown, informal. It

Association in Civil Service matters?—That was our understanding and expectation of the arrangements between us.'

[1] H.C. 118 of 1946–7, qs. 199 and 200.

[2] 'I have said that the whole atmosphere in which these documents were worked out was not an atmosphere in which people anticipated difficulties. . . .' (From Mr. Brown's answer to q. 201).

[3] From Mr. Brown's answer to q. 130.

[4] From Mr. Brown's answer to q. 203.

arose from the close association of Mr. Brown with the Association and expressed his concern and sympathy with it and its affairs. It is upon some such basis as this that all relationships between groups and members must rest, if friction is to be avoided. An attempt to read more than this into the Agreement can only gain justification from its ambiguities and not from any clear expression within it.

One of the difficulties of the Agreement was that it did not provide the Association with any clear means of terminating the relationship in normal circumstances, although it gave to Mr. Brown the right to terminate the Agreement upon six months notice. This was unfortunate in that it gave to the Agreement an appearance of inviolability which was likely to lead to friction, since it restricted the Association's freedom of action. This may have been one of the factors leading the President and Vice-President of the Association to their interpretation of the Agreement. Very naturally they may have assumed that an Agreement in which the Association had so tied itself, at least gave it some definite powers. In fact this provision dates from the previous agreements governing Mr. Brown's tenure of office as General Secretary. He assumed that position at some personal risk, sacrificing his civil service position, and this was one of the measures adopted to give him some degree of security.

Mr. Brown's views upon matters, which were of parliamentary and political interest to the Association, did not always accord with its views. It is true that the Agreement professed to exclude political issues from the relationship, but whatever that was supposed to mean in theory it meant little in practice.

Various problems arose from the very nature of Mr. Brown's political views that clearly concerned the Association. His advocacy of a Liberal candidate to civil servants at Llandudno caused a certain discontent, but led to no trouble since it was clearly one of those matters excluded from the concern of the Association. But issues like the closed shop and the right of civil service unions to affiliate to political parties were not clearly excluded or included by the Agreement. However, if they had been definitely civil service matters, the Agreement made no provision for dealing with any disagreement upon them and it is doubtful if the situation would have been any clearer.

The Executive Committee of the Association felt that Mr. Brown, by publicly expressing views which were contrary to those of the Association, while he remained a paid official of it, was placing the Association in a peculiarly difficult position. They were inclined to attribute, rather improbably, the defeat of Mr. L. C. White, the General Secretary, in his candidacy for the General Council of the T.U.C. to the difficulties brought about by Mr. Brown's views. A statement which was issued to make clear that his views were his own personal ones did not end the embarrassment felt by the Executive Committee and it determined to propose the termination of the Agreement at the national conference of the Association.[1]

Mr. Brown contended that the expression by the Association of its discontent with his views, coupled with the attempt to terminate the agreement in view of the fact that he had not modified those views, represented improper pressure upon him as an M.P. and constituted a breach of privilege of the House of Commons.[2] The fact that the arrangements upon which the Executive Committee intended to propose the termination of the Agreement involved no financial loss to Mr. Brown should be discounted, since he placed great importance on the personal loss that he would experience through the ending of his relations with the Association. Likewise the question of the Association's power to terminate the Agreement did not arise since it was a matter for the courts, not Parliament.

In asking Parliament's protection, Mr. Brown could not hope that it could restore the relationship which had once existed between him and the Association. The relationship had broken down and could not be restored by any parliamentary action. The conditions of agreement and sympathy upon which such relationships must rest had been destroyed. It is this that makes the case so unreal.

There is, however, much in the case that Mr. Brown stated that appears convincing when looked at from a particular angle. The Association would have preferred Mr. Brown to have altered his views and to that extent can be said to have brought pressure to bear upon him. It informed him that if he continued to act in the same way, it would seek to terminate the Agreement

[1] H.C. 118 of 1946–7, pp. v–ix.
[2] Ibid., p. 78.

and this could be said to constitute a threat. But the Association's case was clear. It was Mr. Brown's views that rendered the satisfactory working of the Agreement impossible. In recognizing this, the Association was not trying to force him to change his views but was trying to end a difficult situation.

Associations such as the C.S.C.A. have a proper and legal purpose to fulfil in society. It would be unfortunate if the privileges of Parliament were to accord to an M.P. a special position in outside groups that hindered them fulfilling their proper purpose. Such groups should conduct their relations with M.P.s in the same way as with other persons associated with the group. They must be free to sever or to create relationships on the same principles as they are free to sever or to create other relationships. If an M.P.'s activities are embarrassing an association, then it must have the right to ask him to leave the association unless he stops them. This is a principle that can be extended beyond the type of case here considered. The M.P. is bound to have connexions with many organizations outside Parliament. He may be a member of several clubs, of a union, of a church; he may have a job in a firm or be a director of several companies. He cannot live outside society. His position in those bodies gives them certain opportunities to influence him. The ending of his relationship with them may harm him. Yet that should be no reason for saying that it would be improper for them to end it. A firm can properly sack an M.P. for inefficiency. In the nineteenth century an M.P. was expelled from the Reform Club because of his political views, a matter upon which Parliament decided to take no action.[1] If that club refuse to retain in membership all people who held those views then it should not have to retain one member just because he is an M.P. In the same way, though it may be considered morally wrong for a firm to sack all employees who advocate the nationalization of that firm, it does not seem right that parliamentary privilege should protect the one employee who happens to be an M.P. If such action could be prevented by trade union or legal action then it should be employed, but it would not seem wise to use parliamentary privilege to create a special position for one employee of that firm. By living in the various organizations of society, the M.P. accepts their terms.

[1] *Commons Journal*, 1876, 252, quoted H.C. 118 of 1946–7, p. 2.

It may sometimes be difficult for an outside organization to treat an M.P. as it does other members or employees. His actions as an M.P. may create problems that do not arise with other people. An organization may be well advised to tolerate the M.P.'s actions, but there are bound to be situations where it cannot. In these situations the organization does not act improperly provided the principles upon which it acts do not differ radically from those it would use in dealing with other members or employees.

If these conclusions seem to leave little place for the M.P. to receive parliamentary protection in his relations with outside bodies, it is because I consider that parliamentary privilege should not be a means of taking an M.P. out of the pressures and problems of normal life, however harsh they may at times be.

Parliamentary privilege is complex and it would be difficult to say that it had reached any satisfactory definition on these points. Certain it is that it has not reached the position outlined above. It has been decided that it is a breach of privilege to bring improper influence to bear upon an M.P. Improper influence is clearly involved in an attempt to bribe an M.P. More complex is the attitude of Parliament towards attempts to influence an M.P.'s actions by threats. It will be necessary to examine this subject more closely in the next chapter. Here it is only necessary to point out that in the W. J. Brown case the existence of a threat depends on the way in which one looks at the position. If one regards the severance of relations as the necessary consequence of Mr. Brown's actions, it is difficult to see how a threat can be involved in the recognition of this fact by the Executive Committee of the Association.

At least one M.P. placed in a similar position to Mr. Brown has recognized that the ending of his relationship with a group was a matter to be settled between himself and the group. In 1931 the National Union of Railwaymen terminated its relations with Mr. J. H. Thomas, its Political General Secretary, as a consequence of his joining the National Government.[1] Looked at from one angle it could be regarded as an attempt to bring improper influence to bear upon him, particularly as it represented a financial loss for him. But Mr. J. H. Thomas did not attempt

[1] *The Times*, 1 Sept. 1931.

to challenge the decision on the grounds of parliamentary privilege. He appealed to the Union's annual conference,[1] as he was fully entitled to do, and he accepted its rejection of that appeal as final. He recognized that his actions had made the continuance of his old relationship with the Union impossible, and he did not challenge its right to terminate it.

If the organization's aim is to force the M.P. to change his views or in some way to control him, then the question of improper pressure does arise. The organization is seeking to take advantage of the position of the M.P. But this was not what was happening in the W. J. Brown case. The Association was trying to end a relationship that had become embarrassing.

The Committee of Privileges moved cautiously in its report. It said that some forms of pressure on an M.P. were proper, such as 'a Resolution passed by some national organisation'. But it said that 'it might be a breach of privilege for an outside body to use the fact that a Member had entered into an agreement with it or was receiving payments from it as a means of exerting pressure upon that Member to follow a particular course of conduct in his capacity as a Member' and that 'It would also be clearly improper to attempt to punish a Member pecuniarily because of his actions as a Member'.[2]

These statements raise the difficulties already discussed. When is pressure exerted to compel a member to follow a certain course? When is an M.P. punished by pecuniary loss? The answer to both these questions lies in the intention.

The Committee is on sound ground when it declares that it regards it 'as an inevitable corollary that if an outside body may properly enter into contractual relationships with and make payments to a Member as such, it must in general be entitled to terminate that relationship if it lawfully can where it considers it necessary for the protection of its own interests so to do'.[3] This is the ground upon which it based the rejection of Mr. Brown's case, for it concludes: 'It must be assumed in the Member's favour that having voluntarily entered the relationship he has put himself beyond the reach of any improper

[1] *The Times*, 30 Oct. 1931 and 31 Oct. 1931.
[2] H.C. 118 of 1946–7, p. xiii.
[3] Ibid., pp. xii–xiii.

influence to which either its continuance or its threatened termination might give rise.'[1]

4

To the Government the main issue that arose was whether outside bodies were trying to control members within the House by means of various agreements. The W. J. Brown case had revealed some of the dangers that could arise out of such agreements. The Committee in its report had drawn attention to this problem:

> The relationship between a Member and an outside body with which he is in contractual relationship and from which he receives financial payments is, however, one of great difficulty and delicacy in which there must often be a danger that the rules of privilege may be infringed. Thus it would certainly be improper for a Member to enter into any arrangement fettering his complete independence as a Member of Parliament by undertaking to press some particular point of view on behalf of an outside interest, whether for reward or not.[2]

This provided the basis for a motion moved by Mr. Arthur Greenwood in the House of Commons on 15 July 1947:

> That this House agrees with the Report of the Committee of Privileges, and in particular declares that it is inconsistent with the dignity of the House, with the duty of a Member to his constituents, and with the maintenance of the privilege of freedom of speech, for any Member of the House to enter into any contractual agreement with an outside body, controlling or limiting the Member's complete independence and freedom of action in Parliament or stipulating that he shall act in any way as the representative of such outside body in regard to any matters to be transacted in Parliament; the duty of a Member being to his constituents and to the country as a whole, rather than to any particular section thereof.[3]

The principle of this motion aroused little dissent. There was a division, but that was upon the question of agreement with the report of the Committee of Privileges. Those who disagreed with the report held that to support it and the principle laid down in the motion was inconsistent and would destroy the value of asserting the principle. To most M.P.s the main issue

[1] Ibid., p. xiii.
[2] Ibid., p. xii.
[3] H.C. Deb. 440, cols. 284–5.

seemed clear-cut. Mr. Greenwood in moving the motion merely said: 'It would be undermining the dignity, the stature, and the power of this House if the general public were to come to believe that there were any questionable relationships—I am not using that phrase in this particular case—between outside bodies and Members of this House.'[1] But the main problem was what in fact was questionable. It must be confessed that the House was not at its best in dealing with this problem. Some interesting points were made by Mr. L. J. Callaghan. He argued that most M.P.s had a profession or occupation which was bound to influence them in their conduct, irrespective of any financial considerations. Memories of their past and fears for their future would have an influence upon their conduct. This was inevitable and it would be unreal to ignore it, but it was not the same thing as an actual agreement to represent an interest or organization in the House. Money grants made by unions were proper, although less necessary to the Labour movement than they once had been.[2]

Mr. W. T. Proctor was at pains to point out that it was right and proper for trade unions to sponsor M.P.s:

> If we interfere with it, we interfere with the whole political organisation of the country, and I cannot see how we can differentiate between a political party and anything which operates in a Division on one side or the other, if we limit the rights of organisations to conduct political agitation and pay for it in the manner in which that has been done up to the present time. The only way in which a person without private wealth can come to the House is by being sponsored by an organisation and as a representative of his fellow workers in that organisation. It is important that that right should be preserved,[3]

but he emphasized that

> it is the duty of any Member of Parliament not to pledge himself to act here as a delegate who is instructed on any matter by an outside organisation.[4]

He knew no trade union which claimed the right to mandate the M.P.s it sponsored, and the National Union of Railwaymen, which was his own, certainly did not do so.

[1] H.C. Deb. 440, col. 290.
[2] Ibid., cols. 325–32.
[3] Ibid., col. 336.
[4] Ibid., col. 337.

These two contributions showed some signs of realism, but for the most part members were content with statements like that of Mr. Herbert Morrison: 'the first duty of Members of this House is to their constituents and the nation, and it is wrong that they should be fettered in their judgement by any outside interest.'[1]

While no clear political philosophy was brought forward to justify this statement, it takes its stand in the tradition of Coke, Blackstone, and Burke, with the one modification that whereas they were concerned to protect the member from his constituents in the interest of his duty to the nation, today the constituency has joined the nation as a suitable recipient of the member's loyalty.

It is not certain that this tradition has any meaning in Britain today. It does not fit the political realities. The M.P. is seen as a judge sitting impartially upon the issues before him. He must have no bonds or ties to influence him. These doctrines find their echo in the phrase used in the motion: 'complete independence and freedom of action'.

Mr. Henry Strauss took his stand avowedly upon Coke, Blackstone, and Burke, claiming that an M.P. cannot be bound to any section but must represent the nation. From this principle Mr. Strauss derived his support of the motion.[2] In doing so he quoted the judgement of Lord Justice Fletcher Moulton (later Lord Moulton) in the Osborne case of 1909: '. . . the position of a representative is that of a man who has accepted a trust towards the public, and that any contract, whether for valuable consideration or otherwise, which binds him to exercise that trust in any other way than as on each occasion he conscientiously feels to be best in the public interest is illegal and void. . . .'[3] 'And it is no answer to say that before or at the election he openly avowed his intention to be thus contractually fettered.'[4]

It is a pity that this speech did not make the House consider more carefully the implications of the motion. It was clearly not the intention of the House in passing this resolution to do anything particularly startling or unusual. It was intended to fit the realities of politics and above all to do nothing to hinder the

[1] Ibid., col. 361.
[2] Ibid., cols. 312–25.
[3] Ibid., col. 316 (see T.L.R. 1908–9, p. 113).
[4] Ibid., col. 317.

practice of sponsoring M.P.s for Parliament. Yet the phraseology that is found in this motion and arguments used in the speeches of many of its supporters were precisely those developed by Mr. Henry Strauss. They were closely related to the arguments used by Lord Shaw (later Lord Craigmyle), also in the Osborne case. By these arguments Lord Shaw was able to condemn, not merely the practice of sponsoring M.P.s, but also the standing orders of the Labour Party.[1]

Today every Labour Party candidate for Parliament has to sign a declaration that he accepts the constitution, programme, principles, and policy of the Party and that he will accept and act in harmony with the standing orders of the Parliamentary Labour Party. This is surely to enter into a contractual agreement with an outside body limiting a member's complete freedom of action in the House of Commons. And if, as Mr. Morrison tells us, the standard by which he is to govern himself is to be his duty to his nation and to his constituents, it is difficult to see where the party comes in and above all how the conduct of the Labour Party can be justified. By his own standards (and they appear to be Mr. Morrison's), Lord Shaw was right.

The motion was based upon an unreal position. No useful meaning can be attached to the phrase 'complete independence and freedom of action'. It suggests an M.P. acting in judicial impartiality, whereas, of course, he is subject to a vast variety of influences, prejudices, and pressures. The M.P. cannot contract out of society; he cannot be completely independent. He is influenced by his past and by his present, by his job and by his family, by his club and by his union. So it must be. The phrase 'complete independence and freedom of action' was a very unhappy one.

So, indeed, was the motion. It has had no practical importance, since the literal interpretation of its terms has seemed so dangerous that it has been assumed that they cannot mean what they say. Thus Mr. Morrison implied that under it the Agreement between Mr. Brown and the Civil Service Clerical Association would be dubious,[2] but the National Executive Committee of the Association, after taking legal advice and consulting with

[1] Law Reports, H.L. (E), 1909, pp. 111–15.
[2] H.C. Deb. 440, col. 355.

the Speaker, declared themselves satisfied that Mr. Brown could be recalled to duty (he had been placed on leave while the situation was investigated) until his position was decided.[1]

It is hard to see any necessity for the intervention of Parliament in the question. The building of healthy relationships between groups and M.P.s is not likely to be helped by the creation of formal rules. All that it is necessary to ensure is that an M.P. is perfectly free to terminate when he wishes any relationship into which he has entered. It seems to be of little importance whether the terms of such an agreement stipulate that during its existence the M.P. will represent the association provided he is free to end the relationship.

It is obviously expected that a sponsored M.P. will be available to support amendments promoted by a group just as it is expected that the elected member of a group's executive will support its views in the House. In all these relationships what matters is that they can be easily ended, a condition which induces informality and tolerance. This was the mistake of Mr. Brown—that he sought to perpetuate a relationship, the basis of which had gone.[2]

5

One danger is the possibility of secret relationships. It is desirable that it should be known that an M.P. is connected with the group on whose behalf he speaks. In the House of Commons it is customary for a member to declare an interest in any matter in which he is personally concerned and many members acknowledge their relations with various groups in such a way.[3] Thus Mr. Chuter Ede, speaking on the Luton Corporation Bill in 1954, said: 'I shall not conceal from the House the fact that

[1] *C.S.C.A. Annual Report*, 1947, p. 120. In the end Mr. Brown retired rather than involve the Association in further controversy.

[2] In fairness to Mr. Brown it should be stated that he regarded the Executive as unrepresentative of the membership whose confidence in him, he believed, still continued.

[3] This is not laid down in Standing Orders nor does *Erskine May* give any guidance on the question. In 1956 the Clerk of the House described the position to the Select Committee on the House of Commons Disqualification Bill in these words. 'By custom—and I am deliberately using that word because I think there is no rule of the House, but it is a custom of the House—Members who are pecuniarily or personally interested in a matter on which they are going to make a speech, should declare their personal interest' (H.C. 349 of 1955–6, p. 100).

although I speak for myself in this matter . . . I am President of the County Councils' Association. . . .'[1] Speaking on the National Health Service (Amendment) Bill in 1949, Mr. Hugh Linstead said: 'The last point to which I wish to draw attention concerns the pharmaceutical service and here I must disclose an interest in that I am the Secretary of the Pharmaceutical Society.'[2]

Such declarations are not overcommon.[3] The more frequent form in which an M.P. makes references to outside bodies is not so much a declaration of interest but a statement that he is speaking officially for some group. Sir Thomas Moore on the Dogs (Protection of Livestock) Bill said in 1953: 'The R.S.P.C.A. for whom I have the authority to speak, are warmly in support of the principle of the Bill.'[4] Mr. Cove, speaking in 1949 on the question of the London area allowance for teachers, said: 'I hope to put clearly and definitely the views of the N.U.T., the main body represented on the Burnham Committee.'[5] Sometimes the reference is oblique. The M.P. indicates his connexion with the group by showing intimate knowledge of its affairs or by use of the word 'our'. On the Children and Young Persons (Amendment) Bill in 1952 Mr. (now Sir) Peter Roberts said; 'Our experience in the N.S.P.C.C. is that we must always try to help and encourage by example in order to see that these things do not happen in the home',[6] or, and on the same Bill, Mr. Charles Royle said: 'The matter has been discussed by the Council of the Magistrates' Association, who are interested in the subject.'[7]

Often enough no such preface to an M.P.'s remarks is considered necessary. In the second reading debate on the Mines and Quarries Bill in 1954 none of the N.U.M.-sponsored M.P.s felt it necessary to declare an interest. The reason is obvious. It was already so well known. In 1955 Mr. Reader Harris, when challenged with not declaring his interest in the question of tyre distribution, said: 'I have declared my interest in this

[1] H.C. Deb. 525, col. 705. [2] Ibid. 465, col. 1127.

[3] One reason may be that interest is normally interpreted as direct pecuniary interest. It certainly is for the only question upon which principles have been formulated—divisions; cf. *Erskine May* (15th ed.), pp. 418–19.

[4] H.C. Deb. 512, col. 1767.

[5] Ibid. 464, col. 586.

[6] Standing Committee Debates, Committee B, 1 May 1952, col. 1278.

[7] Ibid., cols. 1258–9.

matter so many times that it should not be necessary for me to do so again.'[1] It would be cumbersome to try and insist upon M.P.s declaring their interest on every possible occasion. Besides, in the case of M.P.s sponsored by the unions affiliated to the Labour Party, the information is readily available to anyone sufficiently interested. If these are the grounds upon which interest is not declared they seem legitimate enough. So long as the information is available, a declaration of interest is not important.

6

Any examination of these relationships must conclude with a recognition of their value. The M.P. must, if he is to play any part at all in the affairs of his country, take cognisance of the existence of important groups which represent large sections of opinion. It may be argued that such representation is imperfect and that an M.P. has in his own constituency opportunities for sounding public opinion. Yet even in his constituency, this opinion will often enough be group opinion. The M.P. will find himself dealing with the affairs of the local branch of the British Legion or the opinions of a member of a trade association. These opinions may not exactly reflect those of the group's national headquarters but neither will they depart very drastically from them. To claim that pressure groups cannot represent public opinion in a way that will help an M.P. is to ignore the fact that what is meant by public opinion is often enough group opinion. Both at the national and at the local level the M.P. can learn from the group.

The M.P. can learn more than opinions. The group is a veritable store of information. It is information ordered and arranged to a purpose. It is information which the M.P. may not be able to obtain elsewhere.

Groups are important in our political system. They exert continuous influence. They are called into consultation by the government. They have access to departments and even to ministers. In many cases they help to formulate government policy.

It is for these reasons that groups are of importance and concern to M.P.s, but the duty of the M.P. goes beyond mere interest.

[1] H.C. Deb. 536, col. 407.

He should assist groups. Parliament, if it is to provide any means of control over the government, must give to the groups an opportunity to express their grievances. For the groups reflect the discontent in their fields of concern. If Parliament were not available to give that discontent expression, a valuable check on the government would be lost. The government is anxious for consultation, but its anxiety is made stronger by the possibility of the groups' appeal to Parliament. Of course, for the most part the group representative in Parliament is not needed to express serious discontent, but merely to bring matters before the House as an aid to consultation. This simple process may be a factor in preventing the growth of discontent.

The views of any particular group will not appeal to one M.P. as readily as to another. It may be that a group will not be able to find anybody to express its views, but this is unlikely unless they run contrary to party principles. If party principles permit an M.P. to support a group, then it is almost certain that an M.P. can be found to represent it.

If it is right for an M.P. to attend to a group's views, then it is right for an M.P. to enter into a more permanent relationship with a group. An M.P. in sympathy with a group and interested in its particular sphere of politics will naturally concern himself with its point of view and seek to express it in the House. By doing so he adds to the knowledge and range of the House. The group, too, gains by these arrangements. They result in the group being helped not merely at crisis point, but even before a crisis develops. If views are to be expressed in the House the group will prefer to have them expressed from experience. So both the House and the groups gain by these relationships. With the growth of sectional politics the group representative has become of great importance to Parliament, although with the growth of consultation he is of less importance to the group.

CHAPTER IX

Lobbying

I

THE need to approach the general body of M.P.s does not normally arise in the routine activities of the group, unless that group is of the type considered in Chapter VII. For the others the need arises only in the campaign. Certain groups, however, maintain a machinery of contact both as a preparation for future campaigns and as a public relations measure.

These are groups which have been forced to campaign in the past, and expect to have to campaign in the future. The National Union of Teachers is an example. Its organization provides for a system of parliamentary correspondents. The function of the parliamentary correspondent is to maintain contact between the local branches and their M.P.s. The theory is that by these means a relationship will be built up which will prove useful at times of crisis. The parliamentary correspondent is an official of the branch elected in the same way as the other officials—treasurer, secretary, &c. Since the branches do not embrace the same areas as the constituencies, one branch may have two parliamentary correspondents, or two branches may have two parliamentary correspondents in the same constituency. Often these posts are combined with other posts, such as press secretary, and even secretary or treasurer in some of the smaller branches. A few branches have not appointed parliamentary correspondents, generally where other branches have already appointed one in the constituency. In Oxfordshire the position in 1947 is shown in the table on p. 206. In Manchester there is only one branch, and it had 2,762 members in 1947. The branch had nineteen parliamentary correspondents, only two of whom were holders of other posts.[1]

This elaborate system does not seem to be worth the trouble taken, since it is difficult for contact to be made between the

[1] *N.U.T. Annual Report*, 1947.

Branch	Membership	Parliamentary correspondent (constituency)	Other posts held
Banbury	104	Banbury	Press secretary
Bicester	51	None	..
Chipping Norton and Charlbury	97	Banbury	None
Oxford City	365	Oxford	Press secretary and Minute secretary
Oxford District	106	None	..
Oxfordshire South . . .	117	Henley	Treasurer, Press secretary, &c.
Witney and Burford . . .	77	Banbury	None

correspondent and the M.P. except upon specific issues, which were the matters with which it was hoped continuous contact would help. It is probable that the M.P. prefers to deal with the official responsible for general branch affairs rather than an official specially appointed to contact him.

The National Farmers' Union has used a system of parliamentary committees which are organized at county level and have to maintain contact with more than one M.P.[1] Contact will be maintained in an informal way by invitations to dinners as well as by formal contact on definite issues.

A number of organizations make a practice of inviting local M.P.s to become honorary vice-presidents of their branches—the British Legion and B.L.E.S.M.A. are examples. These bodies are anxious to maintain favourable parliamentary opinion. They often need to enforce their demands by campaigns. They represent interests which are regarded as national in character, and have little difficulty in persuading M.P.s to hold these positions.

Most organizations, however, have no special machinery prepared for the necessities of the campaign. Bodies like the R.S.P.C.A. and the Lord's Day Observance Society have lists of supporters whose aid can be obtained for campaigns, but they merely take the place of members and branches in other organizations. In most cases, the group merely adapts its routine organization.

[1] e.g. see *N.F.U. Yearbook*, 1944, p. 51, for complaints that not enough branches have set them up, and ibid., 1946, pp. 84–85, for moves to organize them.

2

Lobbying[1] is the main weapon of the group in bringing pressure to bear upon the main body of M.P.s. The most sensational form is the mass lobby. The object of this method is to persuade the M.P. of the degree of feeling in his constituency on an issue and incidentally to put some arguments to him.

It is arguable whether in some cases it is used not so much to indicate opinion as to simulate it. Since lobbying can be the outward sign of deep feeling on an issue, there is a danger that a well-organized group may be tempted to achieve by technique what other groups achieve through a deep discontent amongst their members.

British politics have not advanced to the general use of the telegram as a weapon of the lobbyist. It is true that the National Chamber of Trade encouraged local chambers to send telegrams to their M.P.s before the debate on the second reading of the Rating and Valuation (Miscellaneous Provisions) Bill in 1955[2] and that in 1946 Mr. G. R. Strauss quoted in the House of Commons an instruction which he said had been sent out by the Road Haulage Association before the second reading of the Labour Government's Transport Bill, which read: 'On the morning of 17th December, without fail, send a telegram to your Member as follows, Conservative, Liberal or Socialist, condemning the Bill. . . . You should remember that all Conservative M.P.s are on our side and word your telegram therefore more politely to them than to the supporters of the Government.'[3] But the technique is too expensive for many groups to follow these examples.

Personal lobbying is a method more commonly used, with some effect in annoying M.P.s if not in convincing them. There are two tactics—the mass assault and the steady trickle. It is a little difficult to say which is the more infuriating. The mass assault generally takes place after a meeting held at the Central Hall, Westminster, which is conveniently situated within five minutes' walk of the House of Commons. Since this hall can

[1] 'Lobbying' as it is used in this chapter may have a wider sense than some political scientists are used to. It is used here to describe any approaches made to M.P.s on a large scale by outside organizations. It is not restricted to activities within the precincts of Parliament.

[2] H.C. Deb. 539, col. 1247.

[3] Ibid., 431, cols. 1973–4.

hold over three thousand people it can easily be seen what disruption can be caused when they flood the Central Lobby of the House of Commons and demand to see their M.P.s. The National Federation of Old Age Pensions Associations is one of the bodies which habitually hold meetings in the Central Hall, having held its annual rally there ever since 1947 when they 'outgrew the Caxton Hall', which is also very convenient for Parliament.[1] Although the most regular, it is not the only group to resort to this type of lobbying. It is a frustrating method, since the police have to control the crowd and to limit the number of admissions.[2] The fervour roused in the meeting is damped a little unkindly.

If the mass assault is the expression of disorganized passion, the steady trickle is presumably the expression of a purpose, iron but calm. One example will suffice:

> The Board of Trade was I believe, the first Department to set up its own Equal Pay Committee, a sub-committee of the Staff Side itself. . . . The allocation to Departments of different evenings in which to lobby M.P.s on Douglas Houghton's motion needs good machinery if the evening is to be a success. Active Members in Trade are not convinced that their machinery is infallible, but the faults made clear by our experience of lobbying in November are being rectified. . . . Each building has a central agent whose duty on lobbying is to contact all organisations in the building and ensure that every person, whatever his or her grade, is fully aware of the event and what to do. Central agents and other Committee members then arrange small groups of people to include someone who knows the procedure of lobbying and sallies forth. Accidents do occur. . . .[3]

One of the difficulties inherent in this method is members whose constituencies are far from London. It is possible for deputations to be arranged from the constituencies as was done by the Cinematograph Exhibitors' Association in the course of its campaign against the entertainments tax. Alternatively, arrangements may be made to lobby M.P.s in their constituencies. The Equal Pay Co-ordinating Committee set up local committees which did some work in lobbying in the constituencies. The Equal

[1] E. Melling, *Pensioners' Progress* (undated), pp. 13–14.

[2] e.g. see *C.S.C.A. Annual Report*, 1951, p. 73. There was lobbying for equal pay after a mass meeting, as a result of which the police restricted admission to the Central Lobby.

[3] *Red Tape*, February 1952, p. 139.

Pay Campaign Committee endeavoured to get its supporters to attend M.P.s' surgeries or ask questions at their meetings, but with little success.[1]

Forced personal interviews, which this form of lobbying amounts to, whether carried out *en masse* or not, are not a very useful form of pressure, and it is doubtful whether the return it brings is worth all this organization. There is an irritant in the method whatever form it takes, and some lobbyists are not very effective in putting a case into words when they are face to face with an M.P.

The most satisfactory form of personal lobbying is the approach by branch officials to their M.P.s for an arranged meeting. It ensures a degree of preparation and knowledge on both sides. This was the method used by the British Legion for the Day of Demand.

3

The letter is the basic form of lobbying in this country and yet even it has snags. A large number of bodies attempt to use it. 'Write to your M.P.' is a plausible slogan, but it is surprisingly little acted upon. On many issues the M.P. will receive no more than one or two letters. The Sunday Freedom Association on the occasion of the second reading of Mr. Parker's Bill in 1953 attempted to challenge the Lord's Day Observance Society on its own ground and had printed a large number of postcards with appropriate slogans, which it distributed through member organizations. It was hoped that they would be signed and sent to M.P.s. But no M.P. reported having received more than one or two. In the same way in 1950 the National Association of Schoolmasters asked its members to write to their M.P.s to protest against the character of the recent salary increases and to ask for representation for the Association on the Burnham Committee. Again, a few letters were probably all that most M.P.s got. On many controversial issues the correspondence is surprisingly little. On the cuts in education proposed in 1952 one Conservative M.P. received only four private letters of protest. All this means that it does not need many letters to make an impression on an M.P., because the standard by which they are judged is low. It is a great achievement for any

[1] Allen Potter, 'The Equal Pay Campaign Committee', *Political Studies*, Feb. 1957, p. 56.

group to get as many as fifty letters written to an M.P. by his constituents. In one constituency between 1950 and 1954 there were only two issues upon which so many letters were written. Though fifty letters may not seem very many, it may appear a lot in the individual M.P.'s mailbag. Although the number is not sufficient to overcome the doubts of a member suspicious of the spontaneity of the letters, it is more than sufficient to impress those members who regard their letters as a guide to public opinion.

The two issues which succeeded in arousing this number of letters were Sunday observance and equal pay. The equal pay letters bore the signs of obvious organization, and for that reason bad organization. Great use was made of postcards by the equal pay campaigners. In 1952 one was distributed which read: 'I am only one of many of your constituents who want Equal Pay passed by THIS Parliament. Please be present at the debate in the House of Commons on Friday 16th May. Give satisfaction to a lot of us by voting FOR Mr. Pannell's motion.' This letter, distributed through sponsoring organizations, was then signed and sent off to the signatory's M.P. Amongst those who complained about receiving these postcards were strong advocates of equal pay, for at this stage there was no attempt to discriminate between supporters, opponents, and the uncommitted. However, the postcard is not so irritating as the master letter laboriously copied out. If a constituent is going to take the trouble to write a letter, it would be more impressive if he used his own words, however blunt they were. Instead, many copied out formulas such as this one; 'As one of your constituents keen on seeing Mr. Pannell's motion on Equal Pay passed by the House of Commons on Friday, 16th May, will you please do your best to be present for the debate and I hope vote for the motion.' Perhaps the least impressive example of equal pay tactics that I saw was forty duplicated letters in the same envelope.

One sensible modification in tactics was made in 1954. The Chairman of the Equal Pay Co-ordinating Committee wrote: 'Only Labour M.P.s who have not signed this motion should be written to or lobbied, because those who have already shown their support should be saved from further pressure.'[1]

[1] *Red Tape*, Mar. 1954, p. 186. Conservative M.P.s were to be pressed to sign another motion.

It may be one is wrong to criticize the equal pay movement for its techniques. The postcards and copied letters may have been as genuine and as sincere as original letters. All that can be said is that they do not give that impression. If teachers, civil servants, and local government officials cannot be bothered to write a letter, who can?

The obvious answer is supporters of Sunday observance. Neither the Lord's Day Observance Society nor any other body advocating this point of view has ever made much use of post-cards; although some cards sent out as literature to supporters by the Society in 1941 were sent on to M.P.s. But in 1953 it is probable that all the letters received by M.P.s originated with the sender, at least as far as matter if not inspiration was concerned. Most of the letters were phrased with restraint and courtesy (differing greatly from the thousand letters received by the promoter of the Bill which horrify in their crude hatred). They look completely spontaneous. It is therefore very difficult to say what part the Society had in bringing about this correspondence. The most that can be said is that without the Society's activities many people would probably not know of the threats to Sunday observance and hence take no action.

The actual number of letters received by M.P.s whenever this issue arises is difficult to assess. It varies from area to area and is probably greatest in Scotland and Wales. Exaggerated claims are made by the Society which speaks in terms of hundreds per constituency. Sixty would probably be nearer the mark for the average English constituency.

The old-age pensioners are not able to send a large number of letters. It would be a very great effort for many of them, besides being expensive, so they tend to rely on petitions to their local M.P.s which I have seen signed by as many as 400 people. It is much wiser to do this than to resort to post-cards. This sort of petition can be an impressive communication.

A similar technique was used by the teachers in 1950 in some constituencies using the schools as the basic point. Each school sent out a joint letter setting forth a catalogue of grievances and signed by as many teachers as possible. It is an effective way to secure a large number of signatures. Other subjects which led to a smaller yet significant correspondence between 1950 and

1954 included the abolition of gin traps, earlier pensions for spinsters, divorce reform, and railway fares.

Of the correspondence in general it can be said that it is normally restrained and courteous. Rarely does a writer even hint that his vote may be involved. Rather do they 'hope' or 'trust' that the M.P. will support their case. 'It would be interesting to have your viewpoint', or, a little more strongly, 'Do all you can to see we have a fair deal' and 'I feel if you support this Bill you will not be representing the views of the majority of your constituents'. One almost feels that the lobbyists are concerned to show that they do not want any fuss. That is the British tradition.

Some groups cannot hope to organize a large number of letters; their membership is not large enough to render it possible. That will not itself stop a group encouraging its members to write to their M.P.s:

Dear Sir,

Finance Bill 1953

May we respectfully ask your kind assistance once again with regard to the proposition that Off-Licences should be permitted to sell single quarter and miniature sized bottles of Spirits? This as you know is a very important matter to people of limited means, who sometimes find it necessary to purchase small quantities of spirits for medicinal purposes and have to be told that they must buy at least a half bottle.

Thanking you in anticipation of your very kind co-operation.

There was enclosed in this letter an official statement from the National Federation of Off-Licence Holders' Associations. Letters of this kind cannot hope to convince an M.P. of a widespread feeling about a subject. They come from interested parties, and in very small numbers. What they can do is to arouse the M.P.'s interest in the subject. Before this subject was raised by local firms it is unlikely that many M.P.s had strong views, if views at all, on the question.

Slightly different was the case when several football clubs wrote to their local M.P.s after the 1953 budget to protest against the level of entertainments tax on football. Such a protest could not go uninvestigated by any M.P. who had any sense of the need to look after his constituents. Groups which cannot hope to stimulate mass lobbying may yet achieve influence if their membership includes firms or organizations of importance in the constituencies.

Some groups, including a number which might be able to stimulate or at least attempt a mass lobby, prefer to rely on the influence or prestige of the local branch. Organizations like the local chamber of trade or the branch of the British Legion have a considerable importance in certain areas. It may be preferred to use the branch, implying strongly held opinions without putting them to the test.

In order to show the variety that this form of activity may take, some examples are drawn from a Conservative M.P.'s mailbag during the period 1950–3. The local Chamber of Trade, acting on behalf of the National Chamber of Trade, approached him several times on the subject of retailers' stocks and purchase tax reductions. In 1952 a draft of a proposed new clause was submitted with a note attached which read: 'The foregoing has been drafted for the use of M.P.s to raise the Rebate question.' The local Chamber of Trade also made approaches on the Transport Bill in 1953. The local Licensed Victuallers' Society wrote during 1953 to ask various M.P.s from the district to receive a deputation to protest against the proposal to allow the sale of spirits in miniatures from off-licence premises. The National Pharmaceutical Union's local branch wrote in 1951 to protest against the white paper on resale price maintenance. The British Legion local branch asked to see all the local M.P.s on 22 March 1952, the Day of Demand, giving only two days' notice. N.A.L.G.O.'s local branch wrote to ask for support for the opposition to parts of the Sunderland Extension Bill in 1950. The Association of Assistant Mistresses in Secondary Schools asked for a vote against the Simplified Spelling Bill (1953). Other bodies writing included the local branches of the National Allotments and Gardens Society Limited, B.L.E.S.M.A., and the National Union of Teachers.

The local authority is in a position of special importance. Good relations with his local authority are of considerable value to an M.P.; he feels under a special obligation to respect its views. This was realized in 1955 by the Council of Justice to Animals which was promoting a private members' bill to prevent *shechita*, the Jewish practice for slaughtering animals. The Council wrote to all local authorities asking for their support, with the idea of influencing M.P.s. It made some headway, at least until the Board of Deputies of British Jews put the opposing point of view to the local authorities.[1]

The local authority is used by the various local government associations, which sometimes ask their members to put a case before their M.P. or M.P.s. Some authorities may refuse to do so, others may do it automatically. This has been important on the Bills promoted by Luton and Ilford to secure for themselves the status of county boroughs. Debates on these Bills have served as preliminary trials of strength on the issue of local government reform, the County Councils' Association vigorously opposing the Bills. If one takes the parliamentary division of constituencies into borough and county as roughly corresponding to those areas in which the county borough and the county are the major influences, then it is instructive to examine one of the free votes taken on these Bills in the House of Commons—that in 1954 on the Luton Corporation Bill, for example. The members voted predominantly in accordance with the nature of their seats:

For the Bill:

County members	21
Borough members	69
London members	5

Against the Bill:

County members	75
Borough members	40
London members	12[2]

It is difficult to decide what influence the local government associations had in bringing about this result. Did local authorities or even M.P.s need to be circularized?

4

All these forms of lobbying are believed to have an effect not

[1] *Jewish Chronicle*, 4 Mar. 1955, p. 10.
[2] H.C. Deb. 525, cols. 717–20.

only by those who use them, but also by those who are subject to them. In 1955 Mr. Fred Mulley wrote:

We in the house will do our best and I have great hopes of success. But there is something YOU can do. All our branches should ensure not only that their local M.P.s understand the importance of this Bill to office workers but that they will be present in the House on April 1st to vote for it. Even though it may prove not to be controversial, we must have at least 102 present and supporting it to prevent a single opponent talking it out. And this number is very high for a Friday when so many M.P.s have evening constituency engagements and cannot stay until 4 p.m. quite often on a private members' day it is impossible to maintain a quorum of 40 and the House is 'counted out'. Thus the branches can play their part in what I hope will prove a great triumph.

In these matters, quite rightly most members are more influenced by their constituents than by their colleagues in the House. They will not believe our statements of large public support for a measure unless they have evidence for it in their post-bags.[1]

Mr. C. G. P. Smith, speaking at the 1949 conference of the Civil Service Clerical Association, said: 'In the end it is the local Members of Parliament, the ordinary back-bench Members who have got to feel themselves satisfied on the justice of the claim before it can hope to succeed. That is why I place such emphasis on what has been done by the Branches in the way of explaining our case. . . .'[2]

In 1955 Mr. (now Sir) Tom O'Brien said of the campaign against entertainments tax on the theatre: 'Those who haven't yet written to their M.P.s must do so at once and say frankly that the living theatre will soon be a dead one if it is not rid of this tax. . . . I hear quite a lot of irresponsible talk that everything is in the bag. This is foolish and dangerous complacency.'[3]

Mr. C. W. Black advised the Lord's Day Observance Society in the course of their 1953 campaign against the Bill promoted by Mr. John Parker, and himself wrote to a number of church newspapers asking readers to write to their M.P.s.[4] Sir Ian Fraser claimed some credit for the ideas behind the British

[1] *The Clerk*, Mar.–Apr. 1955, p. 32. This was with reference to the Non-Industrial Employment Bill, introduced as a private members' bill.

[2] *Red Tape*, July 1949, p. 325.

[3] *Stage*, 21 Apr. 1955.

[4] e.g. *The English Churchman*, 16 Jan. 1953, p. 33.

Legion's Day of Demand,[1] while the equal pay campaigners were advised by a number of M.P.s of differing outlook and background.

On the other hand, in 1946 Dr. Hyacinth Morgan at the British Medical Association Council expressed some doubt about the value of letters to M.P.s. But he was speaking with particular reference to letters which urged a policy contrary to that of the M.P.'s party. It was related to his advice that the B.M.A. should not forget to lay stress on those parts of the National Health Service Bill with which it agreed.[2]

All this is evidence from M.P.s, and there is an absence of anything more definite. It is possible to examine the results of various free votes taken in the House, but hard to draw any conclusion from them since one lacks the knowledge of what the vote would have been without the lobbying. It is asserted by Mr. John Parker that in 1941 over thirty of the members who signed a petition to the Home Secretary asking for the Sunday opening of the theatres for the benefit of the forces, voted against this as a result of pressure.[3] But for the most part evidence designed to show a change of opinion is unreliable.

More important is attendance at the discussion of bills about which lobbying has taken place. The normal number of M.P.s present on a Friday for private members' bills is certainly not more than a hundred. Yet the Bill to abolish various forms of hunting was defeated by 214 to 101 in 1949 and Mr. John Parker's Bill on Sunday observance by 281 to 57 in 1953, while Mr. Harold Davies' Non-Industrial Employment Bill had a good attendance in 1955. Lobbying seems to be effective in securing a member's attendance. Since it commands this much attention from members, it does not seem unreasonable to assume that it has some influence on their decisions.

Even where the effect of lobbying is prevented from appearing in the voting figures by party discipline and the necessities of government business, its effect can still be seen in the references that are made to the lobbying and the attention it

[1] *British Legion Journal*, May 1952, p. 1.

[2] *British Medical Journal* (Supplement), 13 Apr. 1946, p. 79.

[3] H.C. Deb. 481, col. 556. Cf. *The Times*, 2 Apr. 1941: 'The number of members who had previously associated themselves with the movement in favour of Sunday Opening was greatly in excess of the 136 who voted for the new Regulations yesterday. Many of them must have changed their minds or abstained from voting.'

commands in the debate. In 1950 a sharp lobbying campaign was conducted by the Association of Cinematograph and Allied Technicians against the new quota figures for British films which had been recommended by the Cinematograph Film Council. The views of the Association were discussed in the speeches of Mr. Harold Wilson, Mr. Tom O'Brien, Mr. Michael Foot, and Mr. Walter Elliot among others.[1] Mr. Walter Elliot summed up the situation by saying: 'I do not think it can be denied that the discussion today is not so much between the two sides of the House as between the right hon. Gentleman and the point of view represented in the memorandum of the Association of Cinematograph and Allied Technicians.'[2] A lobbying campaign commands at least the attention of members.

It is not very surprising that it should. The cynical explanation is that members are afraid for their seats and hence respond to lobbying. If this were so, one would expect to see a strong variation in response as between safe and unsafe seats. If one accepts a majority of 5,000 as the limit of the marginal seat, then 32 per cent. of the M.P.s in the 1951–5 Parliament had marginal seats. If the voting figures on Mr. John Parker's Sunday Observance Bill are taken as a guide, then it is found that 40 per cent. of the votes against the Bill came from those with marginal seats. If one takes the first 108 signatories of Mr. Douglas Houghton's motion for equal pay in 1954 then 43 per cent. had marginal seats.

The desire to safeguard his seat seems to have some influence on a member's response to lobbying, but it is clearly only one factor. It may be argued that the other members are concerned merely to maintain the size of their majorities, but here the cynical approach lacks the realism that gives it its appeal.

One must not be carried away into believing that there are not many members who hold strong opinions of their own and even some who would be willing to express them on a private members' Friday. But upon those with no strong views lobbying may well have an effect, not because members are frightened to lose votes, but because members accept an obligation to their constituencies. There are some members who enjoy their constituencies, who like being what Mr. James Maxton described

[1] H.C. Deb. 473, cols. 572–634. [2] Ibid., col. 586.

as 'a bloody welfare worker.'[1] Where there appears to be a strong expression of opinion, they will naturally attend to it. But beyond this the general principle must be admitted that no M.P. likes going against the prevailing opinion of his constituents.

Members of Parliament exist in a distinctive atmosphere. In it, certain ideas and principles are taken for granted. One of them is that a member has a duty to his constituents. It would be as false to say that this attitude is solely due to the desire to preserve or increase his votes as it is to say that that does not come into the question at all. The M.P. is there to represent his constituents and though this does not mean accepting their views on all issues, it does mean paying attention to them. An M.P. who acts against a strongly held view in his constituency is acting properly, provided he is clear in his own mind; but so is the M.P. who considers the weight of opinion in favour of a certain viewpoint is such that he ought to support it.

An M.P. is not always in a position to assess accurately the feeling in his constituency. He has certain guides to opinion, of which one of the most important is the mailbag. But not all opinion is represented there, and it is possible to simulate deeply held opinion by organizing a comparatively small attack upon the M.P.'s mailbag. Again it is easy for a member to place too much weight on the representations of local organizations. These dangers are not important when the member is protected by the discipline of the party, but are important in a free vote, where the member is left to deal direct with his conscience and his constituents. The answer of the lobbyists to this argument is that other bodies can act in the same way as themselves, and their failure to achieve the same influence is a sign that they do not represent public opinion. However, not all opinions are equally likely to be expressed in lobbying.

It must remain one of the major arguments for party discipline that it controls the lobbyist. The letter in the mailbag still has an effect, but the M.P. through the party can bring to his judgement upon it wider considerations. The issue is seen in better perspective than when left to be settled between the M.P. and the more vociferous of his constituents.

[1] J. Lee, *Tomorrow is a New Day* (1939), p. 128.

5

The constituency provides the group with a sure way of catching the M.P.'s attention. Circulars or other communications received from the national headquarters of the group are likely to go straight into his waste-paper basket unless he is particularly interested in the matter discussed. The group may send out such circulars as part of a routine, not connected with any specific issue. But more often there is a specific intent or a specific criticism of the government. If the issue is important quite a number of M.P.s may read the circular, but as often as not it is uninviting, even unreadable. In July 1953 the National Union of Manufacturers circulated a duplicated copy of 'The case for the raising of the heavy goods vehicles speed limit from 20 m.p.h. to 30 m.p.h.' It looked dull and it was dull. It was badly presented and gave little fresh information on the problem. An M.P. is either going to be interested because of new information or interested by presentation. This document gave him neither.

Equally useless is too polemical a document. In June 1953 the National Union of Teachers circulated an Open Letter to members of the House of Commons. Its tone is indicated by the following paragraph which was emphasized in heavy print:

> 'The fundamental cause of present difficulties is that no Government has allocated sufficient money, labour and materials to meet the needs of the schools and the child population. No Government has ever made arrangements for the building of sufficient new schools nor for adequate improvement of the dilapidated and insanitary old schools. The main responsibility lies with successive governments who, in speeches and manifestos have all declared in favour of better educational facilities but who in practice, have failed to provide the means.'

The net result of such a document is a mild feeling of irritation.

Other groups, such as the British Road Federation, circulate press releases to M.P.s. But, while the press is interested in finding out news, the average M.P. has to be interested and a press release will not normally attract his attention.

If groups were well advised their circulars would be better designed. An M.P. is probably as amenable to good advertising as the rest of us. These circulars rarely subject him to it. A bright little memorandum on earnings issued in 1953 by the Federation of British Port Wholesale Fish Merchant's Associations was a rare exception. It gave useful information, it presented it well both statistically and graphically, it was mercifully short, and it was in good print, thus avoiding all the usual faults.

A circular issued just before a second reading debate to all members of the House or to all members of a standing committee just before a debate on a bill will, provided the group's position is important, naturally arouse interest. It will be quoted in the debate. In the debate on the Rating and Valuation (Miscellaneous Provisions) Bill, 1955, the circular sent out by the National Chamber of Trade was widely quoted in the second reading debate,[1] as was the circular sent out by the Association of Cinematograph and Allied Technicians in the discussion on film quotas in 1950.[2]

It is the natural recognition that the logical opposition to some government proposals comes not from the opposition in the House but from some group outside it.

The principles relating to circulars are simple to grasp. They must be relevant, they must give information, and they must be well presented. If all circulars followed these principles they might not reach M.P.s' waste-paper baskets quite so quickly.

6

The procedures of lobbying are not restricted by any special laws in this country. There have been occasions when the lobbyist has found himself involved in a breach of privilege case, but for the most part he is in no such danger. He has only to observe the normal procedures.

There are certain means of influencing M.P.s which have been ruled to be improper. It would be improper to bribe a member. 'The offer of money or other advantage to any member of Parliament for the promoting of any matter whatsoever, depending or to be transacted in Parliament is a high crime and misdemeanour and tends to the subversion of the English Constitution.'[3]

[1] e.g. the speech by the Minister of Housing and Local Government refuting the charge that he had misled the National Chamber (H.C. Deb. 539, cols. 1293–4).

[2] See p. 217.

[3] *Erskine May* (15th edn.), pp. 122–3, from the Resolution of 2 June 1695.

Erskine May states that it is also a breach of privilege 'To attempt to influence Members in their conduct by threats'.[1] Nevertheless, it is conceded that at least one threat is legitimate. For an elector to attempt to influence a member's vote by threatening the withdrawal of electoral support is not in itself a contempt. 'Anybody, surely, can write to his Member and say, "Look here, if you vote for this, I will not support you at the next Election." That is not intimidation', was the Speaker's conclusion in 1946 on telegrams received by Mr. Hector Hughes.[2] However, he indicated that a telegram received by Mr. David Kirkwood (later Lord Kirkwood), reading: 'Directors, staff mechanics and drivers unanimously regret Transport Bill all support in future will be denied you if you vote in favour', was more serious in that it was collective and contained a kind of intimidatory threat, but he ruled that it did not constitute a prima facie breach of privilege because it was not definite.[3]

However, certain examples of lobbying have been ruled to be breaches of privilege. In 1935 a case was decided by resolution of the House immediately upon the report of the incident by Mr. (later Sir) Herbert Williams:

> During the course of yesterday, in common with many, if not all, the hon. Members of this House, I received a letter from the secretary of the League for the Prohibition of Cruel Sports. This letter enclosed a questionnaire asking my views on five questions. The details are not in themselves a matter with which I need concern you, except to say that . . . they ask my views . . . on blood sports. [The concluding sentence reads], 'If we do not hear from you we shall feel justified in letting your constituents know that you have no objection to cruel sports.' This sentence seems to me to be a particularly objectionable form of political blackmail and moreover, seems to be a gross breach of the Privilege of this Honourable House.

The House so ruled.[4]

It is unfortunate that the House did not consider the matter more fully so that both the purpose and the implications of this resolution could have been made clear. Mr. (now Sir) Winston Churchill, in considering a later case said of the communication from the League for the Prohibition of Cruel Sports: 'It suggests that members who take a certain course are indifferent

[1] Ibid., p. 123.
[2] H.C. Deb. 431, cols. 1967–8.
[3] Ibid.
[4] Ibid. 301, cols. 1545–7.

to cruelty . . . it is a highly injurious, dangerous, insulting, mordaunt attack upon a Member. . . .'[1] It seems, from the remarks of the Clerk of the House, that the gravamen was the nature of the threat: that a slanderous imputation would be spread about. It hardly seems necessary for the House to be protected from such threats, but so it has been ruled.

In 1946 the Face the Facts Association published widely, in London, posters saying: 'Names of M.P.s voting for bread rationing in the Commons on Thursday will be published here as public enemies and dictators.'[2] This was reported to the Committee of Privileges who declared that the wording was improper in that it 'was in effect a threat to hold Members voting in favour of the order up to public contempt',[3] and thereby to attempt to influence members by improper means.

Mr. Churchill, a member of the Committee, disagreed with this conclusion and moved an amendment to the report stating:

> . . . An examination of the precedents and authorities shows that it is plainly a breach of privilege to threaten to molest Members of Parliament or to impute criminal or dishonourable conduct or motives to them. But your Committee find no ground for the view that it is a breach of privilege to seek to influence the votes of members by threatening to make a political attack on them if they vote in a particular way. . . .[4]

This amendment was rejected.

Mr. Churchill was wise in attempting to limit the occasions on which a 'threat' should be regarded as a breach of privilege. He pointed out that threats and political abuse are part of the life of an M.P. He must expect to be held up to public contempt: 'People have got up on platforms and spoken all over the place and urged that I should be turned out of Parliament and have used most abusive terms about me. These are very minor compared to the things that for years I have lived and flourished under the reproach of.'[5] To Mr. Churchill the crucial question was: 'Do you consider that the Privilege precedents and so forth have been built up from the point of view of protecting Members against real intimidation, real injuries, or merely to protect them from vulgar abuse?'[6]

[1] H.C. 181 of 1945–6, q. 49.
[2] Ibid., p. iii.
[3] Ibid., p. iv.
[4] Ibid., p. vi.
[5] Ibid., q. 48.
[6] Ibid., q. 80.

The Committee, on the other hand, took a narrower view of the matter. In effect it said that there is something improper in any threat designed to influence an M.P. There are not proper and improper threats.

The same conception seems to be behind a ruling of the Speaker on a letter sent by Service Equity to Captain H. F. C. Crookshank (now Lord Crookshank), dealt with in 1946. This letter stated that: 'In the event of no reply, we shall be forced to assume that the Member of Parliament concerned is against us.'[1] This was ruled by the Speaker not to contain a prima facie breach of privilege, since the letter contained no definite threat. But, he said: 'It is quite true that it is worded in such a way as to insinuate what I might call a veiled threat. In tone it is disrespectful to Parliament. I think that a repetition of such a letter might justifiably incur the serious displeasure of the House.'[2]

'Threat' is an uncertain word upon which to build a law of privilege. Many actions only appear as threats when viewed from one angle. Some attempt to clarify the situation can perhaps be detected in the Speaker's use of the term 'intimidation' in his decision on the telegrams to Mr. David Kirkwood. This seems to give some importance to the intention of the person making the threat, but this point has not been pursued.

The M.P. is entitled, as is any citizen, to protection from certain threats, but it is surely not necessary to protect him from anything that can be called a threat, and is designed to influence his vote. A distinction should be drawn between threats to do things which are in themselves proper and threats to do things which are improper. A realization of this distinction is presumably the reason why an exception has been made for the threat to withdraw electoral support.

7

There remain to be considered the activities of a group at election time. It may seem strange to class these with lobbying, but they are very similar since they give groups a chance to approach the general body of future M.P.s. They are used by those groups which are the most assiduous lobbyists of the House. What more natural than that a group should seek to

[1] H.C. Deb. 425, cols. 885–6. [2] Ibid., col. 887.

raise with candidates any outstanding issues at election time? The election provides an opportunity for campaigners.

It is not likely to be part of a campaign against a specific government proposal except in so far as this is foreshadowed in the programme of a party, and if in fact this is so, the group is in a difficult position. It can either campaign against the proposal and for the defeat of the party concerned or it can seek to influence the future M.P.s to secure the modification or the elimination of the proposal. The latter indicates the greater helplessness. Yet in the 1951 election[1] several bodies interested in retaining the system of resale price maintenance took measures which would only have been useful if the Labour candidates had been open to conviction on the subject. The Branded Textiles Group circulated to all candidates a brief pamphlet on resale price maintenance—the case for its retention in the textile trade. The Fair Prices Defence Committee also circularized and got member organizations and firms to circularize candidates on the subject. Its covering note, enclosing a memorandum, said a little ingenuously:

> Since Resale Price Maintenance is a subject which may well come up for discussion during the Election Campaign, you may be glad to have the enclosed short memorandum on the subject which has been prepared by the Fair Prices Defence Committee. . . . May I express the hope that you will study the arguments set out in this Memorandum before reaching any final conclusion.

The Committee was a body to which various interested groups such as the National Pharmaceutical Union, the Proprietary Articles Trade Association, the National Chamber of Trade, the Grocery Proprietary Articles Council, and the National Union of Retail Tobacconists belonged. Some of these bodies themselves undertook activities. Through the local branches of the National Federation of Grocers' and Provision Dealers' Associations, the Grocery Proprietary Articles Council circulated its own memorandum: 'Our immediate request is that you will not commit yourself to supporting any proposals for abolition of Resale Price Maintenance at least until there has been opportunity for the whole technical and controversial subject to have been further examined.' A mass of literature

[1] This chapter concentrates on the 1951 election. However, Appendix E provides a list of bodies active at the 1955 election.

was sent out, some of which may have been useful to Conservative candidates (though it is probable they preferred to remain safely within the confines of the Conservative party's own *Campaign Guide*), but none of which was likely to make Labour candidates change their minds in the middle of an election campaign.

Yet what could these groups do in 1951? If it is impossible to influence candidates, it is not easy to influence electors on the basis of a limited issue. Besides any such attempt was beset with legal problems.

Before the 1950 election those industries threatened with nationalization in the Labour Party's programme organized campaigns to arouse public opinion against the proposals. These campaigns have been described by Mr. H. G. Nicholas[1] and a particularly close analysis of the campaign of Tate & Lyle has been made by Mr. H. H. Wilson in an article entitled 'Techniques of Pressure'.[2]

As Mr. Nicholas has pointed out, the sugar refining industry and the industrial life offices were in a better position to make an impact on electors than, say, the Imported Meat Trade Association or the Cement Makers' Federation. Their contact with the electors was direct. Tate & Lyle, by printing on its packets of sugar a picture of Mr. Cube with slogans varying from 'If they juggle with sugar, they'll juggle with your shopping basket' to 'Whatever the party we wish you all a Happy New Year', brought the issue of sugar nationalization before the housewife. A sample poll in November 1949 showed that of those who had seen Tate & Lyle's propaganda 54 per cent. had seen it on the packets, 41 per cent. in the press, 25 per cent. on posters, and 3 per cent. in some other form. Tate & Lyle itself said: 'To put these great thoughts over, our chief medium has been the sides of our packets', but as the figures show, the traditional methods of press and poster were still very important.[3]

Those groups which lacked this direct contact with the public were unable to campaign with the same zest. Although they set up posters and issued pamphlets either at meetings or through shareholders and employees, they did not have the same im-

[1] H. G. Nicholas, *The General Election of 1950* (1951), pp. 71–72.
[2] *Public Opinion Quarterly*, 1951, pp. 225–42.
[3] Wilson, op. cit., *passim*.

pact as the insurance offices and above all not the same impact as the sugar refiners—or to be more precise, Tate & Lyle.

A warning was sounded by Mr. Herbert Morrison in a speech at Birmingham on 26 November 1949 that these campaigns might infringe the laws governing elections.[1] The section of the Representation of the People Act which was at issue read:

> No expenses shall, with a view to promoting or procuring the election of a candidate at an election, be incurred by any person other than the candidate, his election agent and persons authorised in writing by the election agent on account—
>
> (*a*) of holding public meetings or organising any public display; or
>
> (*b*) of issuing advertisements, circulars or publications; or
>
> (*c*) of otherwise presenting to the electors the candidate or his views or the extent or nature of his backing or disparaging another candidate:[2]

The relevance of this clause to these campaigns was explained by Sir Hartley Shawcross in the House of Commons on 5 December 1949 when he said:

> I think it is right to add, however, that whilst I can lay down no binding rule in the matter, which is one to be considered on the facts of each particular case, it is my view that the prohibition of certain expenditure on propaganda calculated to influence an election is not necessarily restricted to propaganda in which any particular candidate is expressly referred to, nor is it necessarily confined to expenditure incurred only after the dissolution of Parliament or the issue of a writ for an election or the nomination of a candidate.[3]

This statement was extended in a written reply to a question on 15 December:

> An intention to promote or procure the election of a candidate is a necessary ingredient of this offence. Intention, however, is not usually capable of positive proof; it can only be implied from overt acts and it is a well recognised principle of law that a person may be presumed to intend the natural and probable consequences of what he deliberately does. If, therefore, in the circumstances existing at

[1] Nicholas, op. cit., p. 73, comments: 'Read now . . . Mr. Morrison's statement wears an appearance of pure scarecrow-ism. There is none the less good reason to suppose that it was seriously meant, and that it was the expression of a deep-rooted conviction on the part of its author as to the potency of pressure groups in swaying the voter's opinion.'

[2] 12 and 13 Geo. VI, c. 68, s. 63 (1).

[3] H.C. Deb. 470, col. 1515.

the time of an election particular propaganda appeared calculated in fact to promote or procure the election of a candidate in the sense that that was its natural and probable consequence,[1]

then an offence might have been committed.

Sir David Maxwell Fyfe and the bodies concerned disputed the relevance of this to the matter at issue. The groups were campaigning against specific points in the party programme. It would be hard, indeed, if they were not to be allowed to reply to the attacks being made upon them.

During the election the actual interpretation to be put upon law remained uncertain, but these statements were sufficient to restrain the bodies concerned. The election of 1951 was remarkably free from this form of activity. Sir Hartley Shawcross's warnings seemed to have had the desired effect and several groups drew the attention of their members to the dangers of activities at election time.

A case came before the courts in 1952 (*Rex* v. *Tronoh Mines Ltd. and others*).[2] After the writs had been issued for the general election of 1951 this company inserted in *The Times* an advertisement condemning the Labour Party's financial policy with particular reference to its proposal to limit company dividends. It continued: 'The coming general election will give us all the opportunity of saving the country from being reduced, through the policies of the Socialist Government, to a bankrupt "Welfare State". We need a new and strong government with Ministers who may be relied upon to encourage business enterprise and initiative. . . .'

The Court held that Section 63 (1) (*b*) of the Representation of the People Act (1949) was designed to prohibit expenditure on advertisements 'supporting a particular candidate or candidates in a particular constituency, which, if authorized by the election agent, would form part of the election expenses for that constituency and thus be subject to the statutory maximum of expenditure for that constituency'. The judgement went on: 'I therefore, accept the submission of counsel for the Times Publishing Co., Ltd., that S 63 (1) does not prohibit expenditure, the real purpose or effect of which is general political propaganda, even although that general political propaganda does incidentally assist a particular candidate among others.'

[1] H.C. Deb. 470, cols. 337–8 (written). [2] [1952] 1 A.E.R. 697–700.

This ruling ran contrary to the interpretation Sir Hartley Shawcross had put upon this section, and in a case that was far more extreme than the ones which gave rise to his comments. In this case there was a clearly stated opposition to the Labour Party. The Court took the law at its face value, and did not seek to examine what were 'the natural and probable consequences' of the action. By doing so they avoided introducing a dangerous element of uncertainty into the law of elections.

In 1952 the National Executive of the Labour Party declared that it was the intention of the Labour Party to amend the law so that it would cover the cases discussed.[1] This is a very dangerous proposal. Unless the means of political expression at election time is to be denied to all organizations except political parties,[2] it is difficult to see how any satisfactory boundary can be drawn between legitimate and illegitimate activity. Most activity, be it only the sending of a questionnaire, will tend to favour one candidate over others.

There is force in the contention that there was nothing improper in the activities of Tate & Lyle. There is a danger of excluding from the public scene views that must have an important bearing on the decisions to be taken in an election. The elementary right of self-defence is hard to deny. There are dangers in the growth of subsidiary organizations as a means of avoiding the legal restrictions on expenses, but until these become a real problem it would probably be better to leave the law in its present state rather than risk greater dangers in legislation. Since it is unlikely that the propaganda of Tate & Lyle had any marked effect on the result of the election it would probably have been wiser for the Labour Party not to have raised the issue, but calm detachment is not to be expected in a political party at election time.

8

The groups threatened by specific proposals in the election programmes of political parties are not the only ones which make use of the opportunities provided by elections. The election

[1] *Labour Party National Executive Report to Annual Conference*, 1952, pp. 7–8.

[2] The theory of the arena cleared for the parties to fight in has certain attractions, but it is not very realistic since it separates off the electoral campaign from the rest of politics.

may catch the swelling of a discontent and give it expression. In 1951 the British Road Federation sent out to all candidates its statement of policy, which was in effect a protest against the failure of the Government to inaugurate a programme for the improvement of the road system. The Standing Joint Committee of the Automobile Association, the Royal Automobile Club, and the Royal Scottish Automobile Club sent to all candidates, both directly and through motor distributors, a statement of policy on much the same lines, though with a greater emphasis on taxation. It also sent a questionnaire.

Elections provide the long-term campaigners with an opportunity. In 1951 the advocates of equal pay were the most persistent. One candidate received communications from the following bodies on the subject: the Council of Women Civil Servants, the National Association of Women Civil Servants, N.A.L.G.O., the National Union of Women Teachers, the Equal Pay Campaign Committee, and the National Union of Teachers. In addition there were various individual letters or duplicated forms.

Other campaigners which took advantage of the 1951 election to state their claims were B.L.E.S.M.A., the National Federation of Post Office Veterans, and the Officers' Pensions Society, all of which were campaigning for better pensions in one form or another. The Joint Committee of the Four Secondary Associations took the opportunity to put forward its views on, among many other things, the need for an examination of the principles that should determine salary scales of teachers.

The Roman Catholic Church (or to be more precise, Catholic Parents' and Electors' Associations) has been an active campaigner at elections on the issue of financial support for Catholic schools, hardly counterbalanced by the leaflets circularized by the Secular Education League or even the more formidable intervention oflocal Free Church Federal Councils, for the simple reason that the latter bodies do not command votes whereas it is considered that the Roman Catholic Church may. These tactics are remarkable in that it is probably the only group which places most weight during a campaign on election activities. If a group's role in an election is regarded as important, then its intervention therein may have as great an effect as months of routine campaigning.

These are groups with campaigns in hand. A few groups ask questions at election time without such specific intent. They are groups which are always prepared for a campaign. Distrust of the government or a belief in the possibilities of the campaign have led them to organize for it. The outstanding examples are the National Farmers' Union, the National Union of Teachers, and the groups representing the licensed trade. They are all bodies which can claim a widespread membership and, especially in the case of the National Farmers' Union, a good deal of influence in certain constituencies. Parliamentary pressure has always come easily to them.

The licensed trade was forced into activity as a measure of protection against the temperance movement. But with the decline in the strength of that movement, there have been signs that the trade would conform to the more normal pattern of groups. In 1945 some groups normally sending out questionnaires did not do so.[1] The Licensing Act of 1949 revived the old campaign spirit. The Conservatives' Licensed Premises in New Towns Act (1952) may have satisfied it, though it has not destroyed the trade's wariness.

Many cause groups send out leaflets or questionnaires. The United Committee for the Taxation of Land Values is a very regular sender of questionnaires, while the Lord's Day Observance Society steadily sends out its one vital question. The League Against Cruel Sports, the National Anti-Vaccination League, the British Field Sports Society, and the Crusade for World Government all sent out some form of literature during the 1951 election. It is important to these groups to know where their support, limited as it may be, will lie in a new House of Commons. The groups probably also hope to influence candidates but that is their perpetual optimism (which is their strength) rather than a cool assessment of the situation.

The decision to take part in an election is not always an easy one, nor does an election always fit into a campaign. In 1951 the British Legion was just about to launch its campaign for a 90*s*. pension, when a general election was announced. Its usual practice was to send out questionnaires or the like, but it was decided that it would not be wise to do so at a time when the

[1] *Wine and Spirit Trade Record*, 16 Aug. 1945, p. 988.

Legion was about to launch a campaign, since it was not allowed for in its plans.[1]

9

The group which has decided to approach candidates has to decide whether to send a pamphlet, questionnaire, or deputation. It is doubtful whether a pamphlet is any use without a letter for a reply on certain points—in other words, unless it is a questionnaire. Electoral campaigns are not suited to a relaxed consideration of the inessential.

A questionnaire is adequate for a group's purposes provided it can be certain of a response. Unhappily this cannot be guaranteed. A number of factors affect the extent of the response. Quite a number of M.P.s will only answer questionnaires received from the constituency. The result is that groups which can ensure that their questions are asked by local members or branches secure a better response than other groups. In 1951 the National Temperance Federation sent out a statement of principles, on the basis of which candidates were asked either by letter or deputation, whether they would support or join a group to be formed in the new Parliament. The approach was made in constituencies by a variety of temperance and church bodies. Only in 312 constituencies had the future M.P.s been approached, but replies had been received from all but 88 of them. The Standing Committee of the motorists' organizations was able to report 445 replies to the 1,375 questionnaires sent out. Most of these were sent out from national headquarters, although some were sent out locally. The United Committee for the Taxation of Land Values publishes figures of the replies received. In 1951 it only received 171 replies to their questions (a number of other candidates either sent their election address or said they only answered questions from constituents).[2] The reason for this is probably the nature of the group, which arouses far less sympathy than the motorists' organizations. Candidates are probably reluctant to send unfavourable replies.

The Lord's Day Observance Society publishes figures after elections which seem to show a large number of replies from

[1] *British Legion Journal*, Oct. 1951, p. 147.
[2] *Land and Liberty*, Nov. and Dec. 1951, p. 94.

future M.P.s. For example in 1951 it published the following table:

Party	No. of M.P.s	Replies				No reply
		Favourable	Favourable (Qualified)	Indecisive	Unfavourable	
Conservative .	321	149	139	16	2	15
Labour . .	295	40	24	90	116	25
Liberal . .	6	5	..	..	..	1
Others . .	3	..	..	1	..	2

But it was explained that these figures were compiled from a variety of sources. Besides the replies returned to the question sent out nationally, the Society endeavours to get its question asked locally. It also uses past records of members, in this case 'especially their manner of voting on the Sunday Opening of the Festival of Britain Exhibition and Funfair'.[1]

One other tendency should be noted. Conservative candidates send a larger proportion of replies than Labour ones. This fact is noted by the National Anti-Vaccination League in its report on the 1951 election.[2] The breakdown of the replies received by the United Committee for the Taxation of Land Values shows that Conservative candidates sent 106 replies and Labour candidates 34 in 1951,[3] and Conservative 95 and Labour 40 in 1950.[4] (The Liberals sent a higher proportion of replies than either of the other two parties, which may well be due to their greater sympathy with the movement.) The reason for this seems to be that the Conservative Party Central Office sends out suggested replies to questionnaires which candidates duly copy, following in this the example of Mr. Churchill himself.[5] The Labour Party only offers advice on a few of the questionnaires.

As far as it is safe to come to any conclusion, it can be said that a group can only be sure of a good response by approaching members in their constituencies.

A number of groups have no choice in the matter. If a group has no well-organized system of local branches, it is difficult for it to use any method except an approach from national headquarters. Some groups attempt to solve this problem by first

[1] *Lord's Day Magazine*, Jan–Mar. 1952, p. 60.
[2] *National Anti-Vaccination League Annual Report*, 1951, pp. 7–8.
[3] *Land and Liberty*, Nov. and Dec., 1951, p. 94.
[4] Ibid., Mar. 1950, pp. 156–8.
[5] Ibid., Nov. and Dec. 1951, pp. 94–95.

sending out their questionnaires on a national basis and then, in addition, trying to get their questions asked locally. The Lord's Day Observance Society sends out its questions direct, and also endeavours to secure answers by getting supporters (and branches where they exist) in the constituencies to ask questions and report back to the Society. The United Committee for the Taxation of Land Values is in the same position. But those groups which have a fully developed system of branches are in a stronger position. This applies to bodies like the National Federation of Grocers' and Provision Dealers' Associations, N.A.L.G.O., or the groups representing the licensed trade. Some groups do not have a national coverage, representing an interest with a more localized membership. The National Farmers' Union confines its attention to agricultural constituencies. It does not endeavour to learn the opinions of the candidates for Wimbledon or the M.P. for Edinburgh West. The National Chamber of Trade only has member chambers in a limited number of constituencies and outside these no questions are asked on its behalf. These groups realize it would be a waste of effort to do more than this.

To be certain to obtain replies a group has to arrange a deputation. Not all groups are able to do this. Candidates cannot deal with too large a number of deputations, and unless a group can guarantee that a fair proportion will receive its deputations, the method is not of much value. Where, on the other hand, the group represents an important element in most constituencies, the deputation provides a reliable method of approach with the additional advantage of giving the group a chance to pierce through the party-dictated answer.

The National Farmers' Union places its faith in deputations. Since the main object is to assess the candidate's own views on agricultural questions and hence to avoid the party answers, careful preparation is made by the Union. Instructions are sent out from the national headquarters as to the type of questions to be asked. Some attempt is made to keep the nature of the questions secret, but this indicates the real difficulty, since the only way this could be done effectively would be by asking questions about subjects in which the National Farmers' Union is not really interested.

The National Union of Teachers relies on interviews in which its local branches seek answers on certain stated questions. Instructions are sent out by the headquarters as to how the interview should be conducted. In 1951 the state of school buildings, the size of classes, the price of books, equal pay, and pensions policy were the matters upon which the branches sought the views of candidates. A full report was to be sent to headquarters on each interview.

10

It is not always clear what a group hopes to gain from these activities. A general election appears as a glorious opportunity for action to a fiery spirit. It is doubtful whether some groups really consider what they are trying to achieve at elections.

To some the obvious purpose of the questionnaire is to obtain pledges from the candidates. But the mere signing of a pledge does not help the group, as the friendly societies found out.[1] If the group does aim at this, it must secure that the conditions which make the candidate accept the group's viewpoint at the election will continue to influence him when, as an M.P., the issue is placed before him.

Electoral strength might give the group this security were a group able to obtain it, but the party helps to protect the member from this type of pressure. Not merely does it force him to say 'No' to groups, but it prevents the group from gaining electoral strength. The party dominates the electoral scene to such an extent that it is difficult to believe that any limited group issue can deflect many people from their customary voting habits.

In 1951 local Catholic Parents' and Electors' Associations asked most candidates to receive deputations on the question of Catholic schools. This deputation normally included any Catholics who held prominent positions in the life of the constituency. What form the interview took and what use was made of the answer depended on the attitude of the deputation and on the feeling in the constituency. Where the constituency contained a high proportion of Catholics, the deputation sometimes took a strong line. It was common for the candidate's answers to be put in a local paper or announced in church. Advice may sometimes have been given on which of the answers were to be re-

[1] See pp. 111–13.

garded as suitable,[1] but it should hardly have been necessary. Much detailed research in constituencies would have to be done before it could be said that many votes are affected by such activities. Indications seem to be that normally not many are affected. Party issues are more important than the limited church issue. Strong campaigns in 1951 or 1955 on this issue do not seem to have affected many votes in such constituencies as Dagenham, Huyton, or Liverpool (Exchange).

This does not mean that the electoral threat is not operative. What counts is not what happens, but what a candidate believes may happen, and it is unusual to get clear thinking on electoral matters by parliamentary candidates in marginal seats. It seems likely, however, that pressure by Catholics is most effective within the local party, especially in the selection of candidates. (This is a method which few groups can successfully use, since it demands a concentration of power within a constituency.)

The Scottish Covenant Association in 1955 declared its intention of sending a questionnaire to candidates at elections. It intended to give its full support to all candidates giving favourable replies.[2] But most groups are unwilling to venture into this uncertain and dangerous field.

The Lord's Day Observance Society, it is true, encloses with its questionnaire a covering letter which says: 'Your response would give great assistance to many electors in the constituency who prize our Sunday heritage.' But the Society has no effective machinery for informing electors of the answer; it places weight on the campaigns leading up to free votes in the House, regarding this questionnaire as a means of clearing the air. The National Union of Teachers branches inform their members of the result of the deputations, but it is extremely unlikely that votes are influenced thereby.

The questionnaire to most groups is a straight questionnaire. It is designed to find something out, combined with a little gentle propaganda. It gives the group a chance to find out where its support in the House will lie. To the cause group seeking a private members' bill this can be of great importance. To the larger groups anxious to build up favourable political

[1] Cf. Ivor Bulmer-Thomas, *The Party System in Gt. Britain* (1953), p. 254, note 3.
[2] *Scotsman*, 26 Apr. 1955.

opinion it can also be important. Permanent records can be set up as a result of the information obtained. The other motive is propaganda. The questionnaire may force a candidate to consider a question to which he does not normally devote attention. It is doubtful whether this helps the group much, but it does the group good to feel that a candidate is in some sense responsible to it.

With these motives it is not surprising that the questionnaire is generally a very mild document. Examples are to be found in Appendix D.

To the student of pressure groups these questionnaires are important because they indicate something of the attitude of various groups. But their importance on the political scene is not very great. In the end it amounts to this; all these forms of electoral activity can lead to no definite result since they cannot hope to bind an M.P. Nor is the group likely to persuade the M.P. of its point of view, since in an election a candidate is subject to automatic responses; he gives answers not from thought but as a lesson learnt; of all moments it is the one when he is least likely to change his mind.

II

There was once a time when the parties were seriously concerned about the number of questionnaires received by candidates and took measures to limit it. Before the general election of 1929 the three major parties agreed on the following statement:

> It is hereby agreed by the Headquarters of the Conservative, Labour, and Liberal parties that each shall send to all its respective Candidates a letter recommending them to refuse to answer all Questionnaires, received from outside the constituencies they are contesting, at the coming General Election, and also to decline to receive Deputations of persons other than electors in the particular constituencies which they are contesting.[1]

An agreed letter was sent to all candidates which emphasized that the action had been taken in view of the growth of the practice of sending questionnaires from outside the constituencies.

The Times was pleased with this agreement. It noted that:

> There exists in this country a host of organisations for the encouragement or prevention of particular practices which have con-

[1] *Labour Party, National Executive Report*, 1929, p. 10.

tracted the habit of circulating questions to candidates under the threat, sometimes avowed and always implied, that unfavourable answers will earn active opposition; and it is almost invariably added that silence will be interpreted as dissent. It is no reflection whatever upon the objects of such organisations to say that this habit is altogether unwholesome.[1]

The Times feared that M.P.s would be bound and circumscribed by election pledges, but that should have led it to attack the agreement as a poor remedy, since it allowed constituency questionnaires, only attacking national ones.

The national questionnaire has survived the attack made upon it although some of the aspects to which *The Times* objected have become less prominent. Party headquarters still advise candidates against answering national questionnaires, but since 1929 no joint action has been taken. There is no real difference between the national and the local questionnaire. The national questionnaire does not necessarily mean that the group which issues it lacks members in the constituencies; it may only mean it does not possess well-developed local branch organizations. But it is probably felt that any reduction in the number of questionnaires to be answered saves the candidate trouble and that it is easier to justify leaving the national questionnaire unanswered.

12

It would be unwise to attack as improper or undesirable any of the tactics discussed in this chapter. They may not always be very effective in achieving the group's aims—indeed, for most groups the only really useful weapon is the letter to the M.P. from its branch or its members within the constituency. But that is a matter for the group to decide. These weapons provide the group with its means of appeal. Without them it would be more dependent on the government than seems desirable. It may be that many of these methods do not seem very elegant and that they would have no place in an ideal political system. But in the present system they provide many groups with their means of campaign which is the safeguard of their position. They are part of the communication of our society and as such valuable and important, even though at times distasteful.

[1] *The Times*, 2 May 1929.

CHAPTER X

Conclusions

I

THERE are a few people who wish to dismiss pressure groups out of hand as bad in themselves. That, however, is unrealistic, for whenever society has developed to that degree of complexity that makes groups of people conscious of sectional needs, pressure groups exist. But criticism of the part pressure groups play in political systems has normally been directed at their influence. The custom has been to assert that groups have too much influence rather than too little—to attempt to build barricades against their further growth rather than to ease their path. But if it is possible to assert that groups have too much influence, there is presumably some level below which it would be unfortunate if the influence of groups were to fall.

It is not easy to place an exact meaning on the term 'group influence'. Since groups compete against each other, it is clearly not a conception which can be reached by adding up the totals of group achievement. The failure of a trade union to secure an act limiting the working day is balanced by the success of an employers' association in its efforts to prevent this.

The use of the term 'group influence' and the assumption that in some political systems it is greater than in others, rests upon the premiss that there are other elements in the process of decision-making. Group influence is high when all that is involved in a decision by the governmental process is a trial of strength between groups.

There are many elements that can enter into the process o decision-making—the members of the legislature, the party, the government as the party in action, and the government as the continuing executive of the state. Where these or any one of them form decisions without considering the representations or activities of the groups, then group influence is low.

For any one decision it is difficult, if not impossible, to say what are the important elements. It is often possible to identify that part of the process of government which formally took the decision, but not to single out the factors which led to that decision being taken.

If it is impossible to make a final analysis of any individual decision, it is not necessarily impossible to say of a political system that group influence is high or low. The activities of the groups themselves, the particular institutional structure, and the cumulative effect of many decisions, enable the tendency of the system to be seen and make probable what on one decision must remain only a possibility. In analysing a political system it is possible to show at what points group activity is directed, and the extent to which those points have the resources and the authority to resist group influence.

An individual member of a legislature, unprotected by party discipline, is not likely to have much authority to resist the influence of pressure groups, although he may have the resources to do so.

A political party, purely concerned to obtain power, lacks the resources to resist pressure groups even though it may have the authority to do so.

Authority is dependent upon the power for independent action possessed by the person or institution, resources upon their willingness and their ability to evolve their own standards and policies.

It would be foolish to attempt to define an optimum level of group influence. Yet there are certain situations which I suggest should be regarded as dangerous. A system which does not give to the government the resources from which to come to a decision on group demands and the authority to enforce it, is dangerous because it is turning the process of decision-making into a struggle between pressure groups, the result of which does not derive from clear judgement upon their demands. A positive outlook is required from within the process of government. It is desirable that in making decisions upon group representations, there be brought into play considerations deriving from a wider view of the political scene than is possible to individual groups. There will never be agreement on what is the national interest, but that there are interests other than those closely concerned in an issue is generally agreed. A group exists to express the views of those closely concerned. But in any decision all are concerned, however remotely.

On the other hand, a system of government which did not recognize the part that groups have to play would be equally dangerous. The views of those closely concerned should play an important part in any decision that is taken. Any difficulty a group finds in expressing these views or bringing them to the attention of the government blocks up the channels of communication upon which the government if it is responsive to opinion, must depend. Though the government should always feel itself able to overrule the groups, a system in which the government overrules an opinion passionately held by a group, without backing from the rest of society, is lacking in tolerance. The group should always be able to appeal from such intolerance.

A balance is required and each system has its own problems in arriving at it.

2

The British system of government might appear to have found a satisfactory balance. In one sense it has. The basic point of decision upon a group's demand is the government, which gains authority both from its position as the party in action and from the power and knowledge that has been built up in the ministries.

The power of the party rests upon so much wider a basis than that of any one group, that the support of that group is not vital to it. It is able to appeal to people beyond the interests into which they divide their lives and to obtain from them a loyalty which gives it strength to challenge the groups.

The party has the authority to resist the group. But it also appears to have the resources. If the only object of the party were to gain power, then it would merely need to act as a broker between competing groups. If, however, the party seeks to gain power for a purpose then it has the resources as well as the authority to resist the groups. Party policies may themselves have been modified by groups, but at the moment of decision they belong to the party. The virtue of a party decision as opposed to a group decision is that the party, in making its decision, can be assumed to have considered more factors than the group. It derives from a view of society, not merely from the view of a group in society.

The ministries also have authority, apart from the party. They can use party discipline even without party theory. In the departments a wealth of knowledge has been built up which should ensure that the government brings to the groups' representations a positive attitude. In the machinery of government there is the means to relate each department's problems to wider issues.

The government has the authority and resources to challenge the groups.

Lest it be thought that the groups are placed in too weak a situation, it should be remembered that the system provides safeguards. Groups have ample opportunity to make their views known. The machinery of consultation is particularly well developed, despite occasional defects. The place of most groups is recognized. Their representatives sit upon government committees. There are long and healthy discussions between groups and government.

There are further safeguards should the groups be treated unfairly. The government accepts the appeal to Parliament or to public opinion in that a decision may be modified in the light of the group's impact there.

3

Along these lines runs the theoretical justification of the position of pressure groups in the British system of government. There are, however, indications that there are certain dangers, and that the system may not be working as well as this analysis makes out.

Over a large field of political activity there is no party viewpoint. This may be inevitable, since many of the problems are essentially group problems.

Professor S. H. Beer has suggested that there has been a weakening in the philosophies of the parties which tends to give more influence to pressure groups:

> From this tactic and these shaping forces results not a politics of class or of social philosophy, but a kind of pressure politics. The term is inexact as applied to British politics if it is suggested that policy is made simply by groups pushing an inert government or

party this way and that, for it is often the government or party which in the competition for electoral support teaches the group what its rights and interests are and excites it to demand them.[1]

An analysis of the 1955 Labour Party election manifesto might seem to give some justification to this point of view. But it is not necessary to accept his full criticism to see that the party does not always bring a positive outlook to pressure group demands. This may not be due to a change in the nature of the party so much as a change in the nature of the problem. The growth of group issues in politics may have overwhelmed the party.

An added burden is thrown upon the ministers and ministries who are expected to evolve their own standards to judge upon and between the representations of pressure groups. Their authority remains unimpaired, but that they have the resources to achieve this without the aid of party standards is doubtful. They are expected to judge every issue empirically, or, if it is preferred, upon its merits. The result of the empirical approach to politics depends upon the attitude with which one starts. To judge a question on its merits depends upon one's conception of merit.

In forming this attitude and this conception the most potent influences outside the department are the groups, and on many issues they are the only outside influences there are. In many cases there will be one or two groups only. For the system tends to give weight to a few dominant groups.

The minister or ministry with which the group is concerned is likely to develop an attitude that is largely sectional. It would be a strange Ministry of Agriculture that did not try and do its best for agriculture and it is only too easy to drift into the attitude of thinking the best for agriculture to be what the farmers through the N.F.U. consider it to be. In any ministry the thoughts and arguments that are heard from outside sources come largely from pressure groups. Civil servants and politicians whose daily routine involves contact with the groups, hearing their viewpoints and their problems, obtaining information from them and co-operating with them on committees, may come to accept the standards of the group as their own. There is a danger that

[1] S. H. Beer, 'The Future of British Politics,' *Political Quarterly*, vol. xxvi, No. 1, pp. 38–39.

departments may become mere pressure groups within the government.

It is probably too much to expect civil servants or even ministers always to impose a mental control on the representations of groups in an attempt to weigh these views against some conception of the national interest. What is necessary is that there be acceptable ideas besides those of groups in the fields in which there are no party views. The contribution that an individual group can make could be rendered more valuable by a challenge. The construction of a ministry will determine the extent to which the views of a group are challenged by other groups. But group battles are not the only thing needed to prevent the Minister of Agriculture from being merely a Minister for Agriculture.

The *Manchester Guardian* has written of the discussion on local government reform:

> It is of course right and proper that the Minister should consult such bodies in advance and that in formulating his own proposals he should bear in mind the divergencies of views between them. But it would be a gross dereliction of duty on his part to leave all initiative to them, to accord them a right of veto or to use their constitutional inability to compose their differences as an excuse for government inaction. For in this matter the local authority associations do not represent the wishes of local electors or the interests of local government; they stand for nothing but the defence and promotion of the particular forms of local authority, whose obsolescence has made reform so urgently necessary.[1]

It is not necessary to accept the full censures of the *Manchester Guardian* on these associations to see the point it is making. There are other views on local government, besides those of the associations, besides those of local authorities. There is a danger that close contact with these associations may make a department place too much importance on their views. It is from this attitude that any possible veto from an association derives its force. Where the groups with which a ministry is closely concerned are divided in opinion, the ministry is very reluctant to act.

The problem of finding the national interest cannot be solved by a minister concerning himself with an abstract ideal. There

[1] *Manchester Guardian*, 2 Mar. 1955.

can be no agreed national interest. But there can be a viewpoint derived from other considerations than those advanced by the groups closely concerned in the problem.

The clash between the sectional and the national interest of which theorists talk is difficult to grasp. The sectional interest, as represented by the group, is clear; the national interest is not. But the impossibility of establishing the national interest does not absolve the government from its task. Two things at least are required of it. These are to try to find out whether there are other viewpoints on an issue besides those of the groups immediately concerned, and to attempt to evolve other criteria of judgement than the ones they advance. The government is given by our political system the authority to impose its conceptions of national interest. What the system cannot give is the initiative to do so.

4

These are the dangers that exist in our system of government. It is well to be aware of them. Such awareness is in itself an important factor in meeting the dangers. However, they should not cloud our judgement of the value of pressure groups in our present system of government. Consideration of these dangers may modify the justification of the pressure group's role given earlier in this chapter, but will not destroy it. They are dangers that must be guarded against, but we should be exaggerating their importance if we were to proceed from that to a wholesale condemnation of the part pressure groups play in our system, which, as has been shown, is often a valuable one.

Pressure groups are necessary to the government of our complex society. The coherent expression of opinion they render possible is vital. They have become a fifth estate, the means by which many individuals contribute to politics. Without them discontent would grow and knowledge be lost. It is important that the system of government be such that their role can be carried out with responsibility.

APPENDIX A

Notes on Sources

1. A small selection is given of American works which are useful guides to theories of pressure groups and methods of research:

A. F. BENTLEY, *The Process of Government: a Study of Social Pressure* (1908).

D. C. BLAISDELL, *Economic Power and Political Pressures*, Temporary National Economic Committee, 1941, Monograph No. 26.

STUART CHASE, *Democracy under Pressure* (1945).

K. G. CRAWFORD, *The Pressure Boys* (1939).

M. E. DILLON, 'Pressure Groups', *American Political Science Review*, June 1942, pp. 471–81.

E. PENDLETON HERRING, *Group Representation before Congress* (1929).

V. O. KEY, *Politics, Parties and Pressure Groups* (1953, 3rd ed.).

D. B. TRUMAN, *The Governmental Process* (1951).

2. The pressure group in Britain has not got a substantial literature. The writer who has given most attention to the subject is Sir Ivor Jennings. In *Parliament* he touches upon the subject very frequently, and though far from giving a comprehensive survey, is suggestive both as to ideas and methods of research. For the most part other writers have touched upon the subject indirectly. A list of some of the more important references is given:

S. H. BEER, 'Pressure Groups and Parties in Britain', *American Political Science Review*, Mar. 1956, pp. 1–23.

R. A. BRADY, *Business as a System of Power* (1944), chapter v.

IVOR BULMER-THOMAS, *The Party System in Great Britain* (1953), chapter xviii.

A. M. CARR-SAUNDERS and P. A. WILSON, *The Professions* (1933).

H. FINER, *Representative Government and a Parliament of Industry* (1923), chapter i.

—— *The Theory and Practice of Modern Government* (1954, British ed.), pp. 463–6.

S. E. FINER, 'The Federation of British Industries,' *Political Studies*, Feb. 1956, pp. 61–84.

—— 'The Political Power of Private Capital', *Sociological Review*, Dec. 1955, pp. 279–94 and July 1956, pp. 5–28.

W. IVOR JENNINGS, *Parliament* (1939), especially chapter vii.
F. M. MARX, (ed.) *Foreign Governments* (1949), pp. 71–76.
W. J. M. MACKENZIE, 'Pressure Groups—The "Conceptual Framework"', *Political Studies*, Oct. 1955, pp. 247–55.
—— 'Pressure Groups in British Government', *British Journal of Sociology*, June 1955, pp. 133–40.
RAMSAY MUIR, *How Britain is Governed* (1930), pp. 304–9.
H. G. NICHOLAS, *The British General Election of 1950* (1951), pp. 71–79 and 246–8.
P.E.P., *Government and Industry* (1952), especially chapter vi.
—— *Industrial Trade Associations* (1957), especially chapter iii.
ALLEN POTTER, 'The Equal Pay Campaign Committee', *Political Studies*, Feb. 1957, pp. 49–64.
SIDNEY and BEATRICE WEBB, *Industrial Democracy* (1897), Part II, chapter iv.
K. C. WHEARE, *Government by Committee* (1955).
H. H. WILSON, 'Techniques of Pressure', *Public Opinion Quarterly* (1951), pp. 225–42.

3. A number of works have been published giving details of individual groups. Often these have concentrated on other than pressure activities, but nevertheless some are useful. Only a selection is given below. The number of books about trade unions is, for example, far greater, but most throw little light on these points.

R. P. ARNOT, *The Miners* (1949 and 1953).
ASSOCIATION OF CERTIFIED AND CORPORATE ACCOUNTANTS, *Fifty Years* (1954).
A. J. BELFORD, *Centenary Handbook of the Educational Institute of Scotland* (1946).
H. A. CLEGG, *General Union* (1954).
G. D. H. COLE, *A Century of Co-operation* (1945).
R. EVANS, *An Account of the Scapa Society* (1926).
LORD EVERSLEY, *Commons, Open Spaces and Footpaths* (revised edn., 1910)
E. HOWE, *The British Federation of Master Printers* (1950).
W. A. LEE, *Thirty Years in Coal* (1954).
M. H. C. HAYLER, *The Vision of a Century* (1953).
B. NEWMAN, *Yours for Action* (1953).
L. H. POWELL, *Shipping Federation* (1950).
UNITED COMMERCIAL TRAVELLERS' ASSOCIATION, *Seventy Years* (1953).
G. WOOTTON, *The History of the British Legion* (1956).

4. Very helpful in research in this field are those directories which publish lists of groups. The following are worthy of mention:

Charities Register for many cause groups.

Directory of Employers Associations, Trade Unions, Trade Organizations, &c. (H.M.S.O.)

The London Telephone Directory.

The Manufacturers Manual (National Union of Manufacturers) and the *F.B.I. Register* for lists of trade associations in membership.

Whitaker's Almanack and *The Municipal Yearbook* for useful general lists.

Any trade directory gives a full list of groups associated with that trade.

5. The main material for this thesis has come from trade and group journals, group reports, and group statements. There is no value in giving a list of journals used. These can be seen in the footnotes. Besides, a person's needs in these matters will vary with the groups he wishes to study. It may, however, be useful to say something of the availability of this material, its value, and its character.

A wide variety of trade journals and directories are taken by every large public library in Great Britain. This is particularly true of those libraries which have commercial branches. It is not possible for such libraries to file many of the journals or even the directories. So though a passing picture may be gained of part of the pressure group world, no thorough research can be done in these libraries.

One is therefore thrown back upon the resources of the major research libraries. All of these stock a large number of trade journals and like material. The position as regards annual reports is less satisfactory. The situation is not entirely in the libraries' hands. This material is not always published. Nevertheless, most groups have no objection to research being done on their annual reports. Further, these libraries do possess a number of annual reports. Its seems possible that if positive approaches were made to most groups these collections could be extended.

This material is designed primarily for the membership of the various groups. This is true not merely of group publications, but of trade journals which have no official connexions with a group. These journals are generally linked with one or two groups in the sense that they devote special attention to their activities. All this material reflects the needs of the group members. The members of a group are more likely to be interested in what it is trying to do than how it is trying to do it. There is, therefore, usually no difficulty in establishing what is the group's official attitude to government proposals and what its own policy is. The methods it pursues as a result of these attitudes are often dealt with in passing references.

Annual reports vary from group to group. In few, if any, is there any attempt to hide group activities. There is no reason why there should be. It is merely that some do not feel it necessary to go into great detail. 'The Association's representatives discussed these points with Ministry officials' or 'The Union sought to have the Bill amended' is enough for them. On the other hand, the annual report of a group like N.A.L.G.O. describes in great detail its negotiations with the ministries and its actions in Parliament, giving full particulars of amendments proposed and measures taken to support them. Cause groups are generally fairly expansive. By contrast with other groups their main, sometimes their only, function is likely to be pressure activities, and it is upon these that they must sell themselves to their members.

Some journals are particularly valuable. They contain reports of monthly or even quarterly meetings of the group's executive council or its equivalent. Even these can vary greatly in character. Some of the local government associations publish supplements to their journals. These give very full details of executive meetings. Professional journals are often helpful in this way. On the other hand, the reports of the Brewers' Society published in the *Brewers' Journal* are very slight.

Even where this type of report is not given, the journal may be quite useful in describing incidental activities or conveying trade opinions. Most journals will carry full reports of group annual general meetings and these can give useful information, particularly when there is a large membership and the executive is liable to come in for criticism.

There are occasions when most groups become very expansive about their activities, in journals, annual reports, or public statements. If anything goes wrong, if the group encounters great difficulties, above all if it needs to campaign, it will want to explain its position not merely to its members but often to the public and to M.P.s. Full statements about any negotiations with the minister concerned will then be made. Full details of the campaign will be printed, because in these circumstances the members do want to know what measures the group is taking. Besides their co-operation will be required and instructions and requests are likely to appear in trade journals—as when the *Wine and Spirit Trade Record* printed a list supplied by the Wine and Spirit Association giving the names of all members of the Standing Committee on the Licensing Bill. Readers were expected to write to them (see p. 102).

Even where material seems slight, much can often be learnt of group attitudes. But there is no need to worry about the gaps in our material. A great store exists. Until it has been worked through there is no problem. Even then it seems likely that group co-operation will be available to help the researcher.

6. The groups play an important part in our political life and it is only fitting that there should be many references to them in the press and in government publications. Both provide useful supplements to the main material.

The Times and the *Manchester Guardian* give fairly full reports of group activities. In particular annual general meetings are likely to be reported and details of campaigns given.

As regards government publications, the *Report of the Committee on Intermediaries* (Cmd. 7904) clearly stands on its own. Apart from that, departmental reports, evidence before committees, and *Hansard* are extremely useful in following up points noted from other material.

APPENDIX B

Group Representation in the House of Commons of 1951–5

1. The following list has been compiled to illustrate the extent to which groups can be represented in the House of Commons. It is a list of M.P.s who had official or recognized connexions with groups at some point during the Parliament of 1951–5. This list is far from complete. There are many groups unrecorded and possibly the groups recorded had M.P.s connected with them who are not listed. For the most part it does not include M.P.s who are on informal parliamentary panels. Nevertheless, it will serve to illustrate the points made in Chapter VIII as to the importance of group representation.

2. In some cases it may be that the M.P. took no action on behalf of the group. Nothing is here stated which implies that because his name is on the list he must have so acted.

3. The list is based upon the House of Commons as elected on 25 October 1951. In a few cases a later date has been used, either because it was not possible to use the earlier date or to illustrate a relationship that developed later. If no date is stated then it must be understood that the M.P. was connected with the group at the time of the election.

4. Sponsored M.P.s are marked with the reference number 1, permanent officials (other than sponsored M.P.s) with 2, and those who had no designation in regard to the group but were recognized as supporters are marked 3. The remainder held some honorary position in the group, elected, co-opted, or appointed. It has not proved possible to subdivide these.

5. The list has been compiled from various sources, of which the most important have been *The Times House of Commons*, 1951, and the *Labour Party Annual Conference Report*, 1951. In addition annual reports, directories, trade journals, and *Hansard* have supplied a few names for the list.

6. Where the group had over thirty representatives in the House, it was felt it would be burdensome to list them. The fact has merely been noted.

7. The Co-operative Party M.P.s have been classed as sponsored

M.P.s of the Co-operative Union; though not quite accurate, it is a rough approximation.

Groups	*Year if not 1951*	*Member of Parliament*	*Reference number*
Amalgamated Engineering Union		A. H. Albu	1
		W. H. Ayles	1
		C. R. Bence	1
		C. R. Hobson	1
		F. Lee	1
		T. C. Pannell	1
		G. A. Pargiter	1
Amalgamated Society of Woodworkers		A. S. Moody	1
		G. Porter	1
		S. P. Viant	1
Associated Society of Locomotive Engineers and Firemen		P. H. Collick	1
		W. Monslow	1
Association of British Chambers of Commerce		J. J. Astor	
		F. J. Erroll	
		Sir Arnold Gridley	
		Sir Walter Smiles	
		W. J. Taylor	
Association of Drainage Authorities		E. A. H. Legge-Bourke	
Association of Health and Pleasure Resorts		J. R. Robinson	
Association of Municipal Corporations		H. W. Butcher	
		H. Butler	
		W. J. Field	
		D. R. Grenfell	
		G. Hutchinson	
		D. T. Jones	
		H. V. A. M. Raikes	
		H. Thorneycroft	
Association of Supervisory Staffs, Executives, and Technicians		I. Mikardo	
Automobile Association		D. L.-M. Renton	
Baptist Union		C. W. Black	
		C. Kenyon	
Board of Deputies of British Jews		B. Janner	
Brewers' Society		P. F. Remnant	
British Commonwealth Producers' Association		A. D. Dodds-Parker	
British Field Sports Society		J. G. Morrison	
		R. S. Clarke	
British Hotels' and Restaurants' Association		C. S. Taylor	

Groups	*Year if not 1951*	*Member of Parliament*	*Reference number*
British Iron and Steel Federation		A. Jones	2
		W. Robson-Brown	
British Iron, Steel, and Kindred Trades Association		J. H. Jones	1
		D. L. Mort	1
British Federation of Master Printers		M. S. McCorquodale	
British Legion		Sir Ian Fraser	
British Limbless Ex-Service Men's Association		R. F. Wood	
British Social Biology Council		H. N. Linstead	
British Union for the Abolition of Vivisection		Sir William Darling	3
		R. Ewart	3
		P. Freeman	3
		J. Harrison	3
		E. Hughes	3
		F. Longden	3
		P. L. E. Shurmer	3
		R. J. Taylor	3
		E. Thurtle	3
		S. P. Viant	3
British Waterworks' Association		G. Hutchinson	
Building Societies' Association		W. G. Hall	
		E. H. Keeling	
		J. R. Robinson	
		C. S. Taylor	
Caterers' Association		W. A. Steward	
Chamber of Shipping		J. S. Maclay	
		L. Ropner	
Church of England		Sir Richard Acland	
		T. E. N. Driberg	
		E. G. M. Fletcher	
		L. W. Joynson-Hicks	
		G. Nicholson	
		M. Stoddart-Scott	
Clerical and Administrative Workers' Union		F. W. Mulley	1
Cold Rolled Brass and Copper Association		J. Grimston	
Congregational Union		D. W. Wade	
Co-operative Union		A. Barnes	1
		F. Beswick	1
		W. Coldrick	1
		P. Daines	1
		G. Darling	1
		N. N. Dodds	1

Groups	Year if not 1951	Member of Parliament	Reference number
Co-operative Union (*cont.*)		J. C. Forman	1
		P. Holman	1
		W. J. Irving	1
		F. Messer	1
		W. Nally	1
		J. Rankin	1
		P. L. E. Shurmer	1
		H. N. Smith	1
		W. T. Williams	1
Council for the Preservation of Rural England		E. H. Keeling	
Country Landowners' Association		R. H. Turton	
		W. M. F. Vane	
		C. York	
County Councils' Association		E. G. Gooch	
		G. A. Pargiter	
Cremation Society		J. Reeves	
Dock and Harbour Authorities' Association		J. R. H. Hutchison	
Electrical Power Engineers' Association	1953	A. M. F. Palmer	2
Electrical Trades Union		T. F. Cook	1
Employers Federation of Cane and Willow Workers' Associations	1954	V. J. Collins	
Engineer Buyers' and Representatives' Association		Sir Herbert Williams	
Federation of British Industries		Sir Peter Bennett	
Federation of Master Cotton Spinners' Associations		W. Schofield	
Federation of Umbrella Manufacturers	1953	Sir John Barlow	
Hire Purchase Trade Association	1955	Sir Harold Webbe	
Howard League for Penal Reform		G. Benson	
		C. L. Hale	
		J. Paton	
Incorporated Association of Preparatory Schools		H. Brooke	
Inland Revenue Staff Federation		A. L. N. D. Houghton	2
Law Society		D. Kaberry	
Machinery Users' Association		Sir Herbert Williams	
Magistrates' Association		C. Royle	
Master Ladies' Tailors' Organization	1954	W. J. Owen	2

Groups	Year if not 1951	Member of Parliament	Reference number
Methodist Church		F. Medlicott R. Richards G. Thomas	
Motor Factors' Association	1954	C. Banks	
National and Local Government Officers' Association		G. Hutchinson	3
National Anti-Vaccination League		S. P Viant	3
National Association for the Prevention of Tuberculosis		W. Elliot Sir Austin Hudson Anthony Greenwood F. Messer J. E. Powell	
National Association of Fire Officers		R. R. Harris	2
National Association of Parish Councils	1954	R. Fort G. O. Roberts	
National Association of Theatre and Kine Employees		T. O'Brien	2
National Chamber of Trade		See Note 6	
National Federation of Meat Traders' Associations	1953	H. R. Spence	
National Federation of Retail Newsagents, Booksellers, and Stationers	1953	G. H. Oliver	3
National Smoke Abatement Society		E. H. Keeling	
National Society for the Prevention of Cruelty to Children		W. G. Hall P. G. Roberts	
National Society of Operative Printers and Assistants		G. Isaacs	
National Temperance Federation		S. Hastings J. H. Hudson	
National Tyre Distributors' Association	 1954	R. R. Harris C. Banks	2
National Union of Agricultural Workers		E. G. Gooch	1
National Union of Boot and Shoe Operatives		A. C. Allen	1
National Union of General and Municipal Workers		J. T. Hall M. Hewitson C. J. Simmons O. G. Willey	1 1 1 1
National Union of Manufacturers		W. Robson-Brown G. D. N. Nabarro G. W. Odey	

Groups	*Year if not 1951*	*Member of Parliament*	*Reference number*
National Union of Manufacturers (*cont.*)		Sir Wavell Wakefield	
National Union of Mineworkers		See Note 6	
National Union of Public Employees		A. G. Bottomley	1
		A. Moyle	1
National Union of Railwaymen		A. J. Champion	1
		J. Harrison	1
		D. T. Jones	1
		C. C. Poole	1
		E. Popplewell	1
		W. T. Proctor	1
		J. A. Sparks	1
		I. O. Thomas	1
National Union of Teachers		W. G. Cove	1
		J. C. Ede	1
		R. Morley	1
		G. Thomas	1
Navy League		R. E. D. Ryder	
Periodical Proprietors' Association		Sir Austin Hudson	
Pharmaceutical Society		H. N. Linstead	2
Poultry Association		R. De La Bére	
		R. J. G. Boothby	
		E. R. Bowen	
		C. Kenyon	
		A. Moyle	
		G. D. N. Nabarro	
		J. P. L. Thomas	
River Boards' Association	1953	Sir John Barlow	
		A. C. Bossom	
		W. N. Cuthbert	
		G. R. Mitchison	
		F. Medlicott	
		M. P. Price	
		D. F. Vosper	
		C. York	
Royal College of Veterinary Surgeons		P. H. Collick	
		J. Henderson Stewart	
Royal Society for the Prevention of Cruelty to Animals		R. De La Bére	
		P. Freeman	
		Anthony Greenwood	
		J. C. Lockwood	
		Sir Thomas Moore	
Rural District Councils' Association		H. W. Butcher	
		A. Colegate	
		A. T. Lennox-Boyd	

Groups	Year if not 1951	Member of Parliament	Reference number
Rural District Councils' Association (*cont.*)		P. F. Maitland	
		R. E. Manningham-Buller	
		F. Medlicott	
		C. E. Mott-Radclyffe	
		H. Nicholls	
		I. L. Orr-Ewing	
		A. Pearson	
		R. H. Turton	
		C. Waterhouse	
		H. White	
		T. Williams	
		G. W. Williams	
Society of Motor Manufacturers and Traders		Sir Peter Bennett	
Sunday Freedom Association		J. Parker	
Transport Salaried Staffs' Association		A. E. Davies	1
		A. Hargreaves	1
		H. Hynd	1
		G. S. Lindgren	1
		P. Morris	1
		G. H. R. Rogers	1
		T. Steele	1
Transport and General Workers' Union		S. S. Awbery	1
		G. A. Brown	1
		G. Deer	1
		W. J. Edwards	1
		C. W. Gibson	1
		W. Keenan	1
		C. W. Key	1
		G. Jeger	1
		F. McLeavy	1
		R. J. Mellish	1
		G. H. Oliver	1
		T. Oswald	1
		J. Paton	1
		P. Wells	1
Trustee Savings Banks' Association	1954	F. J. Erroll	
		J. H. Hoy	
Typographical Association		W. A. Wilkins	1
Union of Post Office Workers		H. W. Wallace	1
		W. R. Williams	1
Union of Shop, Distributive, and Allied Workers		H. Boardman	1
		W. A. Burke	1
		G. Craddock	1
		E. Fernyhough	1

Groups	Year if not 1951	Member of Parliament	Reference number
Union of Shop, Distributive, and Allied Workers (*cont.*)		W. E. Padley	1
		J. T. Price	1
		A. Robens	1
		R. E. Winterbottom	1
United Kingdom Pilots' Association		Sir Peter Macdonald	
United Patternmakers' Association		E. Smith	1
United Tanners' Federation		G. W. Odey	
United Textile Factory Workers' Association		G. Tomlinson	1
Urban District Councils' Association		F. J. Erroll	
		R. V. Grimston	
		D. Griffiths	
		Viscount Hinchingbrooke	
		G. S. Lindgren	
		J. S. B. Lloyd	
		W. H. Mainwaring	
		J. F. W. Maitland	
		G. R. Mitchison	
		L. Ropner	
		G. Tomlinson	
		D. C. Walker-Smith	
		T. Williams	
Water Companies' Association	1955	D. C. Walker-Smith	

APPENDIX C

Additional Agreement made between W. J. Brown and the Civil Service Clerical Association, 1943

ADDENDUM

WHEREAS the Executive Committee duly appointed for the time being has by resolution duly passed appointed *WILLIAM JOHN BROWN* to be Parliamentary General Secretary of the Association instead of General Secretary as expressed in the Principal Agreement dated the Twenty-seventh day of September one thousand nine hundred and twenty-three.

NOW IT IS HEREBY AGREED between the Executive Committee for the time being and the said William John Brown that the Principal Agreement shall be and is hereby varied as follows:

1. THE said William John Brown shall be relieved of his duties as General Secretary of the Association and shall be given the title of Parliamentary General Secretary of the Association.
2. THE said William John Brown shall receive in addition to the salary of One Thousand pounds per annum as provided in the Addendum dated the First day of December one thousand nine hundred and thirty-five a sum of Two hundred and Fifty pounds per annum in respect of travelling and subsistence expenses; such allowance of Two hundred and Fifty pounds shall for the purposes of calculating the superannuation only be considered part of his salary.
3. THE said William John Brown shall be entitled to engage in his political activities with complete freedom.
4. THE said William John Brown shall deal with all questions arising in the work of the Association which requires parliamentary or political action and shall advise the Association from time to time on such matters. The said William John Brown shall further confer and consult with the Association on all problems requiring his assistance and advice thereon if and when so required by the Association.
5. THE said William John Brown shall hold the appointment of Parliamentary General Secretary for so long as he shall remain a member of the House of Commons and so long beyond this period as his Executive Committee of the Association shall

decide in general meeting and at the termination of the Parliamentary General Secretaryship, the said William John Brown if he so desires shall be entitled to resume the appointment of General Secretary.

6. NOTHING herein contained shall entitle the said William John Brown in his political and parliamentary activities to purport to represent the political views of the Association (if any) and shall only represent the Association in so far as Civil Service questions are concerned.
7. IT is agreed between the parties that the terms of this Addendum shall be retrospective and shall be deemed to operate as from the First day of June One thousand nine hundred and forty-two.
8. SUBJECT to the above terms of the Principal Agreement dated the Twenty-seventh day of September One thousand nine hundred and twenty-three and the Addendum endorsed thereon shall so far as they are applicable and so long as they are not inconsistent with the provisions of this Addendum remain in full force and effect until such time as a new agreement is entered into between the Executive Committee or the duly appointed Trustees on behalf of the Executive Committee and the said William John Brown.

(H.C. 118 of 1946–7, pp. 59–60)

APPENDIX D

Questionnaires (1951 Election)

A. *Lord's Day Observance Society*

Dear Sir,

May we respectfully ask the favour of your answer to the question on the enclosed Paper?

Your response would give great assistance to many electors in the constituency who prize our Sunday heritage.

A business reply-envelope is enclosed.

Yours faithfully,
H. H. MARTIN,
Secretary

Question:

Will you if elected uphold the present Law and oppose any Bill which would make legal the Opening of Theatres and Music Halls for Performances on Sundays?

B. *League Against Cruel Sports*

Dear Sir,

We should be grateful for your replies in the following matters:

(*a*) Will you, if elected, support any Bill to prohibit or restrict the cruel sports of deer hunting, fox hunting, hare hunting, otter hunting, badger digging, rabbit and hare coursing, or any one or more of them?

(*b*) Will you, if elected, be prepared to support legislation to give the enclosed Code of Conduct for hunting statutory effect?

A stamped postcard is enclosed for your reply.

Yours faithfully,
J. C. SHARP,
Secretary

C. *The Officers' Pensions Society*

Dear Sir,

The Officers' Pensions Society exists for the sole purpose of holding a watching brief on the question of pensions of Retired Officers of the three Services and of their widows.

The main objects of the Society are as follows:

(i) To press on the Government the principle that whenever a new Pension Code for retired Officers is introduced, such new code should apply to ALL retired Officers, from the date of its inception, irrespective of the date of an Officer's retirement.

(ii) To press on Government (*a*) the need for an immediate review of Pensions for the widows of Officers who die under peace conditions, (*b*) the grant of an educational allowance for young children of such widows, and (*c*) the abolition of the Means Test on Widows' pensions.

The Society would be glad to hear that you are in sympathy with these views; and that, if elected to Parliament, you will support the Society whenever such matters are brought forward in Parliament.

(*signed*) H. DIGBY BESTE,
(*Chairman*)

D. *National Association of Women Civil Servants*

Dear Sir or Madam,

EQUAL PAY FOR EQUAL WORK

This Association, which has been working for women Civil Servants since the year 1901, when it was founded in the Post Office, is extremely anxious to see its major aim—equal pay for equal work—realized at the earliest possible moment.

Equal Pay for women in the Civil Service is not a matter for arbitration or negotiation. It depends on the decision of Parliament. Although the House of Commons has repeatedly expressed its approval, and the recent Government has 'accepted the principle', equal pay has not been given effect.

May we have your assurance that if you are elected to the House of Commons on 25th October, you will actively press for the implementation of the principle of equal pay for equal work?

Yours truly,
H. C. HART,
General Secretary

E. *United Committee for the Taxation of Land Values*

GENERAL ELECTION, 1951

QUESTIONNAIRE submitted to Parliamentary Candidates by the United Committee for the Taxation of Land Values, Ltd., 4 Great Smith Street, London, S.W. 1. For return, neither envelope nor stamp is needed. Fold the paper as indicated and tuck in so that the Committee's name and address stands clear.

(*A Copy of the Candidate's Election Address will also be greatly appreciated.*)

QUESTIONS.	REPLIES.*
1. Do you accept the argument that the value attaching to any land, as distinct from the buildings or other improvements thereon, is due to its situation and other natural advantages and that this land value rightfully belongs to the community?	1. ....
2. Do you agree that the value of land, apart from buildings and improvements, should be appropriated as public revenue before any tax is imposed on the work of man's hands?	2. ....
3. Will you urge that the next Finance Act provides for the levy of an annual tax at a uniform rate per pound on the actual market value of all land whether used or not, the revenue so derived being used to reduce or remit taxes upon wages, buildings, industry and trade?	3. ....
4. Will you promote legislation whereby local rates shall be levied on land values, exempting houses, shops and other buildings and improvements?	4. ....
5. Do you stand for the repeal of the Derating Acts by which at present industrial premises pay only one-quarter rates, and agricultural land, however valuable, is virtually exempt, whereas householders, shopkeepers and other occupiers are heavily burdened?	5. ....
6. Do you agree that the assessments of rateable values now being made under the Local Government Act, 1948, are absurd, inequitable and in fact unworkable, and should be abandoned forthwith?	6. ....
7. Will you press for the immediate abolition of the development charges exacted under the Town and Country Planning Act, 1947, and the consequent repeal of the financial and State monopoly provisions connected therewith?	7. ....
8. Do you advocate the removal of protectionist tariffs and the establishment of Free Trade for British imports whatever may be the fiscal policies of other countries?	8. ....

9. Will you urge the abolition of the purchase tax and of all indirect taxation on necessary consumable goods which by raising prices add to the cost of living and diminish wages? — 9. ....

10. Are you in favour of ending the Exchange Control so that the Pound shall find its own level in a free market thus permitting trade in both imports and exports to adjust itself naturally? — 10. ....

* *On other side of this sheet is space for additional remarks.*

APPENDIX E

Group Activities at the 1955 Election

The following is a list of some of the bodies which approached candidates at the 1955 election either through questionnaires, letters, or memoranda, or through organized deputations. These approaches may have been made either from national headquarters or from some or all of the local branches:

Association of Optical Practitioners
British Dental Association
British Legion
British Rheumatic Association
British Road Federation
British Union for the Abolition of Vivisection
Catholic Parents' and Electors' Associations
Committee for a Royal Commission on Voting
Council of Justice to Animals
Equal Pay Campaign Committee
Fair Prices Defence Committee
Free Trade Union
Imperial Alliance for the Defence of Sunday
Incorporated Association of Assistant Masters in Secondary Schools
Inland Waterways' Association
League against Cruel Sports
League of Empire Loyalists
Licensed Victuallers' Protection Society of London
Lord's Day Observance Society
Married Women's Association
National Anti-Vaccination League
National Association of Master Bakers, Confectioners, and Caterers
National Association of Retired Police Officers
National Association of Schoolmasters
National Association of Women Civil Servants
National Chamber of Trade
National Farmers' Union
National Federation of Old Age Pension Associations
National Federation of Post Office and Other Civil Service Veterans

National Federation of Property Owners
National Forth Road Bridge Committee
National Guild of Civil Servants
National Hosiery Manufacturers' Federation
National Spinsters' Pensions Association
National Temperance Federation
National Union of Bank Employees
National Union of Ratepayers' Associations
National Union of Teachers
National Union of Women Teachers
Nursery School Association
Pedestrians' Association for Road Safety
Pit Ponies' Protection Society
Potato Growers' Association
Prohibition of Coursing Committee
Roads Campaign Council
St. Joan's Social and Political Alliance
Scottish Covenant Association
Standing Joint Committee of the Royal Automobile Club, the Automobile Association, and the Royal Scottish Automobile Club
Status of Women Committee
Ten Shillings a Week Widows' Protest Organization
United Committee for the Taxation of Land Values
United Nations' Association
Universities' Federation of Animal Welfare
Water Companies' Association

Index

PRINTED IN GREAT BRITAIN
AT THE UNIVERSITY PRESS, OXFORD
BY VIVIAN RIDLER
PRINTER TO THE UNIVERSITY